Kevin Bloor is the author of *Introduction to Politics*, *Introduction to Sociology for GCSE* and a set of teaching and learning resouces available online from *tutor2u* and *classroom resources*. He is also a regular contributor to online political forums, a conference speaker and has taught at Manchester University and the City of London Freemen's School.

A-LEVEL POLITICS
MADE EASY

2nd Edition

Kevin Bloor

Book Guild Publishing
Sussex, England

First published in Great Britain in 2006 by
The Book Guild Ltd
Pavilion View
19 New Road
Brighton, BN1 1UF

Typesetting in Times by
Keyboard Services, Luton, Bedfordshire

Printed in Great Britain by
CPI Antony Rowe

A catalogue record for this book is available from
The British Library

ISBN 978 1 84624 275 5

To my Dad.
Thank you for everything.

Contents

Introduction

The aims of *A-Level Politics Made Easy* are to help you fully understand UK and EU politics, and to guide you through the whole of the syllabus. Written by an experienced politics teacher, the book should prove invaluable to your course, and is designed to enable exam success.

Each chapter begins with an outline of the syllabus objectives, in order to clarify what you *need to know*. Several websites are provided for further research, and past exam questions are included so that you can practise them during your revision.

I wrote *A Level Politics Made Easy* with the A-Level student in mind, and I hope it helps you grasp what is a fascinating subject.

Kevin Bloor
Head of Politics and Sociology
City of London Freemen's School, Ashtead, Surrey
September 2006

1

Race and Ethnicity

Objectives from the syllabus

- To develop an awareness of general issues related to race/ethnicity within the UK, in particular a knowledge of party positions and public policy on race and racial discrimination/inequality, and of attempts to promote racial harmony.
- Students should also develop an understanding of the key concepts of racism, discrimination, multiculturalism and minority rights.

Internet websites

www.cre.gov.uk
www.r4rj.org.uk
www.migrationwatchuk.org/
www.jcwi.org.uk/

Old exam questions

15 minutes

What is meant by the term 'multicultural society' in the context of the modern UK?   June 2004

What evidence is there that racism remains a problem in the UK today?   January 2004

1

Why has the issue of race relations moved up the political agenda since 1991?   January 2006

Explain the different initiatives that have been introduced to create better race relations in the UK since 1992.
                                                                                January 2005

Outline how economic and racial issues influence immigration and asylum policies.   January 2003

What measures, other than legislation, have been adopted to improve race relations in the UK since 1979?
                                                                                June 2002

What were the main conclusions of the Macpherson Inquiry into the Stephen Lawrence murder case?   January 2002

45 minutes

Explain what is meant by the term 'multiculturalism' and assess how successfully it has been promoted since the 1960s.
                                                                                January 2003

Outline the main differences between Conservative and Labour approaches to dealing with race discrimination.
                                                                                Spec

HISTORICAL BACKGROUND

Ethnic minorities have lived in Britain for centuries. Research suggests that black people first arrived in Britain during the mid-sixteenth century, and people from Asia have been here since the seventeenth century (Lynch, J.E. 2004: 155). Immigrants from all over the world make a contribution towards Britain's multiethnic society.

In the UK we speak more than 360 languages (Mote 2003: xii), celebrate festivals as diverse as St Patrick's Day,

Divali and Ramadan; and the nation's most popular food is lasagne. But whereas ethnic minorities have made Britain their home for centuries, the issue of race and ethnicity first came to prominence during the 1950s. 1958 saw Britain's first race riot, and during a bitterly fought by-election contest in 1965 for the seat of Smethick, the Conservative Party focused its campaign on the issue of race. It was the first time a major British political party had raised the issue of race.

In 1968, the Conservative MP Enoch Powell delivered an infamous 'rivers of blood' speech that warned of 'the black man holding the whip hand over the white man' in the not too distant future. His inflammatory remarks were condemned by politicians of all parties, and he was later sacked from the Shadow Cabinet, yet there is little doubt his views struck a chord among many white people. The dockers' union even went on strike in support of Enoch Powell, to highlight working-class concerns over immigration.

The Labour government (1964–1970) faced a difficult problem. How could they soothe the fears of their traditional working-class voters, who felt threatened by an influx of immigrants, while maintaining the traditional socialist aims of the Party as a whole? In 1965 Parliament passed the Race Relations Act to legislate against racial discrimination, yet in 1968 the government restricted the right of access to a British passport for Kenyan Asians, who until that point had considered themselves Commonwealth citizens with a right to settle in the UK.

Until the 1980s, governments of both parties aimed to restrict the level of immigration. Both the 1971 Immigration Act, which reduced non-white immigration, and the 1981 British Nationality Act, which was designed to end primary immigration (Mote 2003: 27) limited the number of immigrants arriving into Britain. The Labour Party, and a handful of Tory MPs, also supported measures to prevent racial

3

discrimination against ethnic minorities living in Britain (e.g. the 1976 Race Relations Act).

IMMIGRATION

Immigration: the facts

Average net immigration has more than tripled since 1997 (*Independent*, 7/4/05: 1), although the figures have been on the increase since the early 1990s due to the growth of the UK economy, and the fact that migrants are needed to fill shortages in the labour market. According to the 2001 census, migrants accounted for 1.14 million of the 2.2 million increase in the UK's population over the 1990s (*Times*, 23/9/05: 16).

A Home Office study commissioned in 2003 estimates that the 8% of immigrants who live in the UK contribute 10% more to the economy than they take out in terms of welfare benefits (*Time*, 28/2/05: 41–43). Based on such figures, immigration holds clear economic benefits for the host country (A-Brown 1999: 16; Glover *et al.* 2001). Migrant workers often take jobs that, for various reasons, would otherwise remain vacant; such as cleaners, construction workers, au pairs and nannies. Those at the skilled end of the labour market also perform jobs that cannot be filled by the native British population due to a shortage of skilled labour. For instance, one in four of all doctors were born outside of the UK (*Daily Express*, 3/9/04: 8). Added to our declining birth rate and ageing population, Britain clearly needs migrant workers to fill some of the 600,000 job vacancies that currently exist (*Daily Mail*, 2/5/05: 8).

Public debate on the issue of immigration is stifled by political correctness on the left, and a largely xenophobic press on the right. However, there are pressure groups such as Migration Watch that aim to highlight the potential costs surrounding immigration in a non-racist way. These include the following:

➤ Mass immigration can contribute to racial tension, an issue exploited by the British National Party (BNP);
➤ reduces the job prospects for people already living here, including ethnic minorities;
➤ places an extra burden upon housing and public services;
➤ can lower wages (Mote 2003: 6–7).

Everything said thus far about the costs and benefits of immigration refers to *legal* immigration. Illegal immigration, where people reside in the UK without the official documentation, is undoubtedly one of the key issues of British politics.

Immigrants who arrive into Britain illegally often end up working in the hidden economy. This can range from catering to the sex trade, but one thing common to most illegal immigrants is exploitation. In June 2000, 59 illegal immigrants died on a lorry while entering Dover and in March 2004, 20 Chinese cockle pickers died at Morecambe Bay. Added to the human misery of exploitation, illegal immigrants are not paying income tax or national insurance, thus many of the economic benefits of immigration do not arise.

The public's concern over Britain's immigration and asylum system is, in part, justifiable. The resignation in April 2004 of the Home Office minister Beverly Hughes over visas granted to people from Romania and Bulgaria highlighted the pressure placed upon Britain's immigration service, as did the suspension of Home Office minister Steve Moxon

5

on 8 March 2004, after he exposed the practical difficulties in implementing the government's 'managed migration' policy.

THE ELECTORAL IMPORTANCE OF IMMIGRATION

In a survey undertaken in 2004, immigration ranked higher than crime and education in terms of its importance to voters (*Fabian Review*, spring 2004: 21), and in another poll taken at the end of that year, 80% of voters believed that the government was not 'tough enough' on immigration (Toynbee and Walker 2005: 214). To address those concerns, the government plans new measures to prevent sham marriages and bogus college courses being used as a cover by illegal immigrants (http://news.bbc.co.uk/1/hi/uk_politics/3650133.stm); and the Immigration, Asylum and Nationality Act (2005) introduced a £2,000 penalty for employers who hire illegal workers.

The Conservatives are equally aware of the importance of immigration to the voters. During the 2005 General Election, Michael Howard said that in the first week of a Tory Government, Britain would have pulled out of the 1951 UN Refugee Convention. He also set out plans to enable Parliament to place an annual limit on the number of immigrants coming into Britain, and to introduce an Australian-style points system that differentiates between desirable and undesirable immigrants. As for asylum, the party pledged to change the visa system, and introduce 24-hour surveillance of UK ports.[1]

---

[1] The Liberal Democrats planned to provide all applicants with the necessary legal advice and assistance, offer translation services and implement a fairer benefits system. Unlike the Tories, the Liberal Democrats believe that Britain should fully accept its responsibilities under the 1951 UN Convention on Refugees (Hall 2005: 26).

6

Both main parties also wish to attract desirable immigrants into the UK. The Labour government created the Highly Skilled Migrant Programme in January 2002, and in their 2005 election manifesto the Conservatives proposed to restrict the right to settle in the UK to the highly educated on a stable income.

As one can see, there is a great deal of cross-party consensus between the two main parties. One reason for the consensus is the tendency for Labour to move to the right and adopt Tory positions on issues of major electoral importance. For example, in 2005 the Home Secretary Charles Clarke introduced a points scheme for new arrivals into Britain, similar to the policy adopted by the Conservatives just a few weeks beforehand.

WHITE FLIGHT

It was Mrs Thatcher who first spoke of people's fears that Britain would be 'swamped by an alien culture' (Hall 2005: 151), and there is no clearer demonstration of those fears than 'white flight'. Once a family (or a group of families) from an ethnic minority moves into a neighbourhood, white residents are more likely to move out. When white people leave in high numbers, it contributes to a self-fulfilling prophecy, in that the area will inevitably become more ethnic. It is difficult to avoid the conclusion that white flight is based upon racism.

> **Definition of racism**
>
> 'A generalised attitude which views some racial groups as inferior. It leads to discrimination and sometimes race hatred' (McNaughton 2003: 110).

How much of a problem is racism within British society today?

> Unemployment among ethnic minorities is far higher than that among whites.
> Ethnic minorities face a glass ceiling at work in which promotion is denied on the basis of racist attitudes.
> A substantial earnings gap. A person with a black or Pakistani heritage, in the same line of work and in the same town, can expect to earn £6,500 less than a former white classmate. The earnings gap for an African Caribbean is about £5,000 a year (Reid and Phillips, 2004: 10).
> There is a distinct lack of ethnic minority representation within the higher echelons of the law, the Civil Service and in Parliament.
> Racist crime in England and Wales reached record levels in 2004 (*Independent*, 18/1/05: 16).
> There are more Afro-Caribbean men in jail than attending a university (*Sunday Times* magazine, 10/11/04: 43).
> Whites and Asians living 'parallel lives' (Ouseley 2001). In January 2004, a MORI poll found that 41% of white people, and 26% of ethnic minority people, actually *wanted* the races to live separately (*Guardian*, 19/7/04: 1).
> The growth in support for the BNP.
> The MacPherson Report (1999) claimed that the police force was 'institutionally racist'.

Why is racism such a problem in UK society?

> Competition for jobs, housing and public services may result in negative feelings towards so-called 'outsiders'.

8

➤ The failure of some ethnic minorities to assimilate into British society.
➤ The fear of being overwhelmed on a densely populated island. Britain is twice as densely populated as France (Mote 2003: 5), which does to some extent impact on the standard of living.
➤ Ignorance of other cultures.
➤ Ethnic minorities are falsely perceived to be gaining preferential or special treatment (e.g. positive discrimination).
➤ Negative perceptions of ethnic minorities, in part encouraged by the media.

When a person's view of an ethnic minority is formed upon fear and prejudice, myths often become more persuasive than facts. One such view is that Britain has too many immigrants, but that is based on an exaggeration. In a survey commissioned in 2004, those questioned estimated that 23% of the population were immigrants, yet the actual figure is 8% (*Fabian Review*, spring 2004: 21). The gap between myth and reality is even more striking when one considers the most controversial of all areas relating to race and ethnicity; that of asylum.

Asylum: the facts

The number of asylum seekers seeking refugee status in the UK during 2004 stood at 40,200; down from a peak of 110,000 in 2002 (*Independent*, 23/2/05: 2). Indeed over the past three years, applications have fallen by 60% (*Economist*, 12/2/05: 15), the biggest fall of any European Union (EU) country (Toynbee and Walker, 2005: 209), and the numbers claiming asylum are now at the level they were in 1997. Despite the government's recent progress,

---

Britain has a poor record in implementing the asylum system. Just half of those who fail in their application for asylum are forced to leave the country (*Times*, 16/9/04: 9), and there could be up to a quarter of a million failed asylum seekers in the country (www.timesonline.co.uk/article/0,,21699401, 00.html). It is for these reasons that public concern over the asylum system prevails. The fact that other countries take a considerable number of asylum seekers, or that we host less than 2% of the world's refugees (http://news.bbc.co.uk/2/hi/uk_news/ 2049221.stm), does little to calm the public's fears.

Once an asylum seeker's case is successful, he or she is classed as a refugee. The location of refugees will always prove highly controversial, not least because they tend to be housed in areas of high unemployment and relative social deprivation. According to the government's own Audit Commission (2000), the conditions in which asylum seekers are housed 'are often unsafe and vulnerable to racist attacks, and usually unfit for human habitation'. There have been riots at Harmondsworth, Gosport and Yarl's Wood detention centres; and the Sighthill estate in Glasgow witnessed the first murder of an asylum seeker (Solomos 2003: 73).

Many people hold a negative and even hostile perception of asylum seekers, perhaps due to tabloid stories of refugees being housed in five-star hotels. In reality, there has been just one reported case of an asylum centre having luxury facilities (Mote 2003: 18), yet it cannot be denied that there are cases of asylum seekers who appear to have 'worked the system'. For example, in November 2002, a jet landed in Heathrow from Moscow with 16 passengers demanding refugee status in the UK. They had hired the plane out at a cost of £1,000 each.

The government's response has been to introduce a series of measures designed to address the public's concerns over asylum seekers, which reflect both change, and continuity, with previous Conservative governments.

In terms of change, the 'white list' of approved countries was abolished, as it breached the principle that every individual had the right to have his or her case examined regardless of their country of origin. In terms of continuity with the Conservatives (Solomos 2003: 70), there are several examples of both main parties adopting a 'tough' approach to asylum seekers. Since 1997, the government has implemented the following measures:

➢ In response to media hostility at the arrival of around 800 Roma people from Eastern Europe, the length of appeal awarded to asylum cases was reduced.

➢ The government has increased the number of detentions and deportations, and introduced a one-stop appeal hearing system.

➢ Asylum seekers are now denied a right to council housing unless they stay in the area to which they have been officially dispersed (Toynbee and Walker 2005: 212).

➢ Truck drivers have to pay a fine if found smuggling people into Britain. This is known as 'carriers liability'.

➢ Section 9 of the 2004 Immigration Act allows the authorities to deprive families with children of housing support if their initial claim is refused (*Times*, 5/1/06: 9).

➢ The government plans to introduce ID cards to address the problem of failed asylum seekers staying in the country.

In the 2001 general election campaign, the Conservatives proposed a type of safe house for those awaiting their case to be heard, and at the 2003 Tory Party conference, Shadow Home Secretary Oliver Letwin announced proposals to house asylum seekers on an unnamed island. Both measures were criticised by civil liberties groups and the Liberal Democrats. However, the government's current policy of placing those waiting to hear their cases into dedicated detention centres is not all that different to the Tories' safe house idea.

RECENT LEGISLATION

The concept of citizenship is one measure by which the government aims to ensure harmonious race relations and to assimilate ethnic minorities into British society. The 2002 Naturalisation and Immigration Act states that residents seeking British citizenship must have 'sufficient knowledge about life in the UK'. It is also compulsory for applicants to attend a ceremony in order to receive a certificate of citizenship, which then allows residents to apply for a British passport. Candidates have to live legally in the UK for five years (three if they are married to a Briton) to become a British citizen.[2] Newcomers also have to swear or affirm allegiance to the Queen, her heirs and successor in law. The full text reads as follows:

> I [name] swear by Almighty God/do solemnly and truly declare and affirm that, on becoming a British citizen, I will be faithful and bear true allegiance to Her Majesty Queen Elizabeth the Second, her Heirs and Successors

---

[2] In 2004, the number of people seeking UK citizenship stood at record levels (*Times*, 23/2/05:8).

according to the law. I will give my loyalty to the United Kingdom and respect its rights and freedoms. I will uphold its democratic values. I will observe its laws faithfully and fulfil my duties and obligations as a British citizen.

The government has also addressed the under-representation of ethnic minorities within the police force via positive discrimination, with the Home Office now issuing targets for police recruitment. Positive discrimination raises fears of a white person losing out to a less qualified black person, as in the case of the Avon and Somerset police force, who rejected almost 200 applicants because they were white and male (*Times*, 29/11/05: 14). Targets for the police have therefore been described as 'ridiculous' by the President of the National Black Police Association, Ray Powell, because 80% of all new recruits would have to be black or Asian in order to meet those targets (*Observer*, 22/8/04: 1). Certain pressure groups have also criticised the use of targets as patronising racial minorities. Unlike the Labour Party, the Conservatives have always favoured non-legislative measures based upon a person's merit, rather than positive discrimination based upon someone's ethnicity.

What measures could or have been taken by the government to encourage racial harmony?

- ➤ Legislation is important but it is not enough, as racism is a deeply cultural and psychological mindset.
- ➤ Since the Race Relations (Amendment) Act was passed in 2000, various institutions (e.g. the police, schools, the Civil Service and Parliament) have a statutory duty to promote good race relations, and ensure equal opportunities.
- ➤ To address the problem of 'institutionalised racism' among the police, police forces across the country

use black or Asian agents, posing as victims of crime, in an attempt to identify racist officers.

➢ Deal with the underlying cause of racial tensions, such as whites and Asians leading 'parallel lives'.

➢ A fundamental change in the media's portrayal of ethnic minorities.

➢ Taking racial discrimination more seriously, as with the introduction of a racially aggravated crime category in 2002.

➢ Education clearly has an important role in socialising people towards a tolerant view of ethnic minorities. The assumption here is that children can be taught that racism is wrong.

➢ In September 2005 the Home Secretary Charles Clarke launched a new commission on integration to advise on how – consistent with people's freedom to worship in the way they want and to follow their own religion and culture – to ensure there is a better integration within the UK (*Times*, 20/9/05: 11).

RACE AND EDUCATION

Education is closely linked to social improvement, and ethnic minorities in the UK have undoubtedly made significant progress in the past 20 years. Education is also an important agent of socialisation, playing a key role in establishing a more tolerant society. However, there are three factors that may limit its impact. If a child's parents and peer group hold racist views, it is more likely that they will come to share those beliefs. Another factor may be a lack of ethnic minorities within a school. Finally, one must consider single-faith schools, which have faced criticism from the regulatory body the Office for Standards in Education (Ofsted) for failing to teach tolerance of other faiths.

The educational performance of ethnic minorities differs greatly. On average, Indian and Chinese children do 25% and 50% better than white children at GCSE. One possible reason is that income levels and social class broadly correspond with the wider population. In contrast, Afro-Caribbean children perform 40% below the average (Reid and Phillips 2004: 12).

The problem of underperformance is even greater among black boys, yet as with much else in politics, the deeper question is *why* this should be the case. Is it low expectations within the black community, racism from teachers, the impact of negative images from the media, or a lack of black teachers? A controversial proposal was put forward by the Head of the Commission for Racial Equality in 2005, when he called for black boys to be taught separately from white children.

IMMIGRATION AND THE WELFARE STATE

Immigration today is different to previous generations for four reasons:

1   The rise of low-cost airlines has made it a lot easier, and cheaper, to travel from one country to another.
2   The potential number of people who could enter the country has increased due to the recent enlargement of the EU.
3   The UK has a stable economy.
4   The UK has a relatively generous welfare state.

The final point presents a difficult problem for the government. Legal immigrants contribute to the economy, and fill shortages in the labour market. However, as with the rest of the population; ethnic minorities will get old and sick, their children will need to be educated and of course they need to be housed. The pressure upon the welfare state *may* therefore offset the economic benefits of immigration.

The creation of the welfare state occurred at a time when the population was more homogeneous than it is today. What few immigrants Britain housed were mostly white (e.g. the Irish, and those from the white Commonwealth), and cultural values were broadly similar throughout the population. Today this is no longer the case, and there is a view that certain groups are simply working the system for their own benefit. Asylum seekers and illegal immigrants are two of those groups commonly identified as exploiting the welfare state. However, it must be said that this hostile perception of foreigners is not a universal one. The stereotype of certain ethnic minorities is often a positive one, with an emphasis upon family values and hard work; qualities widely admired within British society.

THE EU AND THE ISSUE OF RACE

Freedom of movement throughout the member states of the EU is a key element of the Rome Treaties, and the potential number of people who could enter the country has increased since enlargement of the EU on 1 May 2004. This has presented both opportunities and potential problems for the UK.

Based on the need to fill shortages in the labour market, the government has been keen to stress the benefits of enlargement. Home Office figures published in November 2004 revealed that 90,000 migrants from Central and Eastern Europe boosted the economy by £120 billion, with just 16 claiming benefit (*Independent*, 11/11/04: 15). Having said this, there could still be an influx of so-called 'benefit tourists', who may be attracted to the UK due to our relatively generous welfare benefit system. One possible solution is the creation of a two-strand welfare state, where immigrants would be allowed only limited welfare benefits. A similar scheme operates in Denmark, a country with a more social democratic tradition than ours.

There are much deeper concerns over a 'clash of civilisations' (a quote from the American political scientist Samuel Huntingdon) between a western, secular approach and an extreme view of Islam. Those concerns have played into the hands of the extreme right in Holland, France and Austria.

Until Pim Fortuyn's party came second in the 2002 Dutch elections, the Netherlands had been widely admired as a good illustration of a harmonious, multicultural society. Campaigning on the slogan 'Holland is full', his views aroused deep controversy, and he was later murdered. The filmmaker Theo Van Gogh was also killed by an Islamic extremist after one of his films criticised the treatment of Muslim women within Islamic societies. Many Dutch people feel that Islamic fundamentalism, and Holland's traditionally liberal approach, could be incompatible.

In France the leader of the National Front, Jean Marie Le Pen, reached the final ballot of the 2002 presidential elections, and in Austria the electoral success of Jorg Haider provoked strong criticism from many EU countries. For a brief time there was talk of sanctions against Austria, but such a measure might have provoked a backlash against the EU's high-handed response. The success of Jorg Haider was ultimately down to the Austrian electorate, and in a club of democratic countries the argument that people's democratic choices should be respected won the day.

One could argue that the success of the extreme right within the EU reflects a concern over the difficulty of integrating racial groups, and it cannot be denied that different cultural values exist over the role of women, free speech and attitudes towards homosexuality. One could equally say that Islamic fundamentalism has brought the issue of culture to the forefront of people's concerns and is therefore an important issue to raise.

Should a major UK political party raise the issue of culture? The determining factor will, in all probability, be public opinion. While the public is deeply concerned about issues that could conceivably touch upon race and culture, the voters do not always support a party that warns of Britain becoming a foreign land.

Although a significant number of people are racist, and the fear of being 'swamped by an alien culture' is shared by many, the electoral appeal of the extreme right is negligible. While the BNP gained nearly a million votes at the 2004 European Parliamentary elections, they remain on the fringe of British politics. However, the presence of the BNP can have a negative impact upon race relations. The BNP was accused of stirring up racial tensions in Keighley over allegations of paedophilia among local Asian men, and at the Caia Park estate in Wrexham, party members claimed that coachloads of Iraqi Kurds from nearby towns and cities were coming into the area, with the intent of causing violence (*Guardian*, 24/6/03: 6).

THE POSITION OF THE POLITICAL PARTIES

In the 2001 general election, the Tory leader William Hague tried to distance himself from Mrs Thatcher's public concerns over multiculturalism. This did not, however, prevent him from warning that Britain was becoming 'a foreign land to many of its inhabitants'. Both Labour and the Liberal Democrats accused the Conservatives of playing the race card. Of perhaps greater significance, the government chose not to highlight the issue of race during the campaign.

The only related issue during the 2001 general election

was the relative success of the BNP. The party did better than expected in some northern cities, and their success proved a precursor for the race riots in Bradford, Blackburn and Oldham during the summer of 2001.

In the 2005 General Election, both major parties were accused of playing the race card. In a poster published on its website, the Labour Party portrayed Michael Howard and Oliver Letwin, both of whom are Jewish, as flying pigs. It was later withdrawn. The Conservative Party was also criticised for planning controversial quotas on immigrants, and for proposals to check all immigrants for TB and other diseases.

There is some evidence to suggest that the Conservatives have become a more socially inclusive party. They now have a black MP and fielded more ethnic minority candidates than any other party in the 2005 campaign. However, when Ann Winterton MP was denounced by politicians of all parties for telling a joke about the tragedy at Morecombe Bay, it did little to help the then Tory leader Michael Howard, himself the son of Romanian immigrants.

As the party that instigated all of Britain's Race Relations Acts, combined with a long-standing commitment to equality and the interests of the less well-off, Labour have traditionally secured strong support among ethnic minorities. Yet in recent years, Tony Blair's alliance with George Bush over the Iraq war has undoubtedly cost the party votes among the Muslim community. The impact of anti-terrorism legislation since 11 September 2001 may have also led to a loss of support for Labour among Muslim voters. The Liberal Democrats have benefited the most from dissatisfaction with the government, as shown by their 2003 by-election victory in Brent East.

THE COMMISSION FOR RACIAL EQUALITY (CRE)

The CRE is the most prominent pressure group on issues relating to race, and ethnicity. It has two main roles:

1   Under the Race Relations Amendment Act (2000), the head of the CRE can issue an enforcement notice against any public body that fails to promote racial equality.
2   The CRE campaigns on a number of race-related issues. The most important case in recent years was the CRE's call for an inquiry into the murder of Stephen Lawrence, which in turn led to the MacPherson Report (1999).

The MacPherson Report

Few reports can match the political significance of MacPherson (1999), which marked something of a watershed in relations between the police and the black community. The reaction of the Metropolitan Police to the Report was threefold:

1   To accept the main charges.
2   To commit itself to removing racist officers.
3   To increase anti-racism training.

The MacPherson Report was accepted by all the main political parties, and welcomed by the CRE. Since the report was published, some Conservatives have argued that street crime has gone up because stop and search powers have been weakened, but there is little evidence to support this charge. Crime has actually fallen in recent years, while the number of 'stop and searches' recorded against black and Asian people rose by a third in 2003, compared to an increase of 10% against white people (*Times*, 2/7/04: 4).

Racism within the police force continues to have a high political profile. A report published by the CRE in 2004 claimed that racism within the police force was being driven underground, with a new breed of 'stealth racists' emerging (*Times*, 9/3/05: 26); and Home Office figures released in January 2006 revealed that ethnic minority officers are twice as likely to resign as their white colleagues (*Times*, 16/1/06: 6).

The factual evidence of racism in the police force does appear compelling. Black people are six times more likely to be stopped and searched than a white person, three times more likely to be arrested and twice as likely to be in prison than attending a university (*Sunday Times* magazine, 10/11/04: 43). Yet as with other political issues, there are several possible explanations for such figures, such as racism within society and poor life chances.

MULTICULTURALISM

Multiculturalism is a confusing, and contested, concept. The term does not invite simple definition, as there are *three* main theories on the issue of multiculturalism: conservative, liberal and the Parekh approach. The debate over multi-culturalism goes to the heart of how to integrate ethnic minorities into British society, and could be said to be the most important issue relating to racial harmony in the UK.

Conservative

The conservative view suggests that ethnic minorities should fully integrate into British society. Assimilation of all ethnic minorities ensures an orderly society, which in turn benefits everyone. Conservatives criticise the liberal approach for leading to a society divided by diffuse cultural values.

The conservative view is, as one might expect, articulated within the Tory party. During the mid 1980s, the then Employment Secretary Norman Tebbit wanted all immigrants to pass the 'cricket test'. He believed that everyone living in Britain should support a British team, rather than holding an allegiance to the country of their parents. Tebbit's view remains one of the clearest illustrations of the conservative approach to multiculturalism.

The conservative approach has also been adopted by Labour Home Secretaries. As a response to the race riots in 2001, David Blunkett wanted all immigrants to speak English at home. He also steered legislation through Parliament that was designed to assimilate new arrivals into British society. In 2005 the then Home Secretary Charles Clarke introduced a points scheme for highly skilled migrants, who will only be allowed to stay permanently if they speak fluent English and pass a 'Britishness test'.

Liberal

Liberals wish to preserve different cultures, protect minority rights and prevent racial discrimination. The liberal perspective believes that all ethnic groups should be tolerated, and in contrast to the conservative view, they should not seek full integration. Far from leading to disorder within society, cultural differences are a welcome sign of a vibrant and pluralist society. Consistent with the liberal view, children should be allowed to attend multifaith schools, although some liberals defend a parent's right to send their children to a single-faith school on the basis of individual choice.

The liberal view can be found within the Labour Party, the Liberal Democrats and the CRE. The government's Race Equality Unit, which aims to ensure ethnic differences flourish, and that each person should be free from discrimination, is an illustration of the liberal view.

Parekh

The third approach to multiculturalism is the Parekh view, which lies somewhere between the liberal and conservative perspectives. This approach emphasises dual cultural identities, where ethnic groups retain their own culture, but also adopt a common British identity.

The Parekh Commission (2000) recognised the worth of individuals from each of Britain's many communities, and the extent of cultural differences within Britain today, while stressing the need to combat racism. It recommended that Britain should become 'a community of citizens' at a local and nationwide level. In practice, this would mean:

➤ rethinking 'the national story and national identity';
➤ understanding the transitional nature of all identities;
➤ achieving a balance between cohesion, difference and equality;
➤ eliminating all kinds of racism;
➤ reducing inequalities within society;
➤ building a 'human rights culture'.

TO WHAT EXTENT IS BRITAIN A
MULTICULTURAL SOCIETY?

Britain is clearly a more multiethnic society than a generation ago. One only has to consider the world of business. Harrods is not considered any less 'British' simply because it is owned by an Egyptian, and half of the biggest British companies are run by foreigners (Sampson 2004: 344). Of more political importance, Paul Boeteng became the first black politician to be appointed to the Cabinet in 2002. Sport also provides a good case study of the growing multiethnicity of British society. For example, in February 2005 Arsenal put out an entire team (including substitutes) without *any* English-born player. As for cricket, the English team is coached by a Zimbabwean, and until recently was captained by an Indian-born player named Hussein. All these examples underline the extent to which Britain is a multiethnic society.

One cannot deny that racism is far less of a problem than when landlords used to put up the sign 'no blacks, no dogs, no Irish'; something unthinkable today. Legislation such as the 2002 Naturalisation and Immigration Act, designed specifically to assimilate ethnic minorities into British society, has to some extent helped to create a more harmonious society. More than half of all Britons believe that immigration has made Britain a better place to live (*Times*, 5/1/06: 32), and there is a far greater awareness of the problem of racism, with an extensive body of laws designed to prevent discrimination on the grounds of race. However, it is also true that racism continues to be a problem affecting contemporary British society.

A recent case in point is the rise in Islamophobia, particularly since the 11 September terrorist attacks on the USA. Clearly Islamic extremists are a problem, as in the case of the Muslim preacher Abdullah el-Faisal, who was imprisoned after calls to kill Hindus and Jews, but it is worth adding that most religions possess extremists. This is shown clearly by the long-standing conflict between Protestants and Catholics in Northern Ireland (see Chapter 7).

Although the UK's racial problems are not as great as say France, the Netherlands or the USA, hostility between ethnic groups remains an unwelcome feature of British society. As recently as October 2005, racial tension erupted in the Lozells area of Birmingham between black and Asian gangs after an unsubstantiated rumour posted on a local website. It is therefore difficult to escape the conclusion that Britain is far from being a society at ease with its cultural and ethnic diversity.

2

Law and Order

Objectives from the syllabus

- Students should gain a knowledge of the main pieces of legislation over the last five years.
- A knowledge of the major events that have shaped political debate over the last five years.
- An understanding of public order, crime and punishment.
- A knowledge of party positions and developing public policy related to crime and public order; this includes changing attitudes towards prison policy and towards police powers and accountability.

Internet websites

www.police.uk
www.met.police.uk
www.ipcc.gov.uk
www.homeoffice.gov.uk/crime/index.html
www.cps.gov.uk
www.polfed.org.uk
www.howardleague.org/
www.nacro.org.uk
www.liberty-human-rights.org.uk/
www.worldserver.pipes.com/crimestoppers

Old exam questions

15 minutes

Explain three ways in which governments have attempted to deal with young offenders since 1992.   June 2004

How have police powers been increased since 1979 and why have these changes been controversial?   Spec

Outline ways in which police powers have increased since 1990.   January 2002

What arguments have the major political parties deployed concerning the effectiveness of prison sentencing since 1992?   January 2003

Explain three ways in which governments have attempted to improve police effectiveness since 1992.   January 2004

45 minutes

In what ways have law and order policies since 1979 eroded civil liberties?   June 2005

Has the Labour government since 1997 been 'tough on crime and tough on the causes of crime'?   June 2002

On what grounds have the Conservatives and the Liberal Democrats criticised Labour policies on law and order since 1997?   January 2005

To what extent has the 'war on crime' been successful since 1990?   January 2006

45 minutes (synoptic)

To what extent have policies on law and order eroded civil liberties in the United Kingdom since 1979?   June 2002

28

'Law and order policy was the subject of fierce party conflict in the 1980s and early 1990s, but since the mid-1990s, there has been a growing consensus over the issues.' Explain and evaluate this statement. June 2003

Assess the extent to which there has been a consensus between the major parties over law and order since 1990.
June 2004

LIBERALS AND AUTHORITARIANS

On the issue of law and order there are two perspectives to consider: liberal and authoritarian.

Liberals take an optimistic view of human nature. People are therefore not inherently bad, but they can become bad due to poor social conditions. Criminals are forced into a life of crime in order to fulfil basic needs, as other legitimate methods are unavailable. This is often due to a lack of job opportunities, particularly in deprived inner cities.

Liberals argue that a breakdown in law and order is linked to divisions within society. This argument was prevalent during the 1980s when crime figures more than doubled, and re-emerged at the time of the 2001 race riots. The Ousley Report (2001), which identified the problem of whites and Asians leading 'parallel lives', is an example of the liberal approach to law and order.

As the name suggests, liberals are deeply concerned about the erosion of civil liberties under governments of both main parties. In order to redress the balance between the state and its citizens, the police should be made more accountable, and the constitution should be codified in order to entrench civil rights.

In contrast to authoritarians, many liberals take a critical view of the police. They argue that the police are the instruments of social control and can be used by the government for political means (e.g. to defeat the National Union of Mineworkers during the 1984/5 miners' strike, and the May Day protestors in the year 2000). The police also preserve the status quo by defending those with property, which could be interpreted as favouring the rich against the wider interests of society.

Unlike authoritarians, liberals argue that prisons are not an effective deterrent because the majority of prisoners reoffend. Even a Tory Home Secretary conceded in a 1990 White Paper that prisons are 'an expensive way of making bad people worse' (Hitchens 2003: 122). Liberals also claim that prisons can often brutalise young inmates.

The liberal alternative to prison is to rehabilitate criminals back into society. For instance, ex-offenders could be given help with basic maths and English in order to complete job applications, and treatment could be given to the 90% of prisoners who have mental health and/or substance mis-use problems (www.policyreview.co.uk/policytracker/policy tracker11.html). The pressure group NACRO actively campaigns for the rehabilitation of offenders, as does the National Association of Probation Officers and the Howard League for Penal Reform.

Those who take an authoritarian (or illiberal) view of law and order are pessimists about human nature. They believe humans are aggressive, competitive and prone to committing selfish acts. Punitive measures are therefore needed in order to keep human nature in check.

Authoritarians such as Mrs Thatcher reject the liberal argument that crime is linked to problems within society. According to authoritarians 'there is no such thing as society', merely families and individuals who should be held responsible for their actions. Crime is therefore caused by a lack of moral responsibility among offenders.

Authoritarians believe that prisons are a necessary deterrent and criticise alternative measures as being 'soft on crime'. Evidence for this was shown in March 2002, when the government revealed that prisoners let out early under the tagging scheme had committed 1,400 crimes (Hitchens 2003: 155). Authoritarians also blame 'Hampstead liberals' (a quote from David Blunkett) for creating an 'excuse culture' (a quote from Jack Straw) among criminals, and for showing greater interest in the perpetrators of crime than the victims. More police resources and greater police powers are needed to combat crime.

Authoritarians also complain that criminals often use their rights (ably defended by 'liberal' lawyers) to gain favourable treatment from the criminal justice system. As an illustration of this point, a prisoner recently claimed the right to access pornography under the Human Rights Act. Thus far from protecting human rights, liberal measures are often exploited by the unscrupulous.

The authoritarian view is expressed by the Conservative Party and government ministers. The last three Home Secretaries (Straw, Blunkett and Clarke) could all be described as authoritarian, as could John Reid. The Prime Minister could also be classed as an authoritarian. The liberal view is aligned to the Liberal Democrats, and most of the Labour Party.

THE ISSUE OF LAW AND ORDER SINCE 1979

The issue of law and order divided the main parties during the 1980s and early 1990s, particularly the accusation that the police were employed as the agents of Thatcherism against the National Union of Mineworkers (NUM). There were sharp ideological differences on many political issues, with Labour and the SDP-Liberal Alliance taking a liberal stance against the government's tough approach to law and order.

Under the Conservatives, public expenditure on the police increased by 88% between 1979 and 1993, yet the number of recorded offences rose from 2.5 million to 5.7 million (Jones *et al.* 2001: 553–546). The prison population also grew, passing the 60,000 figure in 1997.

From a liberal perspective, the rise in crime under the Conservatives was due to divisions within society between the haves and the have-nots. High unemployment was another factor to consider. According to authoritarians, the growth in the level of crime was due to a lack of moral responsibility fostered by the permissive values of the 1960s and 1970s, and although police powers increased, such measures were not enough to combat crime.

THE EMERGENCE OF A CROSS-PARTY CONSENSUS SINCE 1993

Michael Howard was appointed Home Secretary in 1993. He was an old-fashioned authoritarian, more in tune with the self-styled 'party of law and order' than his predecessors. During his time as Home Secretary, the prison population grew by 13,000 (McNaughton 2003: 84), clear up rates improved and the level of crime began to fall. In that same year, Tony Blair was the Shadow Home Secretary. He transformed Labour's stance on law and order by his determination to ensure that the Party would never again be seen as 'soft on crime'. The cross-party consensus on law and order dates from Labour's change of attitude and approach during the mid-1990s.

In the run up to the 1997 general election, the two main parties advocated broadly similar policies to deal with street crime and antisocial behaviour. Since then, there has been something of a 'beauty contest' on the issue of law and order, with both main parties trying to 'out tough' each other.

As 'the fear of crime is greater than crime itself', the public have traditionally favoured a tough stance on law and order. In two revealing examples of the electoral importance of law and order, the then Tory leader Michael Howard replaced the self-confessed liberal Oliver Letwin with the more authoritarian David Davis in November 2003. As if to underline the party's change of tone, Davis immediately announced his personal support for the return of the death penalty. On the Labour side, Tony Blair took charge of the government's 'respect' agenda from Charles Clarke in July 2005, as the then Home Secretary was thought to be too 'liberal' for the Prime Minister's liking.

THE POLICIES OF THE MAJOR PARTIES ON THE ISSUE OF LAW AND ORDER

Conservative

The Conservatives have traditionally been described as 'the party of law and order'. Their approach is based upon two core beliefs:

1 Criminals should be held responsible for their actions.
2 Punishments should be severe enough to deter potential criminals (Roberts *et al.* 1999: 638).

Tory Home Secretaries have consistently favoured tougher sentencing, greater resources and more powers for the police force, and taken the view that 'prison works' (a quote from the then Home Secretary Michael Howard to the 1993 Party conference).

There is a belief within the Conservative Party that crime is caused by a lack of moral responsibility, regardless of one's economic background. If there is a link between crime and social background, it is due to the lack of authority in a child's upbringing, often the result of an absent father. In most cases, criminals have not been taught the difference between 'right and wrong'.

One way to reduce crime is to introduce measures that strengthen the family, which is consistent with the Conservatives' portrayal of themselves as 'the party of the family'. One example would be the creation of the Child Support Agency (CSA) in 1993, which forces absent fathers to pay for the maintenance of their children.

In their 2005 election manifesto, the Conservative Party pledged:

- ➢ 5,000 extra police officers a year;
- ➢ 20,000 extra prison places;
- ➢ to reduce the burden of paperwork upon the police;
- ➢ to scrap the government's early release scheme;
- ➢ to create a Department of Homeland Security;
- ➢ to reform, or repeal, the Human Rights Act.

As such, the Party's manifesto was coherent with an authoritarian approach to law and order.

Labour

Until the mid-1990s the Labour Party did not pay much attention to law and order, as the issue was seen as a vote-winner for the Tories. Indeed the Labour Party's 1992 manifesto contained just one paragraph on the subject (Roberts *et al.* 1999: 639). However, since the mid-1990s, New Labour has adopted a more authoritarian approach, while retaining the party's traditional focus upon social justice.

The Labour Party believes there is a connection between poor living conditions and crime, a view borne out by official statistics (www. homeoffice.gov.uk/docs2/annrep2003sec3.html).

Therefore the solution to crime is to tackle 'the causes of crime' via policies to combat social exclusion. The party is also in favour of rehabilitation. For example, the government has targeted help for juvenile offenders in order to prevent youngsters turning to a life of crime.

In their 2005 manifesto, the government pledged to:

➢   introduce a British FBI;
➢   address the 'causes of crime' via policies such as Sure Start, which aims to reduce the number of young children on the at-risk register;
➢   introduce ID cards;
➢   provide greater stop and search powers to community service officers (CSOs);[1]
➢   introduce tougher laws against drug dealers.

Liberal Democrat

Only the Liberal Democrats offer a liberal approach to law and order. They have opposed the government's attempts to curtail civil liberties and the recent growth in police powers. The party has also criticised the government's emphasis on punishment rather than prevention.

During the 2005 general election, the party pledged to:

➢   scrap ID cards and redirect the money into employing 10,000 more police officers;
➢   introduce the ASBO+ scheme, in which rehabilitation measures would be added to antisocial behaviour orders (ASBOs).

---

[1] CSOs have been criticised by the Conservatives as little more than a 'plastic police force', unable to take effective action where needed.

TO WHAT EXTENT DOES A CONSENSUS EXIST?

During the 1980s there was a considerable ideological divergence between the Labour Party and the Conservatives. Since the mid-1990s and the emergence of New Labour the two main parties have adopted a broadly similar approach to law and order. To take one example, both parties favour detention centres to deal with serial criminals and persistent young offenders. However, there are also slight differences to consider:

> ➤ Labour have targeted youth crime and taken measures to combat social exclusion, whereas the Tories reject any possible link between social conditions and crime.
> ➤ The government has prioritised the protection of ethnic minorities (e.g. the introduction of a new racially aggravated crime category in 2002), whereas the Conservatives argue that the police should not be required to fill out stop and account forms every time they stop someone, as it could deter an officer from searching a suspect who happens to be of an ethnic minority.
> ➤ Voices critical of the police can still be heard on the left of the Labour Party.
> ➤ In November 2005, an attempt by the government to extend the maximum period of detention from two weeks to three months failed to gain cross-party support.

NEW LABOUR SINCE 1997

The government's strategy to deal with law and order took shape while in opposition. In 1993, the Shadow Home Secretary Tony Blair declared that the next Labour government would be 'tough on crime, and tough on the causes of crime'.

Blair knew he had to balance the concerns of the public with the traditional views of his own party. Thus to be 'tough on crime' presented New Labour as in tune with public opinion, while being 'tough on the causes of crime' underlined Labour's belief in social justice.

The issue of law and order was traditionally a strong card for the Tories, but public opinion began to shift in the mid-1990s due to the failure of the Conservative government to prevent a steady rise in the level of crime. Tony Blair seized the opportunity to present new Labour as a party that would deal effectively with crime, and by the 1997 general election the party had abandoned many of its old policies in favour of headline-grabbing 'get tough' measures (e.g. fast-track punishments for young offenders).

Labour's revised approach retained some of the party's conventional emphasis on tackling the social causes of crime while adopting an authoritarian stance on law and order. It marked an alternative to Mrs Thatcher's view that 'there is no such thing as society', and the Old Labour approach that, at times, appeared to condone behaviour which undermined the rule of law (e.g. the 1984/5 miners' strike). It has since been argued that no other policy area demonstrates the distinction between Old and New Labour as clearly as that of law and order (Randall 2004: 179).

The government's 1997 document *No More Excuses* indicated the tone of New Labour's approach towards law and order, and in 1998 Parliament passed the Youth Justice and Criminal Evidence Act and the Crime and Disorder Act. Taken together, those Acts introduced the following measures:

➢ restraints could be placed on individuals who engage in antisocial behaviour;
➢ local authorities could evict tenants from council homes if they had committed frequent crimes;

> parents could be held criminally responsible for the behaviour of their children;
> police could set curfews on persistent young offenders;
> those convicted of child sex offences were to be kept under special surveillance by the police;
> the DNA records of all offenders and suspects could be held by the police.

ASSESSMENT OF NEW LABOUR

Law and order: the facts

The key figure is the level of crime, which has declined by 30% since 1997. The government can also boast an increase in police powers and police numbers which now stand at record levels (www.labour.org.uk/top50achievements/). Yet according to official estimates, a crime is committed every second in England and Wales (*Times*, 29/7/05: 2), and some types of crime have increased since 1997, such as gun crime, youth crime and violent offences against the person.

Why has the overall level of crime fallen since 1997?

If one were to take a liberal perspective, a fall in the level of crime could be due to a series of measures designed to address problems within society, and a sustained fall in the level of unemployment. If one takes an authoritarian perspective, the growth in police powers, combined with the record number of officers, has led to more effective policing. However, the reduction in the level of crime might have very little to do with the government, or the explanations offered by liberals and authoritarians. The decline in theft and burglary offences could be due to improved home security, and it is worth noting that crime levels were already falling *before* Labour came to power.

Despite the fall in the level of crime, people do not necessarily feel any safer, partly because many crimes go unreported, and due to the fact that just 18% of crimes are solved (*Daily Mail*, 11/6/05: 26). It is also worth stating that in March 2005, the Chief Constable of Nottinghamshire blamed a lack of resources for the failure of his force to deal with soaring levels of violent crime. His view may be closer to public opinion than the official statistics. The government clearly has much work to do in order to reassure the public that the battle against crime is being won.

What has the government done since 1997 to reduce crime?

Although the government has introduced some liberal measures (e.g. the declassification of cannabis, lowering the age of consent for gay people), it has taken a largely 'tough' approach to law and order. Here are some of the main policies:

> The Crime and Disorder Act 1998 set up a Youth Justice Board in order to coordinate the government's efforts in the fight against youth crime. It is estimated that a quarter of all crime is committed by those aged 17 and under (Toynbee and Walker 2005: 226).
> The introduction of ASBOs in 1999. Around 40% of ASBOs are broken (*Independent*, 30/6/05: 9), and it could be said that to 'name and shame' children is a step too far. Yet few would deny that they have worked to some extent, and according to a Market & Opinion Research International (MORI) opinion poll, 89%

support the use of ASBOs (*Observer*, 12/6/05: 22). Approximately 6,500 ASBOs have been implemented since they became available (*Economist*, 14/1/06: 31).

➤ The government has introduced parenting orders and increased the maximum fine that courts can impose on parents who let their children play truant (Randall 2004: 181).

➤ Since 2000, known football hooligans have been prevented from travelling abroad to England games.

➤ The government has expanded the number of 'trailblazer' areas designed to tackle antisocial behaviour.

➤ The 2001 Criminal Justice and Police Act gives police the power to issue on-the-spot fines for disorderly behaviour, and if the Violent Crime Reduction Bill is passed, aggressive drunks could be barred from all pubs and clubs in their home area for up to two years.

➤ The 2001 Crime and Public Protection Act introduced mandatory drugs testing, with those on the Sex Offenders Register forced to account for their movements.

➤ In 1998 the government appointed a Drugs Czar to deal with the problem of drug-related crime. It is estimated that addictive drugs fuel almost half of all offences (Toynbee and Walker 2005: 218).[2]

THE ROLE OF THE JUDICIARY

The role of the judiciary is threefold:

---

[2] The issue of drugs divides liberals and authoritarians. Some liberals argue for the decriminalisation of 'soft' drugs, whereas authoritarians take a firm line against all drug use.

1 The primarily responsibility of the judiciary is to enforce the law. Punishments range from a custodial sentence to a variety of non-custodial measures.

2 To interpret the law.

3 The judiciary also plays a political role. It can do this via the process of judicial review, in which a judge decides if a public body took action beyond their powers (*ultra vires*). This can involve a judge challenging the decision of a government minister. Law Lords also participate in Parliamentary debates, judges often head controversial inquiries and the judiciary can act as a pressure group on issues such as the jury system, double jeopardy and human rights. For example, in January 2004, an attempt to end the right of judicial appeal against asylum decisions was defeated in the House of Lords after a campaign led by the Law Lords.

Academics have noted something of a 'silent revolution' within the judiciary, in which judges have become *less* deferential to the government, and more willing to act as a check on the powers of the executive. For example, in December 2004, eight out of nine judges in the House of Lords ruled that the detention of terrorist suspects in Belmarsh prison was unlawful under the European Convention of Human Rights, and in June 2004 the courts ruled that the Home Secretary could not remove the failed asylum applicant Mohammed Ali Razgar under 'fast track' deportation rules (*Times*, 18/6/04: 2).

Since 1997, judges have been increasingly willing to defend individual rights against the government. One of the leading critics of the Labour government is Lord Hoffman, who once described the Home Secretary's challenge to habeas corpus as 'the real threat to the life of the nation' (*Times*, 29/7/05: 18). Even Lord Irvine, one of Tony Blair's closest political allies, voted against the government over anti-terrorist legislation.

There has also been a shift in the political ideology of the judiciary. During the 1980s, a predominantly conservative judiciary tended to support the government of Mrs Thatcher. In the case of Clive Ponting (a civil servant who released sensitive information about the government), the judge defended the right of government ministers to define what was in 'the public interest', and during the miners' strike, several injunctions were imposed on members of the NUM. However, in recent years a more liberal generation of judges has emerged. On several occasions the judiciary has clashed with the government over the rights of asylum seekers, and over anti-terrorism measures.

The judiciary is not above criticism from politicians, with MPs from both main parties having accused judges of being 'too soft' on serious crime. In order to thwart the so-called 'liberal' judiciary, the Conservative Party believes that the government should be more prescriptive over sentencing policy. From the opposite end of the political spectrum, judges are criticised for being elitist, unaccountable and conservative with a small 'c'.[3]

POLICE POWERS AND CIVIL LIBERTIES

The police are a 'civilian organisation established to enforce criminal law' (Budge *et al.* 2001: 506). They have two functions:

---

[3] Even the Prime Minister has said that the criminal justice system protects the accused better than their victims (*Economist*, 14/1/06: 31).

1 To maintain law and order. As the former Home Secretary Kenneth Baker once observed, the police are the thin blue line between order and chaos.
2 To prevent and detect crime. Preventing crime relies a great deal on cooperation from the public through schemes such as Neighbourhood Watch and Crimestoppers, and via the media (e.g. the TV programme *Crimewatch*, and public appeals to catch criminals).

What are civil liberties?

Civil liberties are 'fundamental freedoms possessed by a country's citizens ... that are guaranteed in law, with corresponding obligations imposed on Government for their observance' (Turner 2002: 83).

The relationship between the citizen and the state is central to the issue of police powers and civil liberties. The state holds a monopoly on the legitimate use of force. Only the agents of the state, such as the police and the army, can use coercive means to ensure law and order. We must obey the law, and face the threat of punishment if we do not. In return, the state protects and upholds our rights.

All governments have to balance the need to protect society from those who disobey the law against the need to maintain our civil liberties. Under governments of both main parties, the trend since 1979 has been towards greater police powers and a steady erosion of civil liberties.

WHY HAVE UK GOVERNMENTS BEEN ABLE TO ERODE CIVIL LIBERTIES?

Unlike the USA, the rights and liberties of British citizens are not set out in a codified constitution. Many have appeared as customs and traditions, others as Acts of Parliament. Parliament is of course sovereign, and can take away any civil right simply by an Act of Parliament (e.g. removing the right to trial by jury for certain 'middle range' offences). In Britain, we have little constitutional protection from Parliament undermining our civil rights.

Although legislation has been passed since 1997 designed to strengthen our civil rights, pressure groups campaigning for more 'open' government have dismissed such legislation as insufficient. For example, the Freedom of Information Act was used to score political points during the 2005 election campaign, when the government released details about Black Wednesday (1992) in order to embarrass the Conservatives. The Human Rights Act has also been widely criticised as ineffective.

POLICE POWERS AND CIVIL LIBERTIES SINCE 1979

Under successive Conservative governments (1979–1997), the powers of the police steadily increased. Two of the most significant pieces of legislation were:

- ➤ the Police and Criminal Evidence Act (PACE) 1984;
- ➤ the Criminal Justice and Public Order Act 1994; which banned many public demonstrations and placed tighter controls over raves. It also removed the absolute right to silence.

Although there has been some entrenchment of civil rights since 1997 such as the Freedom of Information Act and the Human Rights Act, police powers have increased in the following areas:

- it is now easier for the police to seize the assets of criminals;
- the police can issue on-the-spot fines for loutish behaviour;
- the police have greater stop and search powers;
- the police have gained greater powers to combat paedophilia;
- curfews and dispersal orders can be imposed;
- the police can now retain DNA records from both criminals *and* suspects.

Pressure groups such as Liberty and Human Rights Watch argue that the massive increase in police powers has undermined civil liberties. New technology such as CCTV has also restricted our right to privacy. There are around four million CCTV cameras in Britain, which represents a quarter of the world's cameras for just 1% of the world's population (*Times*, 16/1/06: 20). However, CCTV did help the police catch those responsible for the 7 July terrorist attacks in London.

TERRORISM

Perhaps the most revealing example of the government's somewhat cavalier approach to civil liberties is habeas corpus, the ancient right that no person shall be detained without some form of trial or jury. The government has tried repeatedly to suspend this fundamental civil right for cases involving terrorist suspects. For example, the Anti-

Terrorism, Crime and Security Act 2002 allows the authorities 'to detain indefinitely and without trial anyone suspected of terrorist activity'. Furthermore, a suspected terrorist can be prevented from using the internet, the phone, or even leaving their homes via a control order (*Economist*, 12/11/05: 32).

Doubts have been raised as to the effectiveness of recent anti-terrorism measures. Between 11 September 2001 and 5 March 2003, 304 arrests were made under anti-terrorist legislation, yet only three resulted in convictions (Norris 2005: 143). It has also been argued that the police have used such powers to discriminate against Muslims. Conversely, anti-terrorism measures failed to prevent the terrorist attacks on London in July 2005.

Whatever view one takes of such measures, the government's response to the 'war on terror' has at least been consistent. No less than four anti-terrorism bills have gone before Parliament in the past five years, and in each case the government has taken a 'tough' approach to the threat of terrorism despite, or even because of, criticism from civil rights groups. In one particularly memorable quote, the former Home Secretary David Blunkett dismissed opposition to the right to detain certain suspects without trial as 'airy-fairy' (Hitchens 2003: 2).

The government's recent plans to prevent terrorism have aroused deep controversy. In November 2005 the government was forced to back down from a proposal to detain terrorist suspects for 90 days. Under the Anti-Terrorism Bill, suspects can now be held for up to 28 days, and must go before a High Court judge every 7 days. Anyone found publishing, distributing or selling literature encouraging terrorism can be imprisoned for a maximum term of seven years. The Bill would also have made the glorification of terrorism an offence, with a maximum punishment of five years.

Critics of the Bill claimed that even Mr Blair's wife could have been guilty for saying that she 'well understood how young Palestinians became terrorists'. The law would also have criminalised anyone who justified the use of violence from the African National Congress (ANC) against the apartheid regime in South Africa. The controversial clause on the 'glorification of terrorism' was defeated in the House of Lords on 18 January 2006, but the Bill was passed on 30 March 2006.

The government has curtailed civil liberties in areas unrelated to terrorism. Examples include access to legal aid, the right to privacy and limits on freedom of expression. To take a recent example, spontaneous demonstrations are no longer allowed outside Parliament.

ACCOUNTABILITY AND CENTRALISATION

The Ancient Greek philosopher Aristotle is quoted as saying that 'politics is the art of compromise'. Allowing the police to fulfil their role within society, while being held accountable to the public, is a difficult compromise to achieve. It is important to ensure that the police are accountable to the public, particularly as their powers have increased enormously since 1979. There are four reasons to consider:

1 to uphold public confidence in the police;
2 to avoid the creation of a police state;
3 to prevent a miscarriage of justice;
4 to identify, and take action against, racist officers.

Accountability can be described as 'a duty to explain one's conduct and be open to criticism' (Heywood 2000: 117). In practice, the accountability of the police has two meanings:

47

1   Political accountability. This means that the police should be answerable to Parliament and the local community for their actions. Under the government's five-year plan (2004), local communities have the power to demand information from the police, and members of local police authorities may be elected rather than appointed (*Independent*, 10/11/04: 20). The Conservatives are equally keen to ensure police accountability, with David Cameron having outlined plans to replace police authorities with directly elected commissioners, and to enable Chief Constables to dismiss underperforming officers (*Times*, 16/1/06: 7).

2   Legal accountability. The police must act within the law when carrying out their duties. As such, a police officer is regarded as a 'citizen in uniform', and is therefore not above the law.

How are the police held to account?

➢   Via elected representatives, who can scrutinise the actions of the police by questioning Home Office ministers.
➢   Via reports and investigations into police activities (e.g. the 2004 Bichard Report into the Soham murders).
➢   Via meetings between the police and community representatives. This is particularly important for the black and Asian communities due to charges of 'institutionalised racism' within the police force.
➢   Via local police authorities.
➢   Via the Independent Police Complaints Commission.

The Independent Police Complaints Commission (IPCC)

The IPCC investigates all serious complaints against the police, and can carry out investigations into allegations of misconduct, as in the case of Jean Charles de Menezes, an unarmed Brazilian shot dead by police who thought he was a terrorist. To guarantee impartiality, the IPCC is independent from the police. Complaints made against the police often fail due to a lack of sufficient police cooperation, such as during the inquiry into the murder of the black teenager Stephen Lawrence. It has therefore been suggested that a police ombudsman would be more effective, and might enjoy greater public confidence, especially among black and Asian communities.

In a study of accountability, the intelligence services warrant a separate mention. All MI5 operations are secret, its budget is not subject to Parliamentary scrutiny and in theory it can target who it likes, when it likes. For example, in 2001 the secret services tapped the phone of Lord Ahmed, a Labour peer who opposed British involvement in Afghanistan. Yet few would deny that an intelligence service could not operate effectively without the highest degree of secrecy.

CENTRALISATION

Since 1979, Conservative and Labour governments have centralised the police force. The key pieces of legislation were the Police and Magistrates Act 1994 (under the Tories), and the Police Reform Act 2002 (under Labour). The whole justification for centralising the role of the police is to improve effectiveness.

Centralisation has had two effects, the most obvious of which has been to increase the powers of the Home Secretary. Through Home Office guidelines, performance targets and legislation steered through Parliament, John Reid exercises considerable influence over the police. The other consequence of centralisation is the alleged 'politicisation' of the police force. Traditionally, police officers were thought of as servants of the Crown, and therefore free from political influence. However, one could argue that the concentration of power into the hands of the Home Secretary has, to some extent, politicised the police.

The trend towards centralisation looks set to continue with the Serious and Organised Crime Agency (SOCA), dubbed 'the British FBI'. SOCA will tackle problems based partly on how often they are mentioned in the media. This could lead to the pursuit of an agenda dictated by public opinion, with potential electoral benefits for the government. SOCA has therefore been criticised by the Police Federation as a further 'politicisation' of the police (http://observer.guardian.co.uk/print/0,3858,5104374-102285,00.html).

PRISON POLICY

Prison policy is one of the most controversial issues of law and order. There are two schools of thought on the subject, and the debate reflects the distinction between a liberal and authoritarian approach to law and order. Most of those who argue for penal reform are liberals, while the opposing view is usually put forward by authoritarians.

Liberals believe that prisons are 'the universities of crime' because six out of every ten prisoners reoffend within two years (Jones *et al.* 2001: 555). Based on such evidence, prisons have been criticised as merely 'an expensive way of making bad people worse', with each prisoner costing the taxpayer £30,000 a year (Toynbee and Walker 2005: 222), money which could go to better use. The former Home Secretary Charles Clarke claimed that prisons have become a hot spot for radicalising young Muslims (*Times*, 14/9/05: 24), which does not help the government's battle against Islamic terrorism.

The counter argument states that 'prison works'. Criminals should be punished for committing an offence, and prison is the most appropriate means of taking away someone's rights and liberties. Prisons also protect the law-abiding public from criminal activity.

Prisons: the facts

When New Labour took office, the total prison population was 60,300. Today, the figure is approaching 78,000 (*Times*, 14/10/05: 13). We now have the largest prison population in our history, and the largest in western Europe (*Independent*, 3/11/04: 34). However, the trend has been upward since 1979. An increase in the prison population is one effect of the government's 'tough' stance on law and order. It has also been argued that there is a link between overcrowding and prison suicides (www.crimlinks.com/June162005.htm). An estimated 64% of UK prisons are overcrowded (Randall 2004: 183), with prison suicides standing at record levels.

How have the political parties addressed the issue of overcrowded prisons?

The government has tried to limit the ever-growing prison population via the early release scheme, and extending its community punishments programme. In contrast the Conservatives pledged to cancel the early release scheme, and provide 20,000 more prison places. On this controversial issue, politicians from both main parties appear to be following, rather than leading, public opinion. Only the Liberal Democrats offer a real alternative by proposing to give prisoners the vote, as a means of making politicians take notice of the problems faced in Britain's overcrowded prisons. However, in a recent test case, the European Court of Human Rights ruled that prisoners who committed a low-level offence should be allowed to vote (*Times*, 7/10/05: 16); thus the Liberal Democrat policy is not as radical as it first appears.

ID CARDS

The dominant issue of the present time is ID cards. The government claims that the introduction of ID cards will help reduce crime, prevent bogus asylum seekers and illegal immigrants staying in the country, and combat the threat of terrorism. The government's proposals to introduce ID cards during peacetime are unprecedented, but after the terrorist attacks of July 2005, the Prime Minister has argued that ID cards are a necessary tool in the 'war against terror'.

The Home Secretary's plans to introduce ID cards are backed by Sir Ian Blair (the Metropolitan Police Commissioner), most of the Cabinet, and according to a YouGov poll, 45% of the public (*Independent*, 4/7/05: 16). However the proposed cost is just under £100 per person, which may in time be perceived as yet another stealth tax, and could therefore damage public support for the scheme.

Although ID cards were first proposed by Michael Howard while he was Home Secretary, the Shadow Home Secretary David Davis dismissed the government's plans as 'illiberal and impractical, excessive and expensive, unnecessary and unworkable' (*Independent*, 29/6/05: 4). The Liberal Democrats also oppose the government, as do the pressure group NO2ID.

In March 2005 the ID Card Bill was defeated in the Lords, but plans resurfaced after the general election. On 28 June 2005 the Bill was passed by 31 votes, after Charles Clarke offered concessions to assuage Labour backbenchers. However, the Bill was once again defeated in the House of Lords on 16 January 2006, but later received royal assent on 30 March 2006.

According to the Home Office, the first to get ID cards

Table 2.1 The ID card arguments

Arguments in favour of ID cards.	*Arguments against ID cards.*
ID cards simply bring together all existing identification documents into one.	Without the protection of a written constitution, ID cards could be used to restrict individual liberty.
Those who have nothing to hide have no reason to object.	ID cards could be used to discriminate against ethnic minorities, which may heighten tensions between minorities and the authorities.
ID cards should help to reduce crime and the threat of terrorism.	What can ID cards do that any other ID document (i.e. passports) cannot?
ID cards should help to combat identity fraud, one of the fastest growing areas of criminal activity.	ID cards in Spain failed to prevent the Madrid bombs in March 2004. Even the US Congress rejected calls for their introduction after the terrorist attacks of 11 September 2001.
ID cards will help the authorities reduce the number of illegal immigrants and bogus asylum seekers entering the country.	Technological problems might increase the cost of ID cards, and make the scheme unworkable.

will be the country's 4.6 million foreign residents in 2006. A year later, British citizens renewing or applying for passports will have the chance to gain an ID card, and by 2013 it is estimated that around 80% will hold an ID card. At that time, the government of the day may make ID cards compulsory for all.

WHAT ARE THE MAIN ISSUES FACING THE HOME SECRETARY?

➢ The threat of terrorism. Since 11 September 2001, the UK government has brought in sweeping powers to deal with terrorism. For example, the Terrorism Act allows the Home Secretary to label any pressure group planning direct action as a terrorist organisation.

➢ The level of unreported and undetected crime is unacceptably high. Detection rates have fallen to such a degree that many people do not bother to contact the police. This may be because there is little point, such as to report the theft of a mobile phone, or they feel that the police and the criminal justice system would not handle the situation in an appropriate manner (e.g. victims of sexual abuse).

➢ The under-representation of ethnic minority police officers, and the disproportionately high number of black suspects and criminals, continue to place a question mark over racism in the police force.

➢ It can take seven minutes of form filling each time an officer stops someone (*Economist*, 23/4/05: 22). In their 2005 manifesto, the Conservative Party pledged to scrap the stop and account forms.

➢ Gun crime, youth crime and violent crime have all increased sharply since 1997, although the overall figure is down.

3

The Welfare State

Objectives from the syllabus

- Students should be able to define the welfare state, social rights, social security, individual responsibility and marketisation.
- Students should demonstrate a general knowledge of the scope and scale of welfare provision and of the changing emphasis of the welfare debate in the UK.
- Knowledge of party positions and developing public policy related to the benefits or social security system, the education system, the health service and housing provision.
- A general knowledge of the principles of the welfare state since the 1940s (but no detailed knowledge is required).
- Detailed knowledge of issues and policies since 1997, and a general knowledge of policies and issues since 1979.

Internet websites

www.socialexclusionunit.gov.uk/
www.dss.gov.uk
www.newdeal.gov.uk
www.cps.org.uk

www.ippr.org.uk
www.cpag.org.uk

Old exam questions

15 minutes

Why has the old age pension been a controversial political issue since 1980?   January 2006

Explain the measures adopted by governments since 1997 to support the family.   June 2005

In what ways has the social security system been used to reduce unemployment?   June 2004

Why has the issue of state pensions become more controversial in the UK since 1979?   January 2003

Why have successive governments been concerned about the dependency culture?   Spec

How have Labour governments attempted to deal with the problem of child poverty since 1997?   January 2002

How have the Labour governments attempted to eliminate the 'poverty trap' since 1997?   January 2004

45 minutes

To what extent has the Labour Party remained committed to the welfare state since 1992?   January 2005

In what ways, and with how much success, have governments sought to tackle the problem of poverty since 1990?
                                                          June 2002

'The welfare state has increasingly been subjected to "market forces" and privatisation since 1997.' Discuss.
                                                          January 2006

INTRODUCTION

The welfare state provides for its citizens a minimum level of social, and economic welfare. This is achieved via public services, and the tax and benefits system. There are five themes that run throughout the welfare state section of the course:

1 Centralisation.
2 Consensus.
3 Cost.
4 Marketisation.
5 The New Right's critique of the welfare state.

CENTRALISATION

Centralisation occurs when central government takes a greater role in the provision of welfare services, such as setting nationwide targets and standards and the creation of regulatory bodies (e.g. Ofsted). The trend since 1979 has been towards a centralisation of the welfare state under governments of both main parties.

CONSENSUS

A consensus is a broad agreement shared among two or more political parties about fundamental principles rather than precise details. While policy differences remain, there is a shared agreement across political parties on the basic issues.

COST

The welfare state is by far the largest source of government spending, and has grown significantly under governments of both parties. Today, the welfare budget stands at £147 billion (*Times*, 6/12/05: 10). Some of the policies we will consider, such as marketisation, should be understood as an attempt to limit, or reduce, the cost of the welfare state.

MARKETISATION

Marketisation can be defined as 'the use of market forces, and market principles, within the welfare state'. Critics have often described it as creeping 'privatisation'. Examples of marketisation include:

- ➢ state schools being taken over by private companies;
- ➢ the publication of league tables in health and education;
- ➢ the Private Finance Initiative (PFI);
- ➢ the use of private sector 'hit squads,' sent in to improve some of the worst-performing social work departments.

THE NEW RIGHT'S CRITIQUE OF THE WELFARE STATE

The New Right is a political ideology that came to prominence during the late 1970s. It consists of a range of thinkers such as Friedrich Hayek (1944) and Milton Friedman (1990), and politicians such as Mrs Thatcher and Keith Joseph. The New Right has also been described as neo-liberalism or Thatcherism.

The New Right criticised the welfare state for creating a dependency culture that traps people into poverty. The New Right argued that individuals and families should be encouraged to take responsibility for their own welfare, rather than relying on the state. This would enable people to work their way out of poverty and help to reduce the burden on the taxpayer.

The New Right had a profound impact on the Conservative governments of Mrs Thatcher and John Major, and many aspects of New Right ideology have been accepted by New Labour since 1997.

A BRIEF HISTORY OF THE WELFARE STATE

The state became involved in providing for the public's welfare needs due to market failure. The private sector simply could not (or would not) provide adequate standards of social security, health, housing and education for the majority of the population.

While the Liberal government of 1906–1911 introduced major innovations in terms of welfare policy, it was the Labour government of 1945–1951 that laid the foundations for the welfare state as we recognise it today. They built the welfare state on a universal basis, funded via taxation. No one could opt-out of providing for the welfare state, although a small private sector was allowed to flourish in health and education.

The distinction between universal and selective benefits

Universal benefits are provided on a comprehensive basis according to need, rather than the ability to pay (e.g. child benefit). In contrast, selective benefits are determined according to income and circumstance. Examples include the Working Tax Credit and the Child Tax Credit. It is worth noting that selective (or

---

means-tested) benefits cost more to administer than universal benefits. They also tend to be more bureaucratic and less popular than universal benefits. Some pressure groups, such as the National Pensioners Convention, have even described the means test as 'demeaning'. However, it is difficult to see how the government can afford to provide for the welfare needs of the population without some element of means testing.

The aim of the welfare state was to provide from 'the cradle to the grave', and the inspiration for it was the Liberal Peer Sir William Beveridge. In 1941 he set out a blueprint that aimed to banish the five evils of squalor, want, disease, ignorance and idleness.

Although the welfare state was the creation of the Left and inspired by a Liberal, Conservative governments of the post-war era did little to reduce the scope and scale of the welfare state. There was a broad agreement among all the main parties on the underlying principles of the welfare state until the emergence of the New Right in the late 1970s.

THE CHANGING SCOPE AND SCALE OF WELFARE PROVISION SINCE 1979

From the post-war consensus (1945–1979) that saw both Tory and Labour governments provide an ever-widening range of welfare services, to the New Right's critique of the dependency culture, the scope and scale of welfare provision has been at the centre of political debate.

There are two fundamental questions concerning the scope and scale of welfare provision:

1   How should the welfare state be funded?
2   How should the welfare state be delivered?

Consistent with the founding principles of the welfare state, the government provides welfare services free to all according to need. No one can opt out of the system, which is funded via taxation. Since 1979, all governments have attempted to reduce the role of the state via marketisation, and a greater use of selective benefit. There are three further trends worth identifying:

1   An increased role for the private sector.
2   A smaller role for local government.
3   The granting of new powers to the devolved assemblies (since 1997).

The private sector now plays an important role in the delivery of welfare services. Since 1979, governments of both main parties have 'marketised' the welfare state in order to limit the burden on the taxpayer. There is also a broad agreement among the leadership of the main parties that the private sector is more efficient than the public sector. However, trade unions are worried about the impact of 'privatisation' on jobs and the standard of public services; and many Labour MPs are uneasy at the direction of recent proposals over education.

Since 1979, many welfare services have been contracted out of the public sector (e.g. local National Health Service (NHS) trusts can now buy private healthcare treatment in order to reduce waiting lists). People have also been encouraged to use the private sector wherever possible, and charges have either been introduced or, in the case of prescription charges, increased.

The role of local government has declined significantly since 1979. Mrs Thatcher weakened the power of local councils because she perceived them to be bureaucractic and opposed to her market-based reforms. One could see this most clearly in the case of education, and in the sale of council homes. In addition, responsibilities formerly held by local authorities have been transferred to charities sponsored by the government since 1979, such as housing associations.

Since 1997, devolution to Scotland, Wales and Northern Ireland has fundamentally changed the provision of public services in the UK. The Scottish Parliament, the Welsh Assembly and the Northern Ireland Executive (when it is functioning) now administer their own domestic policies. The Scottish Parliament can also raise additional revenue via the so-called 'tartan tax', although it has yet to do so. Devolution has led to policy divergence to Westminster on a range of welfare issues. For instance, care for the elderly is free in Scotland and Wales, and tuition fees do not apply for Scottish students taking a course at a university in Scotland.

RIGHTS AND RESPONSIBILITIES

To complete our understanding of the scope and scale of welfare provision, we must consider the relationship between rights and responsibilities.

According to the basic principles of the welfare state, everyone has the right to claim universal benefits. In return, we have a responsibility to provide the resources needed to fund the welfare state. A good illustration of this point is national insurance contributions, which act as a form of state insurance. In this example, the state looks after the welfare of its people by providing a safety net for the unemployed.

From 1979 to 1997 the Conservatives aimed to 'roll back the frontiers of the state'. Both Thatcher and Major emphasised the importance of individual responsibility and increased the role of the private sector in providing for people's welfare needs.

Since 1997, the Labour government has attempted to redefine the relationship between rights and responsibilities. While the broad aim of the government's welfare policy has been to encourage individuals to take responsibility for their own lives, the government has taken a proactive role in trying to reduce child poverty and in addressing the dependency culture.

From 1945 to 1979, welfare services were mostly provided on a comprehensive basis, regardless of a person's level of income. Since 1979, reforms inspired by the New Right have transformed the welfare state. Many benefits are now selective and several bodies are involved in the delivery of public services. A person's right to claim welfare from the state has been curtailed in many areas, and we have been encouraged to provide for ourselves via private pension schemes, and private health care. Yet the most important role for central government – to raise the resources required to fund the welfare state – remains.

THE NEW RIGHT'S CRITIQUE OF THE WELFARE STATE

There are six elements to consider:

1 Benefits are too easy to obtain and too attractive to resist.
2 A handout is often seen as an entitlement.
3 Those out of work receive 'something for nothing'.
4 The welfare state undermines individual responsibility.
5 Welfare services are bureaucratic (e.g. the Children's Tax Credit consists of 56 questions and 47 pages of

advisory notes (Bartholomew 2004: 80), and often inefficient. For example, in July 2005, the Treasury revealed that 2 million families receiving Tax Credits had been overpaid (*Guardian*, 12/7/05: 27).

6 The main criticism from the New Right is that the welfare state creates a 'dependency culture' which forces families and individuals to become dependent on the state. State dependency creates a poverty trap, or poverty cycle, in which claimants have little or no incentive to return to work (McNaughton 2003: 68–72). Thus, far from eradicating want and idleness, the welfare state discourages people from finding a job and damages the economy by placing a high burden on the taxpayer. As Tony Blair once said, 'the welfare state is one which simply pays out benefits, trapping people into long-term or even lifelong dependency' (www.lgcnet.com/pages/news/article.asp? ArticleID=323930).

THE NEW RIGHT'S SOLUTION

The New Right argued that welfare benefits should be reduced and become more selective. This would encourage people to work their way out of poverty, perhaps by accepting low wages in order to get back into the job market. Once in employment, the chance to keep most of their money, rather than losing it in tax, would provide a further incentive. This would help reduce the burden on the taxpayer and limit public expenditure.

Tax cuts would inevitably lead to a rise in consumer spending. This would increase demand for jobs and therefore benefit those out of work. To achieve these objectives a flexible labour market would be essential.

THE CONSERVATIVES (1979–1997)

Heavily influenced by the ideas of the New Right, the Conservative governments of Mrs Thatcher (1979–1990) and John Major (1990–1997) reduced the real value of welfare benefits and subjected some benefits to the means test. For example:

- Family Allowance/Child Benefit was frozen in the mid-1980s;
- the level of Income Support was lowered;
- Unemployment Benefit was limited to the first 12 months, with the Job Seekers' Allowance (JSA) reducing the time scale further to just 6 months.

Throughout their time in office the Conservatives promoted and encouraged individual responsibility as an alternative to state dependency. Two cases are worth considering. One was the creation of the CSA in 1993. The CSA forces absent fathers to pay maintenance for their children, as the government believed that fathers should face up to their responsibilities. Another policy to consider was the introduction of the JSA. The JSA requires claimants to sign a contract stating that they were actively seeking work. If they failed to do so, benefits would be withdrawn. As a result of the changes, those out of work would no longer get something for nothing. The Tories also cut the rate of income tax and promoted a flexible labour market by weakening the power of the trade unions.

How did the Conservatives reform the welfare state?

The Conservatives transformed the welfare state in three ways. The most significant reform was to undermine the original principles of the welfare state. Many benefits shifted towards a selective basis, and radical changes were made to pensions, education, health and housing.

The second theme of the Tory programme was a policy of marketisation. The private sector was encouraged to provide its services through generous tax relief for private pensions, health care and education. The government also transferred the responsibility for providing sick pay from the state to the employer. Thirdly, the value of pensions, Child Benefit and Unemployment Benefit all declined in real terms.

Assessment of the Conservatives (1979–1997)

Despite a vigorous attempt to reduce the role of the state, the Conservatives made little impact on the proportion of public expenditure allocated to the welfare state. This was primarily due to a significant rise in unemployment. As the number of jobless increased, so too did the amount of resources required to fund Unemployment Benefit. Another issue that faced the Tories was an ageing population, which placed an added pressure on the welfare state.

Reforming the welfare state is a difficult task for any government. This is primarily due to the bureaucratic nature of public services. Change of any kind is often resisted, and reforms that are ultimately aimed at reducing the role of the state are highly difficult to implement. One must also consider the electoral popularity of the welfare state, which is down to three factors:

1 The votes of doctors, nurses, teachers etc.
2 Most people use, or are affected by, the welfare state at some stage of their lives. Many people therefore share a common interest in maintaining good public services.
3 Many recipients have a self-interest in the welfare state.

Having assessed the Conservatives, let us now consider the policies of the Labour government since 1997.

NEW LABOUR AND THE WELFARE STATE

The government's approach to the welfare state combines the pursuit of social justice with a desire to utilise market forces and the private sector to improve the delivery of public services. While the Labour Party is firmly committed to the welfare state, the leadership has placed less emphasis on traditional socialist objectives, such as equality and the redistribution of wealth, than previous Labour governments.

How has the government tried to ensure social justice?

In order to establish a more just society, the government has implemented a range of policies that fall into three categories:

1 Measures to combat social exclusion.
2 Attempts to address the poverty trap and the dependency culture.
3 Assistance to families.

Measures to combat social exclusion

Since 1997 the government has focused on the 'causes of crime' via policies to combat social exclusion. This is consistent with a liberal perspective on law and order, which takes the view that there *is* a link between crime and problems within society. There are four aspects to the government's approach to dealing with social exclusion:

1 The New Deal.
2 Welfare to Work.
3 Tackling child poverty.
4 A reduction in the level of unemployment (McNaughton 2003: 76). Under Labour, unemployment has dipped below 1 million for the first time since 1975.

Child poverty

When Labour came to power, Britain had the highest rate of child poverty in the EU. Since 1997, the government has increased the real value of benefits targeted at children by 72% (Toynbee and Walker 2005: 53–55). This has been achieved by raising the level of existing benefits and introducing new benefits such as the Child Tax Credit and the minimum wage. One might also include the Sure Start initiative designed to help disadvantaged children, of which there are now over 500 (*Fabian Review*, spring 2004: 6). The government's target is to halve child poverty by 2010 and eradicate it by 2020. Thus far, they have made some progress. Since 1997, the number of children living in poor households has fallen by 500,000 (ttp://news.bbc.co.uk/1/hi/business/ 4392889.stm).

Why has the government been committed to reducing child poverty?

The priority awarded to the issue of child poverty has been influenced by centre-Left think tanks such as the Institute for Public Policy Research, the Fabian Society and the New Policy Institute. Pressure groups such as the Child Poverty Action Group have also played a role, although one might also consider the relationship between Blair and Brown. The Prime Minister may, to some extent, be mindful of his legacy, while providing the resources to reduce child poverty has galvanised support for Gordon Brown within the Labour Party.

The poverty trap and the dependency culture

The government has addressed the poverty trap and the dependency culture by offering a 'hand up, not a handout'. Specific measures include:

> ➤ the introduction of a minimum wage that benefits 1.5 million people;
> ➤ a reduction in the lowest income tax band to 10%;
> ➤ the very poorest families no longer pay income tax;
> ➤ Welfare to Work.

What is Welfare to Work?

Welfare to Work is simply what it says: getting welfare claimants back to work via changes to the tax and benefit system. It is a broad approach that consists of measures to remove the poverty trap and restore the incentive to work. Since 1997, Gordon Brown has tried to move the notion of the welfare state towards a 'workfare state', where everyone who is able to work is encouraged to do so.

The Working Families' Tax Credit (WFTC) is a notable illustration of the Welfare to Work idea. The aim of the WFTC is to compensate families for the loss of benefits that occurs when a member or members of the family gain employment. It guarantees a set income above the minimum wage, and as a tax credit rather than a welfare payment it has encouraged a higher take-up rate. However, the flagship Welfare to Work policy remains the New Deal.

The New Deal

The New Deal was established in 1998 to help the long-term unemployed find work. It was funded out of a one-off windfall tax on the profits of the privatised utilities such as British Telecom and British Gas. Since then, the government has set up various New Deal schemes. Between 1998 and

2004, 490,000 young people, 260,000 lone parents, 178,000 over-25s, 35,000 disabled people and 110,000 older people returned to work under an assortment of New Deals. Unfortunately, not all jobs have lasted. Of those who gained a job through the New Deal for Young People and the New Deal 50+, 40% were claiming unemployment benefit within six months (Toynbee and Walker 2005: 61). Participation rates have also been disappointing, and the New Deal for Communities proved a flop due to claims of nepotism and waste.

What has the government done to assist families?

The government set up the National Childcare Strategy in order to ease the progress of parents going back to work. The Chancellor has also increased the level of benefits that target help towards families (e.g. maternity pay, Child Allowance and Income Support, which is now available for families in full-time employment). However, the flagship of the government's programme to assist families is Sure Start.

Sure Start

Sure Start is a scheme designed to deliver the best start in life for every child. As part of the scheme all 3- and 4-year-olds are now guaranteed a free early education place, and more than 1.2 million registered childcare places have been created since 1997, benefiting over 2 million children (www.surestart. gov.uk/aboutsurestart/about/thesurestartprogramme2/).

The aim of the Chancellor's pre-Budget report 2004 (the last one before the 2005 election) was to create a 'family-friendly welfare state'. In the report, Gordon Brown pledged:

- to lengthen paid maternity leave to nine months;
- to introduce the Child Trust Fund;
- to create 3,500 children's centres for the under-5s;
- to fund a scheme whereby all parents of 3- and 4-year-olds would have access to 15 hours of free childcare by 2010 (*Independent*, 14/4/05: 22). The Chancellor also gave schools extra resources to allow them to stay open until 6 p.m., principally to assist working parents.

Assessment of New Labour

It was widely assumed that a New Labour government would reverse the Tory reforms of the welfare state and provide additional resources. There has, however, been a considerable shift in policy and ideology from Old to New Labour. While resources have substantially increased, many of the Conservative policies influenced by the New Right have been accepted, and in some cases extended, since 1997.

In pursuit of its welfare objectives, the government has adopted a pragmatic, rather than ideological, approach. The government's stance could best be summarised as 'what counts is what works'. A good illustration is selective universality.

Selective universality

There is a clear distinction between universal and selective, or means-tested, benefits. Traditionally, Labour governments were committed to the former, with the New Right arguing in favour of the latter. Since 1997, the government has tried to gain the best of both via selective universality, which can be defined as 'a focus on those groups who are especially in need' (McNaughton 2003: 73).

The Chancellor considers universal benefits to be both expensive and ineffective. This is because they fail to target help where it is most needed (Fielding 2003: 185–186). In order to spend taxpayers' money more efficiently, Gordon Brown has channelled resources to those he feels are most in need (i.e. pensioners and children), and increased the amount of selective benefits. An estimated 38% of households now receive some form of means-tested benefit (Bartholomew 2004: 80).

The shift from Old to New Labour may, at first, appear obvious; yet it was a Labour government that first introduced prescription charges, just one year after the NHS was set up. Perhaps all governments inevitably choose pragmatism over ideology.

Equality

A further illustration of the government's pragmatic rather than ideological approach to the welfare state concerns the issue of equality. Soon after the 1997 general election, the Chancellor declared that the newly-elected government would promote 'equality of opportunity, not equality of outcome'; and in a *Newsnight* interview during the 2001 general election campaign, Tony Blair argued that 'inequality was not a bad thing'. Such comments reflect a fundamental shift in ideology within the Party's leadership.

Equality: the facts

Under the Conservatives, the number of people living below the poverty line grew from 5 million to 14 million. Thus by the time New Labour came to power, more than one in five of the population lived in poverty (Jones *et al.* 2001: 66). Since 1997 the

---

> government has redistributed wealth to some of the poorest members of society, yet the gap between rich and poor has actually widened (*Economist*, 3/4/04: 35). But as the then Department of Trade and Industry Secretary Stephen Byers said in 1999, New Labour is 'about wealth creation, not wealth distribution' (Grant 2005: 26).

Marketisation

Perhaps the most fundamental distinction between Old and New Labour consists of the role of the private sector in the provision of public services. Not only has the government accepted marketisation across all elements of the welfare state, it has actively encouraged it, as in the case of the Private Finance Initiative (PFI).[1]

> **The PFI**
>
> The PFI is an all-encompassing term that applies to cooperation between the public and private sectors over the delivery of welfare policy. The PFI has changed the scope and scale of welfare provision in several areas such as education and health. Examples range from private companies taking over failing schools, to the use of private hospitals to

---

[1] If Gordon Brown becomes leader of the Labour Party, the government might be less inclined to pursue a market-based agenda. In his speech to the 2004 Party Conference, the Chancellor made clear his dislike for marketisation, and praised the public sector ethos that underpins the welfare state (*Times*, 28/9/04: 1). It is certainly the hope of many in the Party that Gordon Brown would provide a more left-wing approach to government policy. However, the Chancellor has been instrumental in the New Labour project from the very beginning and may be disinclined to pursue those left-wing policies that many of his supporters hope for.

treat NHS patients (Ludlam and Smith 2004: 224). The PFI is a continuation of the Conservatives' Public Private Partnership, and can be seen as an example of both marketisation *and* the extent to which a cross-party consensus exists over welfare policy.

Why does the government support the PFI?

Among the leadership of the Party, there is a belief that the private sector is more efficient than the public sector. A more cynical interpretation might be that the PFI removes the need for the government to borrow money, and therefore helps Gordon Brown maintain his golden rule on borrowing ('no public borrowing other than for investment measured over the economic cycle').

The PFI faces considerable opposition from the Left of the Labour Party, who claim that it will result in higher taxes and worse public services. Trade unions have also voiced concern over job losses, and that PFI hospitals could be asset-stripped. Pressure groups such as the Royal College of Surgeons are concerned that the profit motive is incompatible with patient care, and have criticised the scheme as little more than 'a gravy train' for consultants and external advisers.

TO WHAT EXTENT DOES A CONSENSUS EXIST?

During the 1980s and early 1990s, Conservative reforms to the welfare state were strongly opposed by the Labour Party. Since the emergence of New Labour in the mid-90s, a cross-party consensus has emerged over a shift away from universal benefits and a commitment to the marketisation of the welfare state.

It would be easy to overstate the extent to which a consensus exists between New Labour and the Conservatives. Policy differences between the two main parties clearly remain. One only has to consider the difference in *attitude* towards the welfare state between the Conservatives and the Labour Party.

While they were in office (1979–1997), the Conservatives used the 'stick' approach, in which the real value of benefits was reduced and a more flexible labour market was encouraged, in an attempt to get people back to work. As the then Employment Secretary Norman Tebbit once remarked, people should 'get on their bikes and look for work'. In contrast, New Labour have combined the stick with the carrot. For example, in January 2006, the Secretary of State for Work and Pensions, John Hutton, announced increased support for claimants of incapacity benefit who wish to return to work, and tougher penalties for those who do not. Their benefit will be cut by up to £10.93 a week if they fail to attend a job interview. If they refuse a second time, their benefit will be cut by £20.86 a week (*Times*, 17/1/06: 4).

Party policies at the 2005 general election

In the 2005 general election the government's aim to create a 'family-friendly welfare state' formed the backbone of the Labour Party's manifesto. In contrast the Tories promised more choice and more resources. Their specific pledges were:

➢ to extend the right to choose in health and education;
➢ to scrap various New Deal programmes;
➢ to devote less resources to public expenditure than Labour;

75

➤   to spend more on the NHS and education than the present government.

The Liberal Democrats promised to scrap the Child Trust Fund and redirect the money towards reducing class sizes, and also to scrap fees for higher education. Unlike the two main parties, the Liberal Democrats remain critical of the involvement of the private sector within the welfare state. Their policy is to raise funds for the welfare state via an increase in the top rate of income tax.

PENSION POLICY

The biggest challenge facing the welfare state today is to meet the demands of an ageing population. As people live longer, the pressure on the welfare state grows in terms of health care, services for the elderly and of course the state pension.

The state pension provides a basic minimum income for all pensioners, regardless of the savings they might have accumulated while in work. From 1945 to 1979 successive governments steadily increased the value of pensions. The high point of state provision occurred in 1975, when the Labour government introduced the State Earnings Related Pension Scheme (SERPS), which added an earnings-related element to the system. SERPS was thought to be too expensive, and the New Right were highly critical of such generosity.

Pension policy under the Conservatives (1979–1997)

In 1980 the Thatcher government changed the basis of the state pension. Since then the state pension has been linked to prices rather than earnings. Thus in real terms the value

76

of a state pension has been cut substantially, because earnings rise faster than inflation.

A second major change occurred in 1986, when the Conservative government made it easier for people to opt out of SERPS. The eligibility criteria for benefits claimed mainly by older people was also tightened, such as the notoriously complex Cold Winter Payments. Despite a desire to reduce the scope and scale of the government's role, the Tories were reluctant to dismantle the state pension, due partly to its electoral popularity.

Government policy since 1997

Gordon Brown retained the link between pensions and prices, which proved a political mistake in 2000 when the state pension rose by a mere 75p per week. This somewhat embarrassing blunder should not detract from a substantial increase in the level of state assistance provided to pensioners since 1997. The main measures have been:

> an above-inflation increase in the state pension;
> the introduction of a Christmas bonus;
> a free TV licence and a free passport for the over-75s;
> free bus travel for the over-60s;
> an increase in the Winter Fuel payments to those over the age of 70;
> the introduction of the Pension Credit in 2003;
> state assistance to help pensioners with their heating bills.

As with many aspects of welfare policy, New Labour's approach reflects much continuity with the Conservatives. To take one example, the present government has introduced stakeholder pensions. The scheme is run by companies but

77

sponsored by the state, and allows individuals to make their own tax-free provisions. In the long-term, it is hoped the policy will ease the burden on the taxpayer. However, the state continues to regulate the private sector, and is the provider of last resort for those who cannot afford a private scheme.

The 'grey vote' and the 2005 general election

Pressure groups such as Age Concern and the National Pensioners Convention lobby the main parties in order to protect their members' interests. They are demanding that the state pension be raised to one-third of average earnings, and have highlighted the unfairness of the Council Tax. Centre-left think tanks such as the Institute for Public Policy Research have also called for an increase in the basic state pension.

Council Tax

In recent years the level of Council Tax has become a highly controversial issue. Because pensioners live on a fixed income, many have found it difficult to meet their payments. Perhaps mindful of the electoral impact of the issue, the government placed a limit on Council Tax bills during the run-up to the 2005 general election, and pledged £1,000 extra for those over the age of 70.

The opposition parties have been equally keen to court the pensioner vote. The flagship of the Tory programme is the lifetime savings account, in which money deposited by individuals would be matched by a top-up from the state.

The former Shadow Work and Pensions Secretary David Willetts claimed in the election campaign that the extra resources could be paid for by cancelling several New Deal programmes.

In their 2005 manifesto, the Conservative Party also pledged to:

➤ cut council tax for pensioners by £500;
➤ halt the re-evaluation of Council Tax;
➤ increase the basic state pension in line with earnings;
➤ cap long-term care costs;
➤ provide more incentives for people to save.

The Liberal Democrats pledged to:

➤ restore the link between pensions and earnings;
➤ increase pensions for the over-75s by £100 a month;
➤ scrap Council Tax;
➤ introduce free personal care for the elderly.

Both opposition parties point out that Britain faces a pensions crisis. There are five main causes for this:

1 An ageing population.
2 The incentives for people to save have declined since 1997.
3 The Chancellor has removed the tax perks of many private pension funds.
4 Many pension funds invest on the stock market, which has performed below expectations, in recent years.
5 The government simply does not invest enough resources into the state pension.

Pensions: the government's record

Despite efforts made by the government to reduce poverty among pensioners, its record is hardly impressive. In 2004 the number of pensioners living below the official poverty line was 2.2 million, exactly the same as the figure when Labour took office in 1997 (www.natpencon.org.uk/). Private pension funds have also lost their tax perks under Labour, with the result that private pensions have become relatively more expensive and many firms have failed to introduce stakeholder pensions (Ludlam and Smith 2004: 155). The government also backed down from a confrontation with the public sector unions over pension reform in October 2005, and has been criticised for doing 'too little' in response to the Turner Report (2005).

The Turner Report

According to the Turner Report (2005), Britain faces an 'unpalatable choice' between:

- ➢ saving more, including a compulsory second pension;
- ➢ paying significantly higher taxes;
- ➢ staying in work for longer.

The Report outlined three main proposals. The first option, indexing pensions to earnings, is backed by the Liberal Democrats and the Conservatives. The section option consists of linking pension credits to earnings beyond 2008. Turner also recommended an increase in the retirement age, and making the state pension universal at the age of 75 (*Times*, 1/12/05: 6). We have yet to see how the government will respond, but the Chancellor is not thought to be keen on the Turner Report because of its implications for public expenditure.

4

Education

Internet websites

www.dfee.gov.uk
www.teachers.org.uk
www.nasuwt.org.uk
www.aut.org.uk

Old exam questions

15 minutes

Why has higher education funding become so controversial since 2001?   June 2005

In what ways has control over education been taken out of the hands of local authorities since 1988?   June 2002

How has the measurement of performance been used to attempt to improve educational standards since 1988?
                                                                    January 2005

What have been the main effects of the introduction of the National Curriculum and league tables for schools?
                                                                    January 2002

What are the main controversies that have emerged concerning secondary-school examinations since 1997?
                                                                    January 2004

45 minutes

How have governments sought to improve the performance of the teaching profession since 1979?　　June 2003

Analyse the main ways in which governments have sought to raise educational standards in Britain since 1979.

January 2003

COMPREHENSIVE AND SELECTIVE EDUCATION

The 1944 Education Act, supported by all three main parties at the time, entitled children to free education up to the age of 15. Pupils were selected on the basis of the 11 Plus examination, which sent children to three types of school:

1　grammar schools for the academically able;
2　technical schools for a small number taught in manual skills;
3　secondary modern schools for the majority.

During the 1960s concerns were voiced about the socially divisive nature of selective education. Those who attended grammar schools were usually the children of middle-class parents, while most working-class children went to secondary modern schools. It was also argued that the age of 11 was too young to assess a child's academic ability. Influenced by such thinking, the Labour government replaced most grammar schools and secondary moderns with comprehensive schools.

There are five main characteristics of comprehensive schools:

1　No selection.
2　Mixed-ability classes aimed at 'pulling up' the weaker students.

3   Schools provide equality of opportunity.
4   Schools cater for all abilities.
5   Schools offer a wide range of educational experience
    (McNaughton 2003: 56–57).

Comprehensive education was more popular than education based on selection because the majority of schoolchildren gained a better education, and it was thought to be less socially divisive. While some middle-class parents feared a levelling-down of academic standards, the changes gained a broad level of support among the main parties, and the policy of 'comprehensivisation' continued well into the 1970s from governments of both parties. Independent schools, however, remained unchanged by the move towards comprehensive schools.

THE 1988 EDUCATION ACT

The election of Mrs Thatcher in 1979 brought an end to the post-war consensus. After radical changes to pensions, housing and social security, Mrs Thatcher turned her attention to education shortly after the 1987 general election. While rejecting calls for the reintroduction of grammar schools, she was firmly committed to improving the level of choice available to parents.

In 1988, the Education Secretary Kenneth Clarke introduced legislation that radically changed education policy along Thatcherite lines. There were four aims behind the 1988 Education Act:

1   To improve the choice of schools available to parents.
2   To impose nationwide standards via the National Curriculum (NC). Prior to 1988, teachers had largely decided what was taught in schools.

3   To identify the performance of schools through the use of league tables.
4   The introduction of grant-maintained schools (GMS), which allowed schools to opt-out of local authority control, provided a sufficient number of parents were in agreement. GMS would be funded directly by central government, with the heads and governors managing their own budgets. It is important to note that opting out undermines the universal principle of the welfare state.

The impact of the 1988 Education Act remains controversial to this day, although one cannot deny that it has set the agenda of education reform ever since. There are several elements to consider:

➤   on the positive side, a combination of variety, choice and competition within education has pushed up academic results since the 1980s;
➤   changes since the 1988 Education Act have increased the level of stress on teachers and students alike. British schoolchildren now face a higher number of tests than their European counterparts;
➤   the morale of the profession has deteriorated since 1988 due to an increased workload, greater bureaucracy and a decline in marginal subjects; and with most of the timetable devoted to meeting government targets in maths and English, there is inevitably less time for teachers to stimulate a child's creativity;
➤   the influence of local authorities has declined, participation from parent governors has increased, and there is more variety in the non-comprehensive sector.

LEAGUE TABLES

The most far-reaching element of the 1988 Education Act was league tables, which introduced an element of competition between schools. As schools are increasingly judged by their results, one negative effect of league tables has been the manipulation of exam results. Many schools set 'easier' vocational courses to improve their standing in the league tables, and some of the top-performing schools have even expelled pupils who fail to get the highest GCSE grades (*Sunday Times*, 5/9/04: 9). Critics also claim that exams have become easier, and that schools concentrate on exam results at the expense of an all-round education.

The intention of league tables was to encourage parental choice, yet this has not always been the case in practice. As a result of league tables, good schools are heavily over-subscribed, while schools in more disadvantaged areas have gone into decline. Dianne Abbott's controversial decision to send her child to the City of London School in 2003 once again highlighted the problems faced by parents living in disadvantaged areas. When asked to justify her decision, she said, 'in Hackney schools, only nine per cent of black boys get five decent GCSEs ... I really wasn't prepared to put my son through that system' (Bartholomew 2004: 184).

NEW LABOUR SINCE 1997

Before coming to power, Tony Blair announced that his government would pursue three priorities: 'education, education and education'. New Labour's 1997 manifesto contained the following words: 'Education will be our number one priority, and we will increase the share of national income spent on education as we decrease it on bills of economic and social failure'. Education was seen as the key to eliminating social problems, such as the link between truancy and youth crime, and improving the UK's economic performance. Education policy was therefore placed at the heart of the government's aim to create a more just society.

Since 1997, New Labour have attempted to transform public services from a monolithic one-size-fits-all system to one tailored to the needs of its consumers, modelled on the private sector. Nowhere has this process been more apparent than education. Increasingly, parents are seen as customers, with schools competing with each other in order to offer the most attractive package. Coupled with a significant increase in resources since 1997, the education system is undergoing a period of rapid change which may in time be seen as more far-reaching than those instigated by the Conservatives during the 1980s and 1990s.

As with all areas of welfare policy, the New Labour government has pursued much of what the Conservatives had done before, combined with an element of social justice. The third element of the government's strategy has been an attempt to improve standards.

Continuity with the Conservatives

The government has retained the principle of opting-out and strengthened the main elements of the 1988 Education Act, such as the NC and Ofsted. The government has also accepted a limited degree of selection and retained league tables. However the Left of the party remains opposed to league tables, as they tend to favour wealthy parents able to afford homes closer to the best schools.[1]

---

[1] A house within the catchment area of a good primary school can cost as much as a third more than a similar home in the next street (Bartholomew 2004: 184).

Measures to ensure social justice

> ➢ Three weeks after coming to office, Labour transferred resources from the Assisted Places Scheme in order to reduce infant class sizes.
> ➢ An increase in school provision for the under 5s, such as free early education for all 4-year-olds.
> ➢ Creating Connexions in 2000 to assist young people back into education (or work).
> ➢ Implementing programmes to ensure lifelong learning.
> ➢ Providing an Education Maintenance Allowance for the poorest students.
> ➢ Setting up the Aim Higher Excellence Challenge programme in 2001.

Measures to improve standards

Since 1997, the Labour government has:

> ➢ Set targets for literacy and numeracy and ensured regular assessment of both pupils and teachers.
> ➢ Encouraged specialisation within comprehensive schools.
> ➢ Introduced a degree of performance-related pay in the year 2000. However, a direct link between pay and performance is opposed by teaching unions; thus the government is unlikely to proceed further on this issue.
> ➢ Created the Excellence in Cities scheme, and the General Teaching Council.
> ➢ Rewarded successful schools with additional resources, Beacon status, and greater independence from local education authorities.
> ➢ Took tough measures against failing schools. Within days of taking office, the then Education Secretary

David Blunkett 'named and shamed' a range of failing schools and appointed the confrontational Chris Woodhead as Chief Inspector of Schools. In a more recent example, those schools that have 'serious weaknesses' have to make progress or risk the prospect of facing 'special measures' from Ofsted.

All these measures have been backed up with extra cash. Since 1997 the government had increased resources by 41% in real terms (*Economist*, 19/2/05: 31) and encouraged more graduates into the profession by offering £6,000 a year tax-free for trainee teachers. Golden Hellos are also available in less popular subjects, and some of the top graduates can qualify for a free laptop.

ASSESSMENT OF NEW LABOUR

The Labour government can claim a number of achievements with regard to education:

➢ record levels of literacy and numeracy in schools;
➢ best-ever primary-school results;
➢ over 28,000 more teachers in English schools since 1997;
➢ better pay for teachers;
➢ Ofsted has recorded an improvement in the standard of teaching since 1997 (*Telegraph*, 25/10/05: 2);
➢ 5-, 6- and 7-year-olds are now taught in class sizes of 30 or less (www.labour.org.uk/top50achievements);
➢ the number of teachers is at its highest for more than 20 years (www.labour.org.uk/maps/february_2005. php?detail=1andctid=2254); and the number of teaching assistants has risen by over 100,000 since 1997 (*Teaching Today*, February 2005: 16);

➢ 50% of secondary-school children achieve five or more good GCSEs (Toynbee and Walker 2005: 125);

➢ there is now a record number of students in higher education (www.labour.org.uk/top50achievements).

However, there are several problems facing education in Britain today:

➢ a quarter of all primary schoolchildren leave without the ability to read (*Times*, 5/12/04: 19), and almost half of all primary-school children lack the three Rs (*Times*, 10/10/05: 2);

➢ truancy has increased by more than a third since 1997, despite almost £1 billion in government spending to tackle the problem (*Times*, 22/9/05: 1, 7). It is estimated that more than a million pupils played truant during 2003/4 (*Independent*, 7/4/05: 1);

➢ a report commissioned by the National Audit Office found that more than a quarter of primary schools and a fifth of secondary schools lack a permanent head, and nearly a million children are taught in poorly performing schools (*Times*, 11/1/06: 6);

➢ the UK's relatively low level of participation in post-16 education, and high drop-out rate;

➢ high turnover of newly-qualified teachers. Fewer than half are still in the classroom five years later (Toynbee and Walker 2005: 108);

➢ discipline and recruitment remain a problem, particularly in struggling inner-city areas;

➢ in 2005, concerns were raised over the poor nutritional value of school meals after a high-profile campaign led by the TV chef Jamie Oliver;

➢ perhaps the most significant problem facing the

Education Secretary Alan Johnson is the controversy over the academic rigour of exam. In higher education, 90% of academics believe that A-Levels have become less demanding (*Economist*, 21/8/04: 27), partly because pass rates have risen every year since 1982 (*Sunday Times*, 14/8/05: 1). As for examinations taken in secondary schools, doubts were raised in the Tomlinson Report (2004) over GCSEs, AS-Levels, the use of coursework and the effectiveness of Standard Attainment Tasks (SATs) Key Stages 3 and 4. Tomlinson also recommended the replacement of A-Levels with the baccalaureate, but despite these concerns, significant reform of the exam system is not on the government's agenda (www.bbc.co.uk/nol/shared/spl/hi/education/02/tomlinson_report/html/full_report.stm).

PARTY POLICIES DURING THE 2005 GENERAL ELECTION

Both main parties want to widen choice and improve standards, but the means to achieve these goals differ. Starting with Labour, the government has pledged:

- ➤ to allow primary and secondary schools to gain foundation status. Schools that secure foundation status gain greater freedom over their budgets, assets, recruitment, admissions and syllabus content;
- ➤ schools will be expected to develop one or more specialities and can select by aptitude;
- ➤ the City Academy idea will be extended, and in a move designed to appeal to the voters of Middle England, the government will encourage schools to return to traditional characteristics such as a uniform,

houses and sports days (*Talking Politics*, September 2004: 4–5);

➤ in the 2005 Queen's Speech, the government outlined plans to give parents the right to instigate school inspections and to check their child's progress on a day-to-day basis (*Independent*, 18/5/05: 9);

➤ in a government White Paper commissioned on 24 October 2005, Tony Blair pledged to provide parents with the ability to change the curriculum, replace failing heads and start new schools. Every secondary school would expect to become an independent self-governing academy within five years, popular schools will be allowed to take over failing schools and local councils will be stripped of their responsibility for schools (*Telegraph*, 25/10/05: 1).

In their 2005 manifesto, the Conservative Party pledged:

➤ to enable all schools to become independent of state control;

➤ to create 600,000 more school places;

➤ to abolish targets, the surplus places rule and the regulatory body Office for Fair Access (OFFA);

➤ to remove a parent's right of appeal against expulsion of their child;

➤ to create turnaround schools for persistently disruptive pupils;

➤ to provide all parents with a voucher that could be spent on a state or independent school, in the hope that independent schools would then emerge to meet parental demand.[2]

---

[2] However, parents would not be allowed to top up the voucher, which may mean few private schools taking up the idea. The Independent Schools Council also made it clear that none of its secondary schools would take pupils under the voucher scheme (*Independent*, 15/4/05: 4).

The Liberal Democrats are opposed to targets and league tables, and argue that expenditure should be concentrated on achieving excellence for all schools, so that parental choice becomes an irrelevance (*Talking Politics*, September 2004: 4). They would also cut primary class sizes to 20 (funded by scrapping the Child Trust Fund) and employ more teachers.

The two main parties agree on most issues relating to education, such as raising school standards, greater independence for popular schools and widening parental choice. While policy differences clearly exist, they remain marginal to a broad consensus over education. For example, the government's City Academy idea borrows heavily from the City Technology Colleges introduced by the Conservatives during the 1980s, and even Labour's policy on foundation schools could be described as merely an updated version of grant-maintained schools.

HIGHER EDUCATION

University education was made freely available to students under the 1944 Education Act. Between 1945 and 1979 there was a major expansion of higher education, with the number of universities increasing from 17 to 45 (Cootes 1984: 129). The Open University was also established in order to assist mature students, and less well-off families were provided with government grants. Under the Conservatives higher education suffered in terms of status and funding, yet the number of students gaining a place at university soared from one in eight of young people to almost one in three by the time New Labour came to power (www.conservativemanifesto.com/1997/1997-conservative-manifesto.shtml).

The massive rise in student numbers, combined with years

of underfunding, led the newly-elected Labour government to introduce tuition fees in 1997. Tuition fees broke a basic principle of the welfare state – that public services should be granted free to all. However, that principle had already been undermined by the introduction of student loans under the Conservatives. Tuition fees currently exist throughout England and Wales, but not in Scotland.

The government has continued the marketisation of higher education by encouraging universities to compete against each other to bid for public money. Funding for departments and courses is now determined primarily by research. Colleges of further education have also been forced to compete for funds by expanding more popular courses and scrapping less popular ones.

Top-up fees

The most controversial education policy since Labour came to power has undoubtedly been top-up fees. After a pledge not to introduce top-up fees in their 2001 manifesto, the government performed a u-turn in January 2004.

Labour's target is to get 50% of young people to progress to higher education by 2010, and it is difficult to see how the government could achieve this without some charges for higher education. There is undoubtedly some scope to increase students' contribution towards their own education because graduates earn a great deal more than a person without a university degree (*Times*, 14/9/05: 24). However, critics state that the 50% target will contribute to a 'graduate glut' on the labour market (www.timesonline.co.uk/article/0,,2-1055289,00.html), and many Labour MPs fear the creation of a 'two-tier education system'. Some universities have also criticised the government for their misguided attempt at 'social engineering' (http://news.bbc.co.uk/1/hi/education/3742142.stm).

The government has also tried to broaden access to higher education for less well-off students. One method by which this has been achieved is the creation of the OFFA, a regulatory body designed to ensure fair access for under-represented groups. Universities can also gain extra funding if they admit students from postcode areas with low participation rates. The policy appears to have worked, with the number of students from poor backgrounds entering Britain's top universities having risen by nearly 50% since 1997 (*Independent*, 11/11/04: 15).

The opposition parties offer various alternatives. In the 2005 general election the Tories pledged to scrap tuition fees and targets. Students would be expected to pay back commercial rates of interest on their loans and universities would be funded according to the number of students they attract. However, since the election the Party has dropped its policy. In contrast, the Liberal Democrats promised to scrap all fees and planned to raise the necessary resources through progressive taxation.

THE CENTRALISATION OF STATE EDUCATION

The last issue we will consider is the centralisation of education. Since 1979, the powers of central government have greatly expanded. The powers of local schools have also increased, particularly as a result of the 1988 Education Act, while the main losers have been local authorities. The decline in the power of local government has been due to the following measures:

> ➤ grant-maintained schools, which are directly funded by the government;
> ➤ the creation of Ofsted, which replaced the role of local authority inspection teams;

96

> ministers can now send in improvement teams to local education authorities, close down failing schools and reopen them under the Fresh Start programme;
> building and resource grants are provided directly to schools, thus bypassing local authorities;
> failing councils have been ordered to surrender control of schools to private companies.[3]

Despite these significant changes, education still accounts for almost 40% of council spending (*Economist*, 24/9/05: 41).

---

[3] The influence of local authorities will be reduced even further if the government implements its proposal to take the top 500 state schools out of local authority control (www.timesonline.co.uk/article/0,,2-1158456,00.html).

5

Health

Internet websites

www.doh.gov.uk/dhhome.htm
www.doctorsforreform.com
www.timesonline.co.uk/health

Old exam questions

15 minutes

How and why has the private sector become increasingly involved in public healthcare?   June 2005

How far has the Blair government advanced 'privatisation' within the NHS?   June 2004

45 minutes

'Governments since 1979 have consistently failed to solve the problem of health care provision.' Discuss.
                                                      January 2002

Distinguish between the healthcare policies of the Conservative and Labour parties since the 1980s.   June 2003

How, and with what success, have governments attempted to improve the provision of healthcare in the UK since 1992?
                                                      January 2004

HISTORY OF HEALTH POLICY

The NHS was created in 1948 on the basis of providing healthcare free at the point of use, according to need, regardless of the ability to pay. Funded out of taxation, the NHS was as clear a demonstration of the basic principles of the welfare state as one could wish to see. Once dismissed by Michael Howard as 'Stalinist' (*Daily Mirror*, 4/2/05: 7), no element of the welfare state is as centralised as the NHS.

In 1949, the Labour government was divided over the issue of prescription charges for medicine. The policy was duly implemented, and despite a brief period in the 1960s, prescription charges have remained ever since. This partial use of marketisation was the first breach of the principles of the welfare state, predating the New Right by 30 years.

The main justification for prescription charges was to reduce the cost of the NHS, which currently stands at £90 billion per annum (*Times*, 6/12/05: 10). The NHS is highly expensive because new treatments are always becoming available, and Britain has an ageing population. Both these factors combine to place ever-increasing pressure on the cost of health provision in the UK. In addition, the NHS employs almost 1.3 million people (*Daily Express*, 3/8/05: 7), which makes it the world's third largest employer (Briscoe 2005: xvi). Successive governments have tried to ensure value for money by rationing healthcare, while increasing the level of government spending on such an electorally popular service, even under the tax-cutting governments of Mrs Thatcher and John Major.

WHY REFORM THE NHS?

When anything is 'free' at the point of use, supply cannot possibly meet demand, particularly during the winter months when the pressure on the NHS is at its greatest. This problem was acknowledged by the Health Minister who created the NHS, Aneurin Bevan, when he said that 'expectations will always exceed capacity' (Stadlen and Glass 2004: 64). The dilemma faced by *all* governments is therefore a difficult one: 'How do you achieve efficiency in the NHS when the service is not subject to normal market forces?'

The Secretary of State for Health, Patricia Hewitt, has to deal with a number of powerful organisations such as the British Medical Association (BMA) that wish to protect their members' interests and pressure groups such as Patient Concern that highlight issues ranging from waste to waiting lists. With over a million people receiving treatment of some kind each day (Toynbee and Walker 2005: 42), added to the public's reluctance to pay significantly higher taxation, healthcare resources ultimately have to be rationed. Traditionally, this was achieved via waiting lists and prescription charges. However, since 1979, governments of both main parties have 'marketised' the NHS.

There are several cases of marketisation within the NHS. Private healthcare firms can now take over underperforming general practitioners' (GPs') surgeries, and the private sector is regularly used for treatment where there is spare capacity. Even charges for dental care and eye tests could be described as 'privatisation by stealth', but the most significant example of marketisation is the PFI (see Chapter 3).

Marketisation in the NHS is nothing new, and nor is reform. Large-scale reorganisation of the NHS was first attempted in 1974 and ultimately led to a rise in administrative costs. It is therefore important to note that contemporary issues have their roots in the policies of previous governments, and it is against this background that one can assess the record of both Tory and Labour governments since 1979.

THE CONSERVATIVE GOVERNMENTS (1979–1997)

The New Right argued that the NHS was bureaucratic, inefficient and inflexible. The solution was simple: increase patient choice and introduce market forces into the NHS. This would result in efficiency gains due to greater competition, and less bureaucracy. Such thinking heavily influenced the Conservatives during the 1980s and 1990s.

The twin objectives of the Tory government's approach to the NHS from 1979 to 1997 were to widen choice, and increase the role of the private sector in providing for the nation's health. Mrs Thatcher introduced limited reforms along the lines of marketisation, such as compulsive competitive tendering (which was later scrapped by Labour in 1997), and charges for eye tests and dental checks. Thatcher also tried to reform the NHS (the Griffiths Report 1983), but that only added to administrative costs.

It is highly probable that Mrs Thatcher would have gone much further down the road of 'privatising' the NHS if it was not for the political unpopularity of such a move. It was not until her successor came to power that the Conservatives took the radical step of introducing an internal market.

The internal market

In 1991 the Major government split the NHS into purchasers (health authorities, GP fundholders) and providers (NHS trusts, non-fundholding GPs) along the lines of those who demand and those who supply healthcare. The internal market also established self-governing hospital trusts and fundholding general practices; thus decentralising power away from Whitehall.

The Labour opposition argued that opting out would inevitably lead to a 'two-tier NHS', and was the first step towards NHS trusts becoming private hospitals. The

Conservative government argued that an internal market would result in 'money following patients', and hence lead to greater efficiency because hospitals would have an incentive to attract patients. In practice, improvements in the level of choice for patients did not materialise, as patients followed the money.

NEW LABOUR SINCE 1997

On the eve of the 1997 general election, Tony Blair warned voters that they had 'only 24 hours to save the NHS'. While in office, the Labour government has been committed to four principles:

1   Maintaining the basic principle of healthcare free at the point of use, and according to need.
2   Funding the NHS through general taxation, with only limited charges for some services. This objective was made clear in the Wanless Report (2002), which rejected any alternative to the present system (www.hm-treasury.gov.uk/consultations_and_legislation/wanless/consult_wanless_final.cfm).
3   A massive increase in resources. Since 1997, cash spent on the NHS has doubled (Toynbee and Walker 2005: 12).
4   Labour have not only accepted marketisation, but taken this idea further than the Tories did with 'payment by results' and the PFI.

Payment by results

'Payment by results' was introduced for NHS foundation trusts in 2004. Under the scheme hospitals charge a fixed price for an operation and claim the money back according to the number of patients treated. Efficient well-managed hospitals would therefore expect to make a profit from the system, whereas inefficient hospitals risk facing a tariff (*Times*, 11/10/05: 1).

Under any market-based policy, there will always be winners and losers, and in practice 'payment by results' has not worked in the way the government would have liked. As with the internal market of the early 1990s, 'marketisation' has not always met the aims behind it.

The PFI

Unlike payment by results, the PFI has aroused deep controversy. The government claims that the PFI is an effective way of building new hospitals. They point out that nearly all the 68 new hospitals being built are on a PFI basis (Toynbee and Walker 2005: 34), and many would never have been built without money from the private sector. However, critics point out that the PFI has led to a reduction in beds and a decline in resources away from accident and emergency. There are also growing concerns over the quality and costs of PFI hospitals (*Times*, 12/12/05: 4). The first hospital built under the PFI (the Cumberland Infirmary) has faced major ongoing building problems, whereas Darent Valley Hospital in Kent has earned a return of almost 50% a year for investors (*Independent*, 10/2/05: 18).

The PFI once again underlines the level of New Labour's commitment to marketise the delivery of public services. Ultimately the government will be judged on its improvements to public services, thus the PFI could hardly have greater political significance.

How has the government attempted to raise standards since 1997?

Since 1997 the government has attempted to raise standards by imposing sanctions on those hospitals that fail to meet government targets. The government has also set up the helpline NHS Direct, created high street 'walk-in' clinics throughout the country, and endorsed the management reforms introduced by the Tories during the 1990s. However, the flagship of the government's programme remains foundation hospitals. Once a hospital is given foundation status, it gains an incentive to retain the custom of patients. Popular hospitals are then able to keep some of their surplus, which can be used to improve facilities and services (*Economist.* 'The world in 2005': 34).

Assessment of New Labour

As with education, the government can claim a number of achievements:

> There are 78,700 more nurses and 27,400 more doctors than in 1997.

> 68 major new hospitals have either been completed or have been approved (www.labour.org.uk/top50 achievements/).

> Nurses' and doctors' pay has improved since 1997.

> Improvements have been made to the career structure of nurses and doctors, and working hours have been reduced.

> Maximum waiting lists have halved since Labour came to power. Deaths from cancer and heart disease are also down.

Having said this, the vast increase in resources devoted

to the NHS in recent years has failed to address many of the problems facing healthcare. For example:

➢ There is a considerable shortage of nurses and dentists within the NHS. The British Medical Association claims there are 10,000 GP vacancies, many in deprived areas (*Times*, 17/1/06: 1).

➢ The flagship policy of foundation hospitals has hit problems, with NHS trusts refusing applicants to the scheme due to concerns over their readiness and financial viability.

➢ Deaths from the Methicillin-resistant Staphylococcus aureus (MRSA) superbug doubled between 1999 and 2003 (www.news.bbc.co.uk/2/hi/health/2572841.stm).

➢ In 2001 Tony Blair promised that the amount spent on the NHS would eventually match other European countries, but despite an unprecedented rise in NHS spending, Britain still lags behind most other EU countries.

➢ One must exercise caution when using the figures provided by the government, as the Chancellor has been known to double and triple count the money made available to the NHS (Stephens 2004: 241).

Arguably the government's main problems have derived from the use of targets and league tables. Within the healthcare profession, targets and league tables are criticised for having little to do with the actual state of healthcare in Britain. As with league tables for schools, figures are deliberately manipulated in order to meet government targets. League tables also have an impact on house prices, as people move to good practices whilst incompetent GPs are shunned. Doctors also complain that targets interfere with other priorities, such as taking the necessary care to ensure that MRSA does not spread. As with league tables for schools, the aims behind greater choice and competition have not always matched the results.

POLICIES OF THE MAIN PARTIES

The government's five-year plan (June 2004) for the NHS aims to broaden patient choice and build on the considerable investment made in the NHS since 1997.

The government's five-year healthcare plan

➤ To increase NHS spending to £90 billion by 2008.

➤ To cut waits for treatment to 18 weeks.

➤ To increase patient choice from four to five providers, and to any facility (including those in the private sector) in England by 2008.[1]

➤ To enable patients to see a primary care practitioner within 24 hours.

➤ To expand the 'expert patients programme', whereby patients are trained to become their own health experts, aided by internet and digital TV services that provide healthcare advice (*Times*, 25/6/04: 6).

The cornerstone of the Tories' healthcare policy is the Individual Care Plan, which would allow patients the right to choose any hospital, state or private, for treatment. The Conservatives also pledged to offer vouchers to pay for private healthcare. However, the policy was criticised as little more than a subsidy for those wealthy enough to afford to

---

[1] This pledge has since been scaled down due to lack of capacity (*Times*, 9/9/04: 1).

go private, and has since been ditched by the Tory leader David Cameron.

To encourage greater independence from central government, the Conservatives would enable every NHS hospital to become self-governing. The Tories also pledged to spend more on healthcare than Labour, ensure cleaner hospitals and bring an end to hospital waiting lists. As with most aspects of the welfare state, there is much similarity between the two main parties. Indeed one could argue that 'the two parties' policies are ... hard to tell apart' (*Economist*, 23/4/05: 15).

In their 2005 election manifesto the Liberal Democrats pledged to scrap health charges and replace them with funding paid for out of general taxation. As with education and pensions, the Liberal Democrats offered a policy programme closer to the core values of the welfare state than that put forward by the Labour Party, and provided an alternative to the two-party consensus on marketisation.

THE ISSUE OF HEALTH IN THE 2005 GENERAL ELECTION

During the 2005 general election, the electoral battleground was contested over the issue of who could deliver the best public services, rather than the traditional debate between a more market-based approach from the Conservatives against Labour's preference for a greater role for the state. Fortunately for the government, Labour are trusted to run the NHS better than the Tories (*Economist*, 23/4/05: 33), and in a recent opinion poll, 95% of patients rated their care good, very good or excellent (Toynbee and Walker 2005: 42).

WHAT PROBLEMS FACE THE NHS TODAY?

➢ The gap between growing public expectations and actual delivery of the service. Although the NHS has undoubtedly improved over time, people's expectations have also risen.

➢ How to allocate funds and resources. Should they go on high-cost major operations, or several minor services? Should resources go towards prevention or cure?

➢ As medical care improves, demand tends to increase due to new treatments being made available.

➢ An ageing population. By 2025, it is estimated that 41% of the population will be over the age of 65 (McNaughton 2003: 51). This will inevitably place added pressure on the NHS.

➢ The safety of NHS workers.

➢ Shortages within the healthcare profession.

➢ Healthcare need is greatest among the poor. The government has attempted to deal with this problem via the introduction of Health Action Zones and a Lottery-funded school fruit scheme (*Times*, 4/3/04: 18).

➢ Alcohol abuse. 70% of accident and emergency admissions, and 1.2 million violent incidents are linked to alcohol (*Times*, 29/4/04: 4).

➢ The UK has the fastest growth rate in obesity in Europe, costing the nation £7.4 billion a year (*Times*, 27/5/04: 1). Despite the severity of the problem, any action taken by the government on this issue is often criticised as evidence of the 'nanny state'. It is revealing to note that in 2005 the government climbed down from a proposed fat tax and watered down its plans to impose a smoking ban in public places.

➢ Waste within such a bureaucratic service. Since 1997, the government has set up three health regulators (the National Institute for Clinical Effectiveness (NICE), Monitor and the Commission for Health Improvement) in order to tackle this problem. However, it is difficult to measure performance in the NHS in any meaningful sense, thus the Secretary of State for Health faces a difficult problem. Moreover, there are almost as many administrators in the health services as there are nurses (Bartholomew 2004: 329).

➢ The 'post code lottery', whereby the standard of healthcare varies enormously from one region to another.

➢ The NHS Confederation has claimed that many patients could be cared for at home rather than bed-blocking at a hospital.

➢ Despite a significant increase in resources since 1997, one in four NHS trusts face financial difficulties (*Times*, 11/10/05: 1–2).

➢ Ultimately, demands are infinite but resources are finite. Therefore, hard choices have to be made.

6

Housing and a Summary of the Welfare State

Internet websites

www.england.shelter.org.uk/home/index.cfm

Old exam questions (all 45 minutes)

To what extent have the principles of the welfare state been eroded since 1979?   June 2003

Has the welfare state been 'safe in Labour's hands' since 1997?   June 2004

To what extent has the welfare state been in 'safe hands'?   Spec

Synoptic paper

How, and to what extent, have pressure groups influenced UK welfare policy since 1979?   June 2004

INTRODUCTION

The overwhelming majority of the population will make use of services provided by the welfare state at some point in their lives, literally from 'the cradle to the grave'. The majority of parents send their children to state schools, most people use the NHS rather than the private sector, and most people over retirement age claim a state pension. However, only a minority of the public rely on state housing. The politics of housing are therefore completely different to health, pensions and education.

HISTORY OF HOUSING POLICY

During the Second World War nearly a third of all houses were damaged or destroyed by bombing (Cootes 1984: 109). The incoming Labour government believed that the state, rather than the market, was best suited to resolving the housing crisis facing the country. A major building programme was launched throughout the UK. Council homes provided a decent standard of housing, at an affordable rate to tenants.

Throughout the 1950s and 1960s, 'one nation' Conservatives such as Harold Macmillan placed a high priority on housing policy. Indeed, by the early 1960s the Tories were actually building more new homes than the Labour government of Clement Attlee (1945–1951).

The standard of council homes improved during the post-war years, yet by the 1970s those who could afford to move out of a council house often did so. Council estates gradually became the domain of lower-income groups and the high-rise flats built in the 1960s and early 1970s became plagued by crime and antisocial behaviour.

COUNCIL HOME SALES

Mrs Thatcher was elected in 1979 on a mandate to roll back the frontiers of the state, and the very first target of her attempt to transform the welfare state was the 1980 Housing Act (McNaughton 2003: 35). Under the Act, tenants were given the right to buy their own council homes, often at a substantially reduced rate. Studies of voting behaviour show that people who own their own home tend to support the Conservative Party, thus the government gained a significant degree of electoral support from a group previously aligned to the Labour Party. Councils were also limited on the amount they could spend from those proceeds. Both measures reduced the scope and scale of the state's involvement in housing policy and fundamentally changed its agenda.

The downside of the 'right to buy' policy was a reduction in the country's housing stock. Some 1.6 million local authority dwellings were sold between 1979 and 1999, reducing the country's housing capacity by 10% (Savage and Atkinson 2001: 140). The number of homeless people increased dramatically during the 1980s due to greater poverty and the 1986 Social Security Act, which restricted housing benefit for young people.

By the early 1990s Thatcher's dream of a 'property owning democracy' had faded. As interest rates were raised to support the value of the pound due to our membership of the Exchange Rate Mechanism (ERM) (1990–1992), repossessions rose to record levels. Due to the collapse of the housing market in the late 1980s, many people also faced the problem of negative equity, which restricted the level of labour mobility and was contrary to the government's aim to promote a more flexible labour market.

NEW LABOUR SINCE 1997

As with all aspects considered thus far, New Labour has broadly accepted the main principles of the New Right's

113

critique of the welfare state, alongside a commitment to social justice. One of New Labour's first acts was to allow councils to spend the proceeds of earlier council house sales. The government also created the New Deal for Communities to regenerate some of the most deprived communities in Britain, set up the Neighbourhood Renewal Fund to improve substandard housing, and created the Homelessness Action Programme.

Housing since 1997: the facts

The government has doubled investment since 1997 and improved the overall condition of housing in England. Yet this does little to address the fact that the construction of new houses has halved in the last 40 years (*Guardian* Spending review supplement, 13/7/04: 2). The total number of new houses being built is currently at its lowest peace-time level since the 1920s (Crosbie 2004: 71), with the Town and Country Planning Association projecting a need to supply 175,000 extra houses in the foreseeable future (*Times*, 22/9/05: 29). For a party supposedly committed to creating a more just society, it is perhaps surprising that the number of homeless families has now passed the 100,000 mark; more than double the figure when Labour came to power (*Observer*, 18/7/04: 7; Toynbee and Walker 2005: 81).

First-time buyers

From an electoral point of view, the main problem facing housing policymakers is to meet the demand for affordable low-cost housing. In 2005, a Royal Bank of Scotland survey claimed that nine out of every ten towns in the UK are unaffordable to first-time buyers (*Observer*, 23/1/05: 1).

To combat this problem the government introduced the Keyworkers Scheme, where public sector workers and those in essential services receive help towards buying their first home. The government has also enabled first-time buyers to purchase a home for £60,000 under the Shared Ownership Scheme, and has extended the Shared Equity Scheme for young people in order to help them get onto the property ladder (*Times*, 12/11/04: 4).[1]

THE SCOPE AND SCALE OF THE GOVERNMENT'S ROLE

The state came to play a role in the provision of housing because the market had failed to meet people's needs. Over the years, one could argue the need to build council homes has declined due to an overall rise in the standard of living and a rapid growth in owner-occupation.

The desirability of council homes has declined in relation to growing affluence within the population, and housing therefore remains a marginal political issue. It is highly unlikely this situation will change in the foreseeable future.

No other policy area has witnessed such a radical transformation in the scope and scale of the government's role as that of housing. From a major building programme immediately after the Second World War, to a far more limited role today, the frontiers of the state have undoubtedly been rolled back since Mrs Thatcher came to power.

---

[1] In his 2005 pre-Budget report, the Chancellor set a target of building half a million extra homes over the next decade, and pledged a 25% increase in Shared Equity Schemes in order to help first-time buyers.

RELATIONS BETWEEN LOCAL AND CENTRAL GOVERNMENT

The trend since 1979 has been towards a reduction in the role of local government in the delivery of welfare services. Governments of both main parties have aimed to centralise power in all areas of the welfare state. Perhaps the most dramatic example has been in the field of education, but housing also reflects this trend.

Until 1979 local authorities were directly involved in the provision of public sector housing. Both the Thatcher and Major governments centralised elements of the welfare state, and a number of high-profile disputes with left-wing councils added political impetus to the Tories' desire to curtail the role of local government. Despite regaining some resources since 1997, the power of local authorities remains much reduced from the situation pre-1979.

Changes to the housing market have also weakened the position of local authorities. The general trend has been away from the public sector. Indeed the provision of council homes was in decline *before* Thatcher came to power, and since then the percentage of private homes has grown rapidly. Britain now has one of the highest rates of owner-occupation in the world, with over 18 million owner-occupiers (*Independent*, 22/3/05: 21).

Other legislative changes that have reduced the power of local government in terms of housing since 1979 include:

➤ the introduction of compulsory competitive tendering in 1980;
➤ the 1985 Housing Act, which enabled local authorities to transfer council houses to the private sector. One of the justifications for the change was that private sector housing authorities are considered more responsive to the needs of the tenants than local authorities;

116

➤ the 1988 Housing Act enabled private landlords and housing associations (after a vote by the tenants) to take over the management of a council estate and allowed tenants to choose their own landlord;

➤ the 1989 Housing and Local Government Act forced local authorities to cut back on their provision of council houses and reduce subsidies for council houses;

➤ in 1998 the Labour government created a Housing Inspectorate, which can recommend the takeover of failing councils.

SUMMARY

The welfare state has not been dismantled, but it is certainly very different to that outlined in the Beveridge report (1941). The days of universal provision are on the wane, and the building of council homes has been virtually abandoned by the present Government. However the NHS remains free at the point of use, and the majority of parents still send their children to state schools.

The welfare state underwent a major transformation during the 1980s and 1990s, although the results of those market-based reforms did not always match the intentions behind them. Since 1997, the government has attempted to combine social justice with an acceptance of the need for market forces in the delivery of public services. It is a combination that has achieved mixed results.

On the plus side, the government has used tax receipts from a stable economy to ensure greater social justice. This has included a significant reduction in child poverty, the introduction of a minimum wage, and a substantial increase in resources for health and education. However, with resources targeted towards ending child poverty and helping working families, the numbers of working-age adults (with no children) in poverty has actually increased by 300,000 since Labour came to power (*Independent*, 1/12/04: 8).

What cannot be denied is that New Labour has increased resources, particularly in health and education, and targeted help via a policy of selective universality. The 'welfare to work' strategy should also be considered as a vital part of the government's attempt to create a more just society. Yet the marketisation of the welfare state continues to undermine the core principles of the welfare state, and it is unlikely the broad direction of government policy could be reversed if (and when) Gordon Brown becomes Prime Minister.

7

Northern Ireland

Objectives from the syllabus

- Students should gain an understanding of the origins of the problem dating back to the partition of Ireland, and detailed knowledge of the period leading up to, and following, the Good Friday Agreement.
- Students should also gain an understanding of the meaning of nationalism, sovereignty, unionism, republicanism and terrorism, and knowledge of the position of the Northern Ireland parties on any proposed settlement.

Internet websites

www.ni-assembly.gov.uk
www.sdlp.ie/
www.sinnfein.ie/
www.uup.org/
www.grandorange.org.uk
www.dup.org.uk/

Old exam questions

15 minutes

On what grounds have different groups in Northern Ireland opposed the Good Friday Agreement?   June 2005

What are the main sources of conflict between Unionists and Nationalists in Northern Ireland?   January 2003

Explain the main features of Unionism in Northern Ireland.
January 2006

In what ways have religious divisions played a part in sectarian conflict in Northern Ireland?   January 2005

Outline why weapons decommissioning has been a stumbling block to a lasting peace settlement in Northern Ireland.
June 2002

45 minutes

'The divisions within the two main communities in Northern Ireland have proved as significant as the conflicts between them.' Explain and discuss this statement.   June 2004

How successful has the Good Friday Agreement (in Northern Ireland) been?   January 2002

Analyse the main difficulties in implementing the Good Friday Agreement.   Spec

What were the main issues left unresolved when the Good Friday Agreement came into effect in Northern Ireland?
June 2003

Why has it proved so difficult to create lasting peace in Northern Ireland?   January 2004

45 minutes (synoptic)

In what ways does nationalism in Northern Ireland differ from nationalism elsewhere in the UK?   Spec

How and why does the devolution process in Northern Ireland differ from its counterparts in Scotland and Wales?
June 2002

120

THE BACKGROUND TO THE CONFLICT IN NORTHERN IRELAND

The origins of Northern Ireland's divisive society lie in the social, economic and political consequences of British involvement in Ireland. During Tudor times, both the Monarchy and Parliament were determined to ensure that Ireland should not come under the influence of the major Catholic powers. Zealous Protestants, mainly from Scotland, were encouraged to settle in Ireland. The majority settled in the north east of Ireland, because the land was more fertile. This is commonly known as the plantation of Ireland.

From the very beginning, relations between the two communities were antagonistic. The wealthy, land-owning Protestants hired native Irish Catholics to work for them, which over time created something of a 'them and us' mentality. Irish Catholics rebelled against the authority of what they saw as British dominance of *their* country, whereas Protestants remained loyal to the British Crown.

During the eighteenth century, Protestants sought to gain political influence to protect their way of life from Catholic mobs by forming the Orange Order.

The Orange Order

The Orange Order is an organisation named after William of Orange, who led his troops to victory over the Catholic King James at the Battle of the Boyne in 1690. The Order claims to be a religious organisation that defends the rights of the Protestant people. Its membership is restricted to Protestants, and its political strength is based on the ability to appeal to all Protestants, regardless of social class. To

Catholics, they are little more than a sectarian group celebrating Protestant victories over them. As such, their presence in Catholic areas has created tension between the two communities, as in July 2004 when riots broke out in North Belfast after Orangemen marched through a Catholic area. Clashes between the Orange Order and the police have also been a feature of recent times, reflecting a growing discontent within the Unionist community over the Good Friday Agreement (GFA).

During the nineteenth century, the issue of Home Rule for Ireland aroused considerable controversy within British politics. The Liberal Party supported Irish Home Rule and tried to pass legislation on three occasions. The Conservative Party opposed the plans on the grounds that 'Home Rule means Rome rule', a reference to the influence of the Catholic Church over an Irish Government. Protestants in Ireland, the majority of whom lived in Ulster, wanted to maintain the Union with Britain (hence the title Unionist). Yet ironically, some of the leading advocates of Irish Home Rule, such as Charles Parnell, were also Protestants.

Frustrated by the inability of the British Parliament to secure Home Rule, a small band of Irish rebels led an uprising on the streets of Dublin. It became known as the 1916 Easter Rebellion. Albeit unsuccessful, they became martyrs to the Republican cause after their assassination by British troops.

Republicanism

Republicanism is an ideology that advocates a united Irish republic. But unlike Nationalists, who also wish to see a united Ireland, Republicans have justified the use of terrorism to promote their aims. Loyalists, a group of Protestant paramilitaries who wish to maintain the Union with Britain, were in conflict with Republicans throughout 'the troubles' (1969–1993). During the Peace Process, two distinct groups have emerged within the Republican movement. Sinn Féin/the Irish Republican Army (IRA) believe that the GFA represents a gradual step towards a united Ireland, whereas a number of smaller republican groups (such as the Real IRA, Continuity IRA and the Irish National Liberation Army) oppose the GFA, believing the armed struggle to be the only course of action open to Republicans. The history of Republicanism is one of factionalism, and this has undoubtedly weakened its impact. The most powerful Republican group remains Sinn Féin, widely considered to be the political wing of the IRA.

KEY DATES IN THE HISTORY OF THE CONFLICT IN NORTHERN IRELAND

1688   Reformation
1690   William of Orange leads Protestant forces to victory over Catholic King James at the Battle of the Boyne
1916   Easter Rebellion in Dublin
1921   Partition of Ireland
1969   British troops are sent into Northern Ireland
1972   Internment and Direct Rule
1993   Downing Street Declaration
1998   Good Friday Agreement (GFA)
2002   The Northern Ireland Assembly was suspended

over claims of an IRA spy ring. It has not met since

2005   IRA calls an end to the armed struggle

PARTITION

The partition of Ireland in 1921 was little more than a messy compromise between a British government keen to resolve 'the Irish question' and the acquiescence of Irish Nationalist politicians. After partition, Ireland was split into North and South:

Northern Ireland	Southern Ireland
6 counties	26 counties
Majority of Protestants	Overwhelmingly Catholic
Sizeable minority of Catholics	Independent, sovereign state
Part of the United Kingdom	Later became the Republic of Ireland

Partition left two minorities living side by side. It created a Catholic minority within Northern Ireland, which felt threatened by the Protestant majority, and a Protestant minority within the whole of Ireland, which felt threatened by the prospect of a united Ireland. Although far from perfect, it was probably the best option available at the time.

THE STORMONT YEARS (1921–1972)

A devolved Assembly was empowered with a limited range of responsibilities, most notably control over its own police

124

force, the Royal Ulster Constabulary (RUC). The new government was based at Stormont, and the opening words from the first Prime Minister of Northern Ireland, Viscount Craigavon ('we are a Protestant state for a Protestant people') set the tone for the Unionist hegemony of Stormont for the next 51 years.

There were just two concessions made to Catholics during the Stormont years. The government in Northern Ireland gained agreement from Westminster to ensure parity with the level of welfare payments in Britain. Thus the post-war welfare state operated in Northern Ireland, offering a level of state assistance far beyond that offered to Catholics in Southern Ireland. Secondly, Catholic schools gained state support, which helped to placate the powerful Catholic Church.

These concessions did not alter the fact that the best jobs and the best housing went to Protestants. Even in terms of political representation, Catholics were discriminated against. Many districts were gerrymandered to ensure Protestant/ Unionist control, such as the notorious case of Londonderry. In a city with an overwhelming majority of Catholics, the electoral districts were drawn deliberately to ensure there would always be a Unionist majority on the City Council. The criminal justice system was also biased against Catholics due to Protestant domination of the judiciary and the police force, and a widespread assumption that all Catholics held Republican sympathies.

THE POLITICAL IMPORTANCE OF FEAR AMONG THE UNIONISTS

The possibility of a united Ireland being imposed on them contributes to a 'siege mentality' among Unionists. Effectively, if just 11% of Protestants voted for a united Ireland, the North could be submerged into an overwhelmingly Catholic country. Protestant Unionists also tend to emphasise the worldwide influence of the Catholic Church, in contrast to their much smaller faith, and the reluctance of the British government to defend their interests. Protestants are also concerned that the birth rate among Catholics is greater than their own, and thus Catholics will eventually be in the majority.

One needs to first understand the siege mentality of Protestant Unionists in order to fully comprehend their response to the most significant event of the 1960s, the Civil Rights Movement. Many would argue it was fear among Unionists that led to Stormont's reluctance to reform, and ultimately gave the British government little choice but to send troops into Northern Ireland.

CIVIL RIGHTS

During the late 1960s, support for civil rights in Northern Ireland grew among Catholics and a small number of middle-class Protestants. Inspired by black people in the USA, the Civil Rights Movement demanded an end to discrimination based on religion in areas such as political representation, housing, the criminal justice system and employment.

After violence between protestors and loyalists during a civil rights march in Burntollet, the opportunity to gain real progress appeared to be lost. Loyalists felt threatened by any change to the status quo, while the IRA infiltrated the Civil Rights Movement and so destroyed any credibility the demand for civil rights might have had among moderate Unionists. The Northern Ireland Prime Minister, Terrence O'Niell, was one such moderate. He was prepared to reform the voting system, but faced bitter opposition from hardline Unionists, and was later forced to resign. His replacement, Major James Chichester-Clark, could do little to stop the escalating violence.

126

During the summer of 1969, violence in Northern Ireland spiralled out of control. The Provisional IRA, or 'Provos', engaged in a campaign of terror and violence that was later matched by the activities of Protestant paramilitaries such as the Ulster Volunteer Force (UVF), the Ulster Freedom Fighters (UFF) and the Ulster Defence Association (UDA). The conflict became known as 'the troubles'.

1969–1972: THE HEIGHT OF THE TROUBLES

In 1971, the Stormont Assembly imposed a policy of internment. Anyone found on the streets after curfew was arrested without trial. It was a fundamental breach of civil rights that further antagonised the Catholic minority. In that summer alone, 300 were interned, almost all of them Catholics. Faced with the heavy-handed approach of British troops, Protestant paramilitaries and the Protestant-dominated police, many of the Catholic population awarded legitimacy to the IRA as their only real defence against 'the Brits' (a combination of the army, the RUC, the government and the UDA/UFF/UVF). Internment has since been described as the 'best recruiting agent for the IRA'.

One of the worst events of the troubles occurred in January 1972, when 13 unarmed Catholics were shot dead by the British Army in Londonderry. It became known as Bloody Sunday. To exacerbate the situation, the report that followed was widely seen as a cover-up. No British soldiers were convicted and it was the first of many high-profile cases of injustice (e.g. the Birmingham six and the Guildford four) at the hands of the British judicial system.

ATTEMPTS AT PEACE DURING THE 1970s AND 1980s

In April 1972 the Prime Minister Edward Heath closed down Stormont, and imposed Direct Rule from Westminster. The government of the time favoured some form of devolution for Northern Ireland, yet the difficulty faced was how to create a devolved structure acceptable to both communities. Indeed, it is perhaps symptomatic of the problems inherent in Northern Ireland that Direct Rule was retained until 1999.

The Sunningdale Agreement (1974)

In 1974, the UK Government appeared to reach a breakthrough. Having gained agreement from the main political parties, a power-sharing Assembly was created on the basis of proportional representation. It was widely hoped that the new Assembly would gradually assume responsibilities for the affairs of Northern Ireland. A Council of Ireland was also established with representatives from Westminster and Dublin, in order to ensure the support of Catholic Nationalists.

The power-sharing Assembly collapsed due to a series of strikes organised by the Ulster Workers Council, a loyalist group who felt threatened by any involvement from Dublin in the affairs of Northern Ireland. Despite the early hopes, the Sunningdale Agreement lasted just five months.

Rolling devolution (early 1980s)

In the early 1980s the Secretary of State for Northern Ireland James Prior began an experiment based on the idea of 'rolling devolution'. He proposed a new Assembly that would gain greater responsibility over decision-making, as trust between the two communities gradually improved. Again the assembly

128

failed to gain cross-community support, this time due to opposition from the moderate Nationalist party (the SDLP) and Sinn Féin, and was gradually dissolved.

The Anglo-Irish Agreement (1985)

In 1985, the British Prime Minister Mrs Thatcher and the Irish Taoiseach Charles Haughey signed the Anglo-Irish Agreement (AIA) at Hillsborough Castle. The AIA was the most important peace initiative up to the Downing Street Declaration of 1993.

The AIA was based on the idea that the constitutional status of Northern Ireland could only change with the consent of the majority. The British government also recognised the right of the Dublin government to be consulted over Northern Ireland affairs, establishing ministerial meetings via a consultative intergovernmental conference. A permanent secretariat of civil servants from both Britain and the Republic was also created to deal with Northern Irish affairs (Budge *et al.* 2001: 644–645).

Unionists were outraged at the AIA's unprecedented level of consultation with a foreign country, one that still claimed a constitutional right (under Article 2) to the whole of Ireland. A massive campaign was launched with the slogan 'Ulster Says No'. Perhaps more surprisingly, Sinn Féin rejected the AIA, as it meant recognition from Dublin over the legitimacy of partition.

The AIA differed to previous efforts to secure peace because it entailed a much greater level of cooperation between the British and Irish governments. Although the AIA failed to secure a lasting settlement, it did demonstrate the desirability (from the Irish Catholic side) of Anglo-Irish cooperation, which has been one of the founding principles of the Peace Process (1993–present day).

THE POSITION OF THE BRITISH GOVERNMENT DURING THE 1970s AND 1980s

The Conservative Party was traditionally more sympathetic to the Unionists, whereas Labour adopted the pro-nationalist view of 'unity by consent'. Yet in practice there has been a cross-party agreement since 1969 on how the government should approach the conflict in Northern Ireland. During the troubles, the policy of the UK government was based on five principles:

> ➤ defending Unionists against any move towards a united Ireland;
> ➤ a broad commitment to the principle of consent;
> ➤ an attempt to limit the conflict to an 'acceptable level' of violence;
> ➤ working towards a peaceful settlement achieved with the agreement of the political parties of Northern Ireland;
> ➤ defeating the IRA.

By the early 1990s it had became clear that Britain could not beat the IRA militarily, but nor could the Republicans enforce a united Ireland by the use of terrorism.

What is terrorism?

The term 'terrorism' is defined under Section 1 of the Terrorism Act 2000 as 'the use or threat of action ... designed to influence the Government or to intimidate the public ... and the use or threats made for the purpose of advancing a political, religious or ideological cause' (Norris 2005: 142). A broad range of threats and action fall under the

---

category of terrorism. They include violent acts directed against agents of the state (such as the Army and the RUC), and bombing campaigns targeting economic and financial centres such as Canary Wharf in 1996. Illegitimate means are also used by 'terrorists' to raise money, such as extortion and robbery. Indeed, it is widely believed that Sinn Féin are one of the wealthiest political parties in Europe.

Throughout the troubles, over 3,000 people were murdered (Peele 2004: 428). This appalling level of bloodshed proved the catalyst for renewed attempts to bring an end to the troubles. This became known as the Peace Process, of which there are two elements to consider:

➢ the Downing Street Declaration (1993);
➢ the Good Friday Agreement (1998).

THE DOWNING STREET DECLARATION

In the summer of 1993, the British government, led by John Major, took a bold and courageous step. In partnership with the Irish government, the Prime Minister began to discuss proposals for a power-sharing executive that would include terrorists and political extremists. This was based on the view that peace could *only* be achieved with the support of those who use political violence and terrorism. What was needed was a form of words that would allow Sinn Féin/IRA and Loyalists into mainstream politics, while establishing some form of power-sharing among *all* the political parties. The result was the Downing Street Declaration (DSD), announced on 15 December 1993.

The wording of the DSD was deliberately vague, designed to appeal to both Unionists and Nationalists, while allowing some room for manoeuvre over the exact detail of a future peace agreement:

It is for the people of the island of Ireland alone, by agreement between the two parts respectively, to exercise their right of self-determination on the basis of consent, freely and concurrently given, North and South, to bring about a united Ireland, if that is their wish ... the democratic right of self-determination by the people of Ireland as a whole must be exercised with, and subject to agreement and consent of a majority of the people of Northern Ireland.

It also added that Britain had no 'selfish strategic or economic interest in Northern Ireland', and that the Republic would drop its territorial claim to Northern Ireland.

After eight months of debate among Republicans, during which it came under pressure from the Dublin government and prominent Republican supporters in the USA, the IRA announced a cessation of hostilities on 31 August 1994. The IRA's statement was made much easier by the DSD, which contained the words 'the UK government has no selfish strategic or economic interest in Northern Ireland'. So rather than Her Majesty's Army protecting the Unionists/Protestants, the 'Brits' were there simply to keep the peace.[1]

On 13 October the Loyalist paramilitaries followed suit, and talks soon began under the chairmanship of the former US senator George Mitchell, as anyone from the British or

---

[1] The annual subsidy from Westminster to Northern Ireland is estimated to be £2 billion (*Economist*, 26/11/05: 38).

Irish sides would have proved unacceptable. As a neutral arbiter, he managed to gain the trust of both sides during many months of tough negotiations.

Why did the DSD fail?

The DSD stalled on the issue of decommissioning. Both sides blamed the other for this, although the position of John Major's government was probably the main cause of the problem.

With a small and dwindling majority, Major needed the support of the Unionists to ensure the government's policies would get through Parliament. Perhaps with this in mind, he demanded that the IRA surrender its weapons before there could be progress in Northern Ireland. He was also keen to stress the word 'consent', designed to placate the Unionists who had always feared a united Ireland being imposed on them due to a combination of British disinterest and Irish duplicity.

It was the pro-Unionist position of the Major government that undermined its claim to neutrality. Despite concessions to Republicans (and loyalists) over the release of political prisoners from the high security Maze prison, and a softening of the British government's position on the terms of the ceasefire, the IRA refused to surrender its weapons. Nationalists and Republicans alike blamed the British for playing the 'Orange card', a reference to the favourable treatment given to the Unionists.

There were other problems with the DSD. From the Catholic side, it did not go as far as John Hume (leader of the moderate SDLP) and Gerry Adams (leader of Sinn Féin) would have liked. Adams in particular wanted the British to persuade the Unionists to embrace the idea of Irish unity, which was clearly a political impossibility. The DSD was also ambiguous. Did it mean 'national self-determination' for the people of

Ulster or the whole of Ireland? Clearly the answer to this question is going to work for *either* the Unionists *or* the Nationalists.

In February 1996 the IRA resumed violence and set about a large mainland bombing campaign targeting London and Manchester. Talks did reopen in June 1996 after elections to the Forum for Peace and Reconciliation, but when Sinn Féin were admitted in September the Democratic Unionist Party walked out on the grounds that the IRA had not been required to give up one bullet (Mulholland 2002: 139). Once again, the Peace Process had stalled.

THE GOOD FRIDAY AGREEMENT

In May 1997 Tony Blair was elected Prime Minister with a massive Parliamentary majority, and by July that year a glimmer of hope had been raised by the restoration of the IRA's ceasefire. Progress once again seemed a possibility.

By the following year, Tony Blair and the Irish Taoiseach Bertie Ahern unveiled a blueprint for progress that would later form the basis for the Good Friday Agreement (GFA). They proposed:

➢ a devolved Assembly for Northern Ireland, with legislative and executive functions, elected by single transferable vote. Legislation would need to be approved by a majority of both communities and issues would be conducted on a non-sectarian basis;
➢ a prisoner release programme for both Loyalists and Republicans;
➢ reform of the RUC and the creation of a Human Rights Commission;
➢ a Parades Commission to rule on the controversial issue of marching;

➤ an intergovernmental Council for the Isles;
➤ the creation of cross-border authorities, such as the North-South Ministerial Council and the British-Irish Council.

Due to a perceived bias towards the Catholics, the Prime Minister tried to reassure Protestants by stating that he 'cherished the Union'. The then Secretary of State for Northern Ireland, Mo Mowlam's, visit to the Maze Prison, in order to persuade Loyalist prisoners to agree to the Peace Process, also won over some of the sceptics.

Against the backdrop of tough and dramatic negotiations, in which Tony Blair declared 'the hand of history is upon us!' agreement was finally reached 17 hours after the deadline. It became known as the GFA, or the Belfast Agreement, and was signed on 10 April 1998.

The GFA was put to a referendum on 22 May 1998. The result was a massive majority from the Catholic population and a small majority among the Protestant community. A vote was also held in the Republic, with an emphatic 95% saying yes.

Result of the 1998 referendum in Northern Ireland on the GFA

YES	71%
NO	29%
TURNOUT	81%

Elections to the new Northern Ireland Assembly soon followed. The Ulster Unionists emerged as the main party and their leader, David Trimble, became First Minister for Northern Ireland. In the summer of 1998, the GFA's prospects looked promising.

Implementation of the GFA

Delays in establishing a multi-party executive beset the early days of the Northern Ireland Assembly. As with the DSD, the main stumbling block remained the issue of decommissioning. The text of the GFA reads: 'the resolution of the decommissioning issue is an indispensable part of the process of negotiation', but it does not define the word 'decommissioning' precisely. Inevitably, Republicans and Unionists chose to define it differently. To Sinn Féin decommissioning meant 'taking the gun out of Irish politics'. To the Ulster Unionist Party, it meant the final destruction of IRA weapons. The Unionist position therefore became 'no guns, no government', whereas Sinn Féin stuck to the line 'no government, no guns'. As both sides offered a different interpretation of decommissioning, it is hardly surprising that progress proved so difficult (www.nio.gov.uk/index/key-issues/the-agreement.htm).

Both the British and Irish governments demanded that all the paramilitaries place their arms 'completely and verifiably beyond use'. But the IRA's initial response, stating that it would secure its arms dumps and allow for some of those dumps to be inspected by agreed third parties, was simply not acceptable to the Unionists. The stalemate was broken temporarily on 27 November 1999, when the leader of the UUP, David Trimble, managed to get his party's ruling body to agree to limited concessions on the issue of decommissioning. This compromise enabled the multi-party executive to go ahead. In return, Sinn Féin sent a representative to negotiate with General John de Chastelain (who by that time had replaced Mitchell) over the issue of decommissioning. The Northern Ireland Executive then become operational in November 1999, almost 19 months after the GFA had been signed.

The Northern Ireland Assembly stumbled along against

the backdrop of disagreement between Sinn Féin, and the Ulster Unionist Party. With no progress on the issue of decommissioning, the Secretary of State for Northern Ireland Peter Mandelson (who had replaced Mowlam) suspended the structures of the GFA on 19 January 2000. Mandelson feared that Trimble would resign anyway, and the Executive would fall apart. Eventually the Ulster Unionists did walk out, and the Assembly lost all credibility without its First Minister and representatives from the biggest party.

The deadlock was finally broken in May 2000, when an agreement was reached on the sequencing of IRA decommissioning, along with an agreed timetable for the return of the devolved powers revoked by the British government. The Northern Ireland Assembly met once again on 5 June 2000, but as the first deadline for decommissioning ran out, and in the absence of details or a timetable for further action, the Ulster Unionist Party once again walked out during August 2001.

For the next year or so, the Ulster Unionist Party and Sinn Féin could not find common ground on the divisive issue of decommissioning. The British government therefore had no alternative but to suspend the Assembly on 14 October 2002, and to finally dissolve it on 28 April 2003.

Plans to revive the power-sharing Assembly were tabled in October 2003. Despite limited decommissioning from the IRA, the Ulster Unionists refused to cooperate because the IRA did not specify *what* arms had been put beyond use.

Since 2003 there has been a demilitarisation of the security forces and some decommissioning (*Independent*, 9/12/04: 6), but problems remain due to the vagueness of the GFA, which unfortunately allows Sinn Féin and the Ulster Unionists to offer a different interpretation of the 'd-word'.

Talks at Leeds Castle in December 2004

The latest attempt at all party peace talks did not offer much hope for a peaceful resolution of the situation in Northern Ireland. At the start of the negotiations, the leader of the Democratic Unionst Party (DUP) Iain Paisley demanded the complete decommissioning of IRA weaponry, and a guarantee that the IRA would disband. In return, Sinn Féin wanted assurances that the Unionists would enter into government with them. On the thorny issue of decommissioning, the Democratic Unionists insisted on 'photographic evidence' that the IRA was putting weapons beyond use, whereas Sinn Féin complained that this was little more than 'a process of humilation' for the IRA. This view was fuelled further when Paisley said that the IRA should 'wear sackcloth and ashes', and show repentance for its violent actions (*Independent*, 9/12/04: 7).

Assessment of the GFA

While the GFA has failed to secure a lasting peace in Northern Ireland, its achievements should not be underestimated. They include the following:

➤ the main paramilitaries remain on ceasefire, and have taken some small steps towards decommissioning. On 26 September 2005, the head of the international decommissioning body declared that the IRA's arsenal of weapons was now 'permanently unusable';

➤ no soldier or policeman has died as a result of the conflict in Northern Ireland since 1997 (*Independent*, 15/4/05: 26–27);

➤ since 1998 the Orange Order has toned down some of its marches, so as not to offend Catholic neighbours;

➤ the IRA called an end to the 'armed struggle' on 29 July 2005, and apologised for some of the murders committed during the troubles;

- the British Army has scaled down its presence in Northern Ireland as a response to a decline in the threat of terrorism;
- warmer relations have been established between the British and Irish governments, and perhaps more importantly...
- ...the GFA has led to a safer Northern Ireland, with many people's lives having been saved since 1998. However, the GFA is nowhere near establishing a long-term peaceful solution to the conflict.

OBSTACLES TO PEACE IN NORTHERN IRELAND

- The main obstruction is decommissioning. For the Unionists the IRA simply cannot be trusted, whereas from the Republican perspective, it remains an unresolved issue due to the intransigence of the Ulster Unionists.
- Tensions between the communities are a constant problem. Riots in North Belfast during 2002 and 2004, ongoing feuds among loyalist paramilitaries and Protestant animosity against Catholic children attending Holy Cross school in 2001 provide evidence of the continual divide between the two communities. Ultimately, the GFA can do little to change that mindset.
- Intimidation and criminal activity also remain a problem. A report published by the Independent Monitoring Commission confirmed there had been 1,700 punishment attacks since 1998 (www.sundaylife. co.uk/news/story.jsp?story=551691), and in April 2004 both Sinn Féin and the Progressive Unionist Party were fined for punishment attacks.
- 179 people have been murdered by terrorists during the so-called Peace Process (*Independent on Sunday*, Sunday Review, 12/9/04: 11).

The GFA has achieved more than all other attempts at peace since the troubles began. It has contributed to a somewhat fragile and imperfect peace, but it has yet to resolve the underlying causes of religious hatred within Northern Ireland. Perhaps the most realistic summary came from David Trimble, who described the GFA as 'the only show in town'. A more pessimistic assessment was offered by Seamus Mallon of the Social Democratic and Labour Party (SDLP), who depicted the GFA as 'Sunningdale for slow learners'.

THE STATE OF THE PARTIES

On the Protestant/Unionist side, the moderate party remains the Ulster Unionist Party. Its influence within Unionism has declined significantly since 1998, primarily due to its identification with the GFA. After David Trimble's defeat in the 2005 general election, the Party appointed Sir Reg Empey as leader.

The Democratic Unionist Party, led by the Reverend Iain Paisley, is now the main Unionist party. It continues to oppose the GFA claiming it was a sell-out to the men of violence. The Orange Order is also opposed to the agreement, as is the UK Unionist party.

The electoral success of the Democratic Unionists, and the demise of the Ulster Unionist Party, reflects a hardening of attitudes among the Unionist community. Unionists have always been suspicious of the motives of Sinn Féin, and those doubts were confirmed by the arrest in Columbia of three Republicans who were alleged to have been working for that country's left-wing rebels. Claims of an IRA spy ring in the Northern Ireland executive, and an independent report in November 2004 that confirmed the IRA was in a 'state of readiness' (*Independent*, 24/5/05: 12–13) have added to Unionist anger. Unionists are also unhappy at the reform of the police service since the GFA was signed.

Policing in Northern Ireland

Policing Northern Ireland has always been difficult due to the religious and sectarian divide between the two communities. The very word 'Royal' in RUC was, of course, anathema to Nationalists and Republicans alike, and for many years Catholics were persecuted by the RUC. In addition, very few Catholics became members of the RUC, which only reinforced the widespread perception of the RUC as a Protestant force. The GFA instigated a major reform of the police service by the former Governor of Hong Kong, Chris Patten. His report led to the creation of the Police Service of Northern Ireland (PSNI). The PSNI is held to account to both communities by a Police Ombudsman and a Policing Board. Protestants are aggrieved at the change of name, because it reflects a shift in the loyalty of the police in Northern Ireland, and Sinn Féin have yet to recognise the PSNI. Since the reforms were enacted many Unionists have grown disillusioned with the GFA.

Among Catholic voters, a substantial majority favour the GFA. The moderate Social Democratic and Labour Party (SDLP) continues to advocate a United Ireland through constitutional and peaceful means, and unification by consent. However, the electoral appeal of the SDLP has been eclipsed by Sinn Féin since the GFA was signed.

Sinn Féin is widely seen as the political wing of the IRA. By adopting political and terrorist means, often described as the 'Armalite and the ballot box strategy', it is now the second biggest party in Northern Ireland. Its support for the GFA was crucial to its survival, and any further progress on the issue of decommissioning is likely to prove dependent on the IRA's willingness to cooperate.

Of all the major parties, Sinn Féin has moved the furthest along the road to peace. Abandoning the armed struggle was a bold, and ultimately rewarding, strategy for the leadership to take. However, the Peace Process has caused division within the Republican movement. Splinter groups such as the Continuity IRA, the so-called 'Real' IRA and the INLA oppose the GFA, and continue to use terrorism. It was the Real IRA who claimed responsibility for the Omagh bomb in 1998, an act of violence that caused widespread revulsion on both sides.

The murder of Robert McCarthy outside a Belfast bar, and the 2004 bank robbery that most informed opinion suspects the IRA of carrying out, have proved something of a turning point in the recent fortunes of Sinn Féin. The powerful Irish-American lobby in Washington has called publicly for the IRA to disband. George Bush has also added his support for such a move. However, Sinn Féin remains the leading political party within the Catholic community.

THE BRITISH AND IRISH GOVERNMENTS

A review of the political situation in Northern Ireland would not be complete without a consideration of the position of the two governments. Both want a peaceful agreement, but are burdened by the expectation of standing up for 'their' side. This is a particular problem for the British, who face a delicate balancing act. Move too far towards the Nationalists and they are accused of selling out, which can (and has) provoked militant Loyalist groups, and angered the Unionist/ Protestant community. This was Mo Mowlam's mistake, who was considered biased towards the Catholics and labelled 'too green' by the Democratic Unionist leader Iain Paisley. Move too far towards the Unionists and they are accused of playing the 'Orange card', a charge that fatally undermined the DSD during the mid-1990s.

ELECTIONS SINCE 2001

In the June 2001 general election, Sinn Féin made gains at the expense of the Social Democratic and Labour Party (SDLP), reflecting a hardening of attitudes among Catholic/Nationalist voters at the procrastination of David Trimble, and the interference of Peter Mandelson. Among Protestants, the picture is much the same. The hardline Democratic Unionists made significant gains, reflecting a more uncompromising attitude among Unionists disappointed at Trimble's willingness to compromise, and a lack of progress on decommissioning.

In the Northern Ireland Assembly elections held on 26 November 2003, the Democratic Unionists and Sinn Féin once again increased their share of the vote at the expense of their more moderate opponents. In the 2005 general election the once dominant Ulster Unionists were reduced to just one MP, whereas Iain Paisley's party won half the Westminster seats. Sinn Féin continued to progress at the expense of the SDLP, and can now claim to be the dominant voice among Catholics within Northern Ireland. The Democratic Unionists and Sinn Féin took almost 60% of the combined vote, therefore any credible power-sharing agreement has to include these two parties.

WHAT DOES THE FUTURE HOLD?

The predictable failure of the peace talks at Leeds Castle in 2004, over what would appear to be a technical matter, is symptomatic of a huge lack of trust between the two communities. It would appear that whatever the details of a possible deal, and whatever the political pressure placed on the parties involved, all attempts at peace in Northern Ireland

143

ultimately fail due to a lack of trust and confidence between Catholics and Protestants.

The fundamental problem in achieving peace is a conflicting view of sovereignty. Unionism and nationalism are two irreconcilable goals, with fundamentally different views.

In Northern Ireland, politics is often understood to be a case of one side winning with the other losing out. It is, in short, a zero-sum game, because there is almost no common ground between them. Furthermore, it is always difficult for people to compromise their beliefs when religious identity plays such a vital role within society.

One must be careful when using the terms Irish Catholic and British/Ulster Protestant, as they imply an omnipresent religious and ethnic identity. There is a small minority of Catholics who identify with Northern Ireland and wish to remain part of the United Kingdom. Similarly, there has always been a small number of Protestants who would accept a united Ireland, provided the rights of Protestants are guaranteed. Yet it would be hopelessly naïve to suggest that such views are anywhere close to the mainstream, or hold any chance of becoming the majority view within Northern Ireland. The most optimistic scenario is that North and South will gradually integrate, as regional and cultural differences become less prevalent in an ever-widening EU. Yet at the time of writing there is little cause to be so optimistic. A more realistic assessment would be that the Peace Process is a hostage to fortune.

Peace in Northern Ireland can only occur if the political parties are willing to accommodate on certain issues, and are able to persuade their natural supporters that their interests are being defended. This is an extremely difficult task. Splits within the Republican and Loyalist movements, divisions between the leadership and rank-and-file members of the Ulster Unionists and opposition to the GFA from groups as diverse as the Democratic Unionists, the Orange Order and

Republican terrorists continue to prevent any long-term chance of peace. Northern Ireland therefore remains a society divided by religion and politics.

8

The Economy

Objectives of the syllabus

- An awareness of the overlap between this module and the EU module taken later in the course. However, questions specifically addressing EU policy and issues will only appear in Unit 5A.
- Students should be aware of the changing policy agenda in the UK since 1945, and the policies of major parties over the period. The main focus will be on the post-1979 period.
- A knowledge of the general relationship between the state and the market in economic policy, and of debates about the role of economic management, as well as specific knowledge of policies in relation to nationalisation, employment, exchange rates, prices and incomes, and the unions.
- An understanding of interventionism, the free market, Keynesianism, monetarism, nationalisation and privatisation.

Internet websites

www.hm-treasury.gov.uk
www.number–10.gov.uk
www.cabinet-office.gov.uk
www.bankofengland.co.uk

www.adamsmith.org
www.iea.org.uk
www.iod.co.uk
www.cbi.org.uk

Old exam questions

15 minutes

Explain the main political conflicts that have arisen over taxation since 2001. January 2006

Explain the term 'stealth taxes' and describe the ways in which they have been used since 1992. January 2003

Why was control over Bank of England interest rates passed to its Monetary Policy Committee in 1997? June 2002

Outline the main ways in which the Labour government has sought to create greater economic equality since 1997.
January 2005

45 minutes

To what extent is Labour still a 'tax and spend' party?
June 2005

To what extent is there a consensus between the three main parties over economic policy? June 2004

'Prudence with a purpose.' Explain what Gordon Brown meant by this statement and analyse how he has attempted to achieve it. January 2003

In what ways, and with how much success, has the Labour government maintained economic stability in the UK since 1997? January 2005

Analyse the Conservatives' approach to state intervention after 1979 and outline Labour's response since 1997. Spec

How, and to what extent, has economic stability been achieved in the UK since 1997. January 2006

'Economic growth brings as many political problems as dealing with recession.' Discuss with reference to the development of economic policy since the late 1980s.
June 2002

To what extent has control of economic policy passed from elected British governments to non-elected bodies at home and abroad? June 2003

To what extent has Gordon Brown been a 'prudent' Chancellor of the Exchequer? January 2004

Synoptic

How has the UK's membership of the European Union affected domestic economic policymaking? June 2002

To what extent has the development of the UK's economic policy reflected consensus rather than adversary politics?
Spec

To what extent have the economic policies of Labour governments since 1997 differed from the principles of economic management practised by the previous Conservative governments, 1979–1997? January 2002

Basic economic terms

Inflation

Inflation is a measure of the rate of increase in prices within the economy. It occurs when demand for a good or service rises, but firms are unable to increase supply. The price of goods and services therefore

---

goes up because of excess demand. The rate of inflation is expressed as a percentage, and is based on a basket of goods for the average family. The control of inflation has been the central plank of British government policy since the mid-1970s (Lyons 1999: 51). The need to control inflation is accepted as the key economic objective by *all* the main parties, as is the means to achieve it: interest rates.

Interest rates

Interest rates are expressed as a percentage, and could be described as the cost of borrowing money. When interest rates go up, people will usually spend less. This is because the payments on a variable rate mortgage will increase, and loans will become more expensive. This tends to result in less consumer demand in the economy. Raising interest rates is therefore designed to slow down economic growth and reduce the rate of inflation, whereas reducing interest rates helps stimulate economic growth and raise employment. Interest rates are set by the Monetary Policy Committee of the Bank of England on a monthly basis. If we adopt the euro, interest rates would be set by the European Central Bank in Frankfurt.

Exchange rates

Exchange rates measure the value of national currencies on the foreign exchange markets. Governments can either adopt fixed exchange rates (e.g. the gold standard), floating exchange rates or a hybrid of the two. From 1990 to 1992 Britain was a member of the European Exchange Rate Mechanism (ERM), which combined elements of a fixed and floating exchange rate. The current policy is to adopt a floating exchange rate, allowing the value of the pound to rise or fall according to the level of demand in the financial markets with little or no government intervention. The value of the pound changes rapidly, and is often expressed as being either too strong or too low. If the pound's value is considered too strong, the price of British goods abroad will be relatively expensive. This can damage British industry because it makes exports less competitive, and encourages consumers to purchase more imports. If the value of the pound is too low, the price of British goods abroad will be relatively low. This tends to encourage more exports and leads to less imports.

Balance of payments

The UK's balance of payments is a measure of the difference between the value of imports and exports. When the value of exports is greater than the value of imports, Britain has a balance of payments surplus. When the value of exports is less than the value of imports, Britain will have a balance of payments deficit. The latter is more common in the case of the UK economy.

Government debt

When the government raises more money than it spends, the Chancellor can pay off debt accumulated in previous years. In practice, the government often spends more than it generates in tax revenue, particularly in recent years. This is called, for obvious reasons, the level of government debt.

The distinction between macro-economics and micro-economics

Macro-economic policy consists of measures taken to deal with the overall management of the UK economy. The government's macro-economic policy consists of various objectives, such as:

➢ low inflation;
➢ reducing unemployment;
➢ promoting economic growth;
➢ improving the competitiveness of British goods and services.

Macro-economic policy is of major political importance because the performance of the UK's economy determines the ability of the government to pursue its policy objectives, be it to increase public expenditure or reduce taxation. Micro-economic policy consists of measures to encourage small businesses.

Monetary and fiscal policy

Monetary policy consists of any macro-economic decision affecting the money supply, interest rates and exchange rates. Monetary policy is decided by the Bank of England. Fiscal policy involves decisions affecting government spending and the level of taxation. Fiscal policy is the responsibility of the government, who have to balance the desire to improve public services against the reluctance of voters to pay higher levels of taxation. In general terms, a Labour government will increase taxes in order to fund public services, whereas a Conservative government will attempt to cut taxes and reduce the role of the state.

THE POLITICS OF TAX

In recent years the level of income tax has become an important political symbol. Since 1979, the basic and higher rate have been reduced by governments of both parties. With income tax considered sacrosanct, successive Chancellors have found different ways of gaining revenue for public spending. This has led to a surge in stealth taxes since the 1992 general election.

Stealth taxes are taxes raised by indirect taxation, and are less visible to voters than a change to income tax. The 1992–1997 Conservative government introduced 22 tax rises, but it is New Labour that has really exploited the opportunity to raise tax by stealth.

The trend towards indirect taxation reflects the influence of the New Right, who argued that direct taxation (i.e. tax taken directly from source, such as income tax) is harmful to personal initiative and thus has a negative effect on the economy. The present government has avoided raising the 'politically sensitive' rate of income tax. Instead, New Labour have reduced the basic rate and kept the top rate unchanged, while raising revenue by implementing 66 stealth tax rises since coming to power.

WHY IS THE ISSUE OF TAX OF SUCH POLITICAL IMPORTANCE?

During their lengthy period in opposition in the 1980s and 1990s, the perception among voters of Labour as a 'tax and spend' party caused immense damage to the Party. For this reason, the present government has been understandably reluctant to raise income tax. A dramatic illustration of the importance of tax occurred in 2000, when the fuel tax protests caused havoc to Britain's already strained transport system.

Perceptions over the 'excessive' rate of taxation on petrol duty led to the most serious bout of social unrest since Labour came to power. The political importance of tax therefore cannot be underestimated.

TAX AND THE 2005 GENERAL ELECTION

The issue of tax and public services was a key electoral battleground during the 2005 general election. After increasing the tax burden to fund a significant rise in public spending, the government highlighted improvements in those public services, set against the Tories' desire to cut public services.

The Conservatives offered a long-term aim to reduce public expenditure by £12 billion, but the Party's plans did little to excite the public's imagination and have already been criticised by those on the Right of the Party for not going far enough down the road of tax cuts. Just £4 billion was earmarked for tax cuts, which worked out at less than £200 per household (*Times*, 19/1/05: 25), and was a billion less than the level outlined by the Liberal Democrats in their manifesto (*Times*, 21/9/05: 31).

The Conservatives also claimed that New Labour were simply a 'stealth tax and spend party', and criticised the government for wasting taxpayers' money. To outmanoeuvre the Tories, Gordon Brown claimed he could save more than £20 billion by sacking over 100,000 civil servants (http://news.bbc.co.uk/1/hi/ukpolitics/3887053.stm). This leads to an important question in relation to tax: 'Is the government wasting taxpayers' money?'

The James Report (2005), commissioned by the Conservatives, identified £35 billion of waste in public spending. Thus for every £1 the government spends, just over half a penny is wasted. Yet whatever the figures, it is what the public *believe* that ultimately matters, and there is a perception that

Labour have had enough time, and spent enough of our money, to vastly improve public services (www.conservatives.com/pdf/thejamesreport.pdf).

NATIONALISATION AND PRIVATISATION

From 1979 to 1997, the Conservative government aimed to 'roll back the frontiers of the state' by pursuing four related objectives:

1 lower taxation;
2 lower public spending;
3 weaken the role of the trade unions;
4 privatisation.

Privatisation consists of 'the transfer of assets from the public sector to the private sector'. Privatisation reduces the role of the state and promotes the free market ('free' that is, from government intervention). The traditional debate between the state versus the market has always divided Left and Right. 'Old' Labour governments always favoured nationalisation, with the Attlee government (1945–1951) taking several industries into public ownership, such as coal and steel.

Arguments for nationalisation

➤ Nationalisation promotes cooperation rather than competition.
➤ Nationalisation ensures important industries receive the required level of investment.
➤ It is consistent with the broader socialist aims of Old Labour.
➤ Nationalisation is a means towards achieving full

155

employment. This argument was more prevalent during the post-war consensus (1945–1979).

➤ Monopolies can be run for the good of society, rather than simply to pursue a profit.

➤ A nationalised industry can be held accountable to Parliament. In contrast, many of the privatised industries lack political accountability because they are removed from Parliamentary scrutiny.

Those on the Right have traditionally favoured privatisation based on *laissez faire* economics, where the government does not intervene in the market. The most enthusiastic supporters of privatisation were the Thatcher and Major governments, principally from 1984 to 1994. However, since 1997 New Labour has embraced the policy of privatisation with some enthusiasm, going even further than Thatcher and Major. There is now a broad agreement on the front benches of the two main parties over the desirability of transferring assets from the state to the private sector, although dissenting voices can be heard on the Labour benches.

Arguments for privatisation

➤ Most nationalised companies were transformed by privatisation from loss-makers soaking up taxpayers' money to profit-makers generating substantial tax revenues. One academic estimates the revenue generated from privatisation to be £90 billion (Fielding 2003: 168).

➤ Customers have often benefited from improved services due to greater competition and more choice (e.g. telecommunications). However, this has not always been the case in practice.

➤ Privatised industries are more efficient than nationalised companies.

- Privatisation helps to lower public spending and therefore reduces taxation, which the New Right believes is desirable for economic growth.
- Privatisation removes the government out of the problematic area of industrial relations, and weakens the power of public sector trade unions. This goal was particularly important to Mrs Thatcher (Coxall and Robins 1994: 177).

WHO MAKES ECONOMIC POLICY?

Fiscal policy is ultimately the responsibility of the Chancellor of the Exchequer. It is the Chancellor's job to decide how much public money should be raised and how much should be spent. Economic success can often mean electoral success; therefore the Chancellor's job is of major political significance.

Another role performed by the Chancellor is to formulate and present the budget, in which the government's intentions for the next 12 months are outlined. The Chancellor is supported by a team of junior ministers, civil servants and advisers. The Chief Secretary to the Treasury is also involved.

The Prime Minister also plays a role in the making of fiscal policy. There can be three types of Prime Minister in relation to the Chancellor: the dominant Prime Minister (e.g. Thatcher and Blair), the equal Prime Minister (e.g. Major) and the reluctant Prime Minister (e.g. Callaghan). No matter what the type, the relationship between the Prime Minister and the Chancellor is of vital importance to any government (Naughtie 2003).

The Treasury has three important functions: providing senior ministers who can offer policy advice, maintaining the budget and designing policies for the financial markets and international institutions. The Chief Secretary to the Treasury conducts the meetings with each minister in charge of a government department. It is at these meetings that the allocation of money for each department is decided on, and later published in the government's *Comprehensive Spending Review*.

As the name suggests, the Monetary Policy Committee (MPC) of the Bank of England is in charge of the UK's monetary policy. It is an unelected body headed by Mervyn King. Since May 1997 the MPC has been independent of the government, and has set monetary policy in order to meet the government's target rate of inflation (2%). Its most important function is to decide on the level of interest rates. In recent years interest rates have been at historically low levels, and the MPC has met the government's inflation target since it gained independence. The Bank of England also has the power to issue bank notes in England, and is the agent for the government's exchange rate policy. The Bank of England is, in common with its US counterpart the Federal Reserve, regulated by an independent body. While the MPC is unaccountable to the public, it is partly accountable to the Chancellor. It is not widely known that the government can, under 'extreme economic conditions', or war, opt out of the arrangement with the MPC (Crosbie 2004: 44).

Other influences on economic decision-making include:

> the EU;
> multinational companies;
> insider pressure groups such as the Confederation of British Industry (CBI), and outsider pressure groups such as the fuel tax protestors;
> economic advisers such as the former Head of the US Federal Bank, Alan Greenspan;
> think tanks such as the Institute for Public Policy Research (IPPR). It is widely believed that the IPPR is the Prime Minister's favourite think tank.

158

THE IMPACT OF GLOBALISATION ON ECONOMIC POLICY MAKING

We live in a globalised economy in which transactions worth trillions of pounds are dealt with every day. The UK economy is heavily reliant on international trade, and the government's economic policy can easily be thrown off course by the foreign currency markets. The simple fact is that in a globalised economy no national economy is immune from fluctuations on the currency markets, and all governments have to adapt to the demands of a globalised economy. In recent years these have included the 1998 Asian monetary crisis, the Russian government defaulting on its debt payments, the rise in the price of crude oil during 2005, the spectacular success of the Chinese economy and the shock to the US economy immediately after the terrorist attacks of 11 September 2001.

The limitations placed on the British Chancellor by globalisation are considerable. While Britain is the fifth largest economy in the world, Gordon Brown has little influence over multinational corporations who can simply relocate to other countries if they dislike domestic economic policy. Many investors can also switch from one currency to another, which can result in a depreciation of the pound's value. There is also little a Chancellor can do to mitigate the effects of a dramatic event outside these shores. For example, the unification of Germany in 1990 led to a crisis within the European monetary system. The Chancellor Norman Lamont was eventually forced to withdraw the pound from the ERM due to events for which he (and the government) were blamed, but over which they had no control.

A political issue to consider is the extent to which economic policy is made by non-elected, and largely unaccountable, bodies. These include the MPC and the supranational institutions of the EU such as the European Commission. Perhaps more importantly, no Chancellor can ignore the

159

influence of multinational companies, the International Monetary Fund (IMF), the World Trade Organisation (WTO), the G8 and the financial markets. All such actors have a major bearing on economic policymaking, regardless of who is in power.

HISTORY OF ECONOMIC POLICY 1945–1979

Both Conservative and Labour governments have adapted to the economic orthodoxy of the day. From the 1940s until the mid-1970s, the economic orthodoxy was Keynesianism. *Laissez faire* economics and monetarism formed the core economic principles of the Conservative governments (1979–1997). Since 1997, New Labour has been influenced by a political and economic philosophy called the Third Way (Giddens 1998; Hutton 1995).

Keynesianism

From the 1940s to the mid-1970s, governments were committed to a Keynesian economic policy. Keynesianism was based on the work of John Maynard Keynes, a brilliant economist at Cambridge University who advocated a form of managed capitalism, which combined a mixed economy with a commitment to full employment.

According to Keynes, the problem of high unemployment could be overcome by government intervention. Public spending would stimulate the economy, with new jobs created and more money in people's pockets. As a result, aggregate demand would increase and benefit the economy. Thus when economic growth slowed down, the government should inflate the economy via increasing public expenditure, and/or lowering interest rates. Conversely in times of high inflation, the government should deflate the economy.

The economic policy of Keynesianism offered an alternative to unfettered free market economics that many blamed for the recession of the 1930s, and to the planned economy which had been adopted by the Soviet Union and its satellite countries in Eastern Europe. It also meant that governments could intervene to reduce the level of unemployment. Naturally, this would hold major electoral benefits. Full employment became the number one economic priority for all governments from 1945 to the late 1970s. It was measured at 2–3% of the total workforce unemployed, and both Labour and Tory governments achieved this target throughout the 1950s and 1960s.

Keynesianism was also associated with corporatism, whereby the government sought to manage the economy via cooperation with businesses and the trade unions. Wage restraints were agreed on with the trade unions, in return for certain concessions to their members. This was commonly known as a prices and incomes policy, and its aim was to curb inflation.

During the post-war era Britain experienced a period of relative economic decline, with lower growth rates than our major trading partners. British industry lost its competitive advantage, and the economy faced repeated balance of payments deficits, with periodic devaluations in the value of the pound in 1949, 1967 and 1976.

Economic problems were not just limited to trade and the value of sterling. In 1975 inflation passed the 25% mark, and a year later unemployment broke the 1 million barrier for the first time since the Second World War. The post-war consensus fell apart due to the failure of Keynesianism to resolve the twin problems of growing inflation and an increase in unemployment. The high number of days lost to strike action during the 1970s did not help either. This problem culminated in the 1978/1979 'Winter of Discontent', in which the dead were left unburied.

As well as failing to deal with rising inflation and high unemployment, Keynesianism was criticised for leading to stop-go economics, in which the government inflated the economy in the run up to a general election but was later forced to deflate it after a rapid increase in the rate of inflation.

Laissez faire economics

Supporters of this theory, first put forward by the eighteenth-century Scottish economist Adam Smith, believe the state should leave the economy alone, hence the French phrase *laissez faire*. Producers should be allowed to supply products at the price consumers are willing to pay. The Conservative leader Mrs Thatcher believed that if the state limited its role, the free market would help reduce inflation, improve customer choice and restore Britain's economic status.

Monetarism

Monetarists argue that the primary goal of any government should be to reduce inflation. It can achieve this through controlling the money supply, measured as the total amount of money circulating in the economy.

Monetarism is based on the traditional quantity theory of money, which states that inflation is caused by a growth in the amount of money and the speed it circulates around the economy. One of its leading advocates is the American economist Milton Friedman (1990), who argued that the economy was unaffected by the level of government expenditure or the level of taxation. He believed that the economy was simply affected by the money supply. Therefore, the *only* job of the government should be to control the amount of money in circulation.

Monetarism, along with *laissez faire* economics, is closely associated with the New Right. Based on such ideas, the

Conservative governments of the 1980s and 1990s reduced direct taxation, implemented a major programme of privatisation and promoted free-market economics.

Monetarism fell out of favour due to difficulties in measuring the money supply, and because it was perceived to have contributed to the 'boom and bust' of the late 1980s/early 1990s. Monetarism was eventually replaced by targeting the exchange rate in relation to the German Deutschmark, a policy which later led to Britain's ill-fated membership of the ERM. Gordon Brown has repeatedly warned against Britain going back to the boom and bust era that discredited the Conservative governments, which suggests the term still forms part of the public's perception of the Tories.

KEY DATES IN BRITAIN'S ECONOMIC HISTORY SINCE THE 1970s

1973	Britain joins the EC
1975	Inflation tops 25%
1976	Unemployment reaches 1 million for the first time since the Second World War
1978/1979	Winter of Discontent. Trade unions clash with the Labour government of James Callaghan
1979	Mrs Thatcher is elected Prime Minister
1981/1983	Recession. The level of unemployment goes past 3 million
1984	The Miners' Strike
1984–1993	Privatisation of major companies such as British Telecom and British Gas
1987	Stock Market crash ends the Thatcher/ Lawson boom
1990	Poll Tax riots. Major replaces Thatcher
1991/1992	Recession. Interest rates reach 15%

1992	Black Wednesday
1997	New Labour elected. Bank of England gains independence
1999	Gordon Brown abandons Tory spending plans
2000	Fuel tax protests
2001	Euro adopted by most European countries. Britain stays out, for now...
2005	New Labour re-elected for a third term

NEW LABOUR AND THE THIRD WAY

To understand the thinking behind New Labour's economic policy, we need to begin with two significant events from 1992.

Until that time it was widely assumed that *the* decisive factor in a general election was the state of the economy. When the economy was doing well and people felt optimistic, it would result in greater levels of support for the governing party. This was sometimes known as the 'feel-good factor'. When the economy was doing badly, a governing party would often be unpopular with the electorate.

This assumption was shattered at the 1992 general election. In one of the deepest recessions since the Second World War, the Conservatives were unexpectedly returned to power. It seemed the public still lacked confidence in Labour's 'tax and spend' approach to deal with the economy.

Traditionally, the Conservatives were thought to be the party best suited to run the economy. Three devaluations of the pound under Labour governments also contributed to this view, as did fears about high taxation. All this changed after Black Wednesday.

164

The Importance of Black Wednesday

After raising interest rates to a crippling 15%, and spending vast amounts of foreign currency reserves in order to prop up the value of the pound, the Conservative Chancellor Norman Lamont had to withdraw Britain from the ERM on Wednesday 16 September 1992. It proved a turning point in British politics. No longer were the Tories seen as the party that could manage the economy better than Labour. Since then, New Labour has established itself as the party most trusted to manage the economy.

Despite an improving economy, the Conservatives lost the 1997 general election by a landslide. Black Wednesday had discredited the Tories' reputation for sound economic management, yet ironically it could be argued that sterling's devaluation benefited the economy in the long run. Cheaper sterling led to a surge in export profits, wages rose steadily without leading to high inflation and unemployment gradually fell. New Labour thus inherited a sound economy and a golden opportunity to establish itself as the party of prudent economic management.

The Third Way combines an acceptance of the current economic orthodoxy for supply-side economics, with a desire for social justice. It reflects Labour's traditional objectives with the reality of a globalised economy, in which Britain has to compete in a global market by maintaining low inflation, a flexible labour force and high levels of investment.

Supply-side economics

Supply-side economics consists of four elements:

1   The government's role should be to improve the skills of the labour force, rather than the Keynesian approach of influencing demand in the economy.
2   Improving the UK's competitiveness by maintaining low direct taxation.
3   Advocating the merits of a flexible labour force.
4   Promoting investment by prudent economic management.

According to this view, the role of the government is not to increase aggregate demand, or to make the economy 'go' with policies to stimulate growth, but to concentrate on the supply side of the economy. This view first took hold during the mid- to late 1970s, when New Right think tanks such as the Adam Smith Institute, the Centre for Policy Studies and the Institute of Economic Affairs began to influence the direction of Conservative policy. It has since been incorporated into the Third Way.

The idea of rights and responsibilities is a key element of the Third Way. According to this approach the state provides a 'hand up not a hand-out', as demonstrated by the Welfare to Work programme. Welfare to Work ensures that a person will always be financially better off *in* work than when receiving unemployment benefit. It is a clear attempt to address the dependency culture and remove people from the poverty trap.

Unlike old Labour governments, who aimed to achieve

'equality of outcome', the Third Way rejects this approach as leading to conformity and mediocrity, and the imposition of electorally unpopular tax burdens that proved so costly to the Labour Party in the 1992 general election. Instead, New Labour is committed to 'equality of opportunity'.

Another element of the Third Way is stakeholding. This is the idea that businesses have a responsibility to various groups such as employees, customers and the wider community, rather than just their shareholders. Stakeholding is closely associated with the author Will Hutton and his best-selling book *The State We're In* (1995).

The Third Way is the defining economic and political philosophy of New Labour. The first, and most important, sign of the shift from Old to New Labour occurred when the Party scrapped their old Clause 4 attachment to nationalisation. Clause 4 of New Labour's Constitution (1995) commits the Party to achieving 'a dynamic economy, serving the public interest' rather than old-style nationalisation. The party is also pledged to ensure 'the rights we enjoy reflect the duties we owe', and the creation of 'a just society'.

Many criticise the Third Way as little more than repackaged Thatcherism, part of a cynical attempt to convince voters that New Labour is more competent to run the economy than Old Labour. Hutton himself describes New Labour as 'cherry picking' from both the left and the right to construct a new set of values under the title 'Third Way', and trying to make it consistent. Thus it's the party of both enterprise *and* regulation, of flexible labour markets *and* trade unions, of change *and* no change (Hutton 2002: 14). In short, the Third Way is all things to all people, part of an electoral strategy designed to ensure that the Labour government retains power.

HOW DIFFERENT IS NEW LABOUR FROM OLD LABOUR?

The Labour Party traditionally had a reputation as a 'tax and spend' and high inflation party. After four election defeats, Tony Blair and Gordon Brown were anxious to show that New Labour could be trusted to run the economy and avoid the economic problems that had dogged previous Labour governments. New Labour has achieved this transformation via the following:

- ➢ The commitment to public ownership (Clause 4) was ditched in 1995.
- ➢ By 1997 the party had accepted most of the Conservatives' tax changes, and industrial relations laws.
- ➢ Labour is a broadly pro-European party, and in favour of joining the Eurozone. Only a generation ago, the party wanted to withdraw Britain from the EC.
- ➢ Gordon Brown has won plaudits from all quarters on his well-judged stewardship of the economy. None of his Labour predecessors could claim that.
- ➢ With most of the key indicators moving in the right direction, the economy was Labour's strongest card in 2001 and 2005. Labour is now trusted to run the economy better than the Conservatives (Seldon and Kavanagh 2005: 414), a transformation of profound electoral significance.

PRUDENCE WITH A PURPOSE

Gordon Brown has been the Chancellor of the Exchequer since New Labour came to power on 1 May 1997. He has a reputation for being an Iron Chancellor committed to 'prudence with a purpose'.

As Chancellor, his first move was to grant independence for the Bank of England. Whereas Old Labour had nationalised the Bank of England, New Labour granted it independence from the government. It remains by far the most important economic decision taken by the government, and was a shrewd political move on the part of Gordon Brown.

Gordon Brown's decision to grant the Bank of England independence placed monetary policy out of the hands of politicians and into those of professional economists. He believed that the Bank would be more likely to take a long-term view of the UK economy, as it was free from political constraints such as the electoral cycle and party politics. Independence for the Bank also reflects Brown's commitment to the economic ideas of the New Right, and met one of the criteria required for European Economic and Monetary Union. It therefore kept the door open to British membership of the single European currency, or euro.

By enabling the Bank of England to set monetary policy, Gordon Brown cannot be held accountable to the public (or trade unions and Labour MPs) for the level of interest rates in the economy. It also removes any temptation he might have to inflate the economy in the run-up to a general election, thus effectively cancelling any possibility of a return to stop-go Keynesian economics, or the boom-bust cycle that damaged the Conservatives' reputation for sound economic management.

Independence for the Bank of England has certainly improved the prospects for long-term stability and growth in the economy, and gained the approval of the City of London, the CBI and the previous two Conservative chancellors. Brown also hoped it would mark a contrast between the irresponsible Conservatives, associated with boom-bust and Britain's humiliating withdrawal from the ERM, and New Labour's 'prudent' approach.

THE CHANCELLOR'S FIRST TWO YEARS

From 1997 to 1999, Labour kept to the Conservatives' spending plans. After consultation with Cabinet Ministers, government departments and focus groups the Chancellor launched the *Comprehensive Spending Review* in 1999.

The aims of the *Review* were to plan for the next three years, and to scrutinise departments' spending commitments. The key features were:

- an increase in public spending of £50 billion;
- the NHS received £21 billion, and education received £19 billion;
- departments would know how much money they would be getting for the next three years;
- conditions were placed on the new money.

THE CHANCELLOR'S GOLDEN RULE

Another factor in Gordon Brown's claim to be a prudent Chancellor is the golden rule of borrowing ('no public borrowing other than for investment measured over the economic cycle'). The Chancellor introduced the golden rule to counter fears of a Labour government borrowing at an irresponsible level in order to fund a major expansion of the welfare state.

From a deficit exceeding £50 billion in 1993–1994 under the Tories, government finances were transformed into a surplus of £15 billion in 2000. This was due to stringent controls on public spending. Such prudence enabled the government to pay back some of the debt they inherited from the Conservatives, and kept public spending to a relatively low level. Since then the Chancellor has funded a major increase in public expenditure; and inevitably the government's finances are now in deficit.

Based on such a turnaround, one might argue that the Chancellor has not been prudent with the public's money. Some economists have warned that the economy is in worse shape than the Chancellor believes, and the Conservatives have criticised Brown for the black hole in the government's finances, estimated to be in the region of £10 billion (*Economist*, 10/12/05: 34).

Clearly the biggest economic (and political) decision facing the Chancellor is whether or not the UK should join the Eurozone. The five economic tests to determine this are symptomatic of Brown's cautious approach, and his desire to hold on to power.

The Chancellor's five economic tests

1   Would joining create better working conditions for firms making long-term decisions to invest in the UK?
2   How would adopting the single currency affect our financial services?
3   Are business cycles and economic structures compatible, so that we and others in Europe could live comfortably with euro interest rates on a permanent basis?
4   If problems do emerge, is there sufficient flexibility to deal with them?
5   Will joining help to promote higher growth, stability and a lasting increase in jobs?

There was evidence of the Chancellor's prudence in the run-up to the 2005 general election, when he resisted the temptation to significantly increase public expenditure despite pressure from within his own party and refused to reduce taxation to win short-term popularity with the voters. By gaining a wide level of political support for his prudent approach to the economy, Gordon Brown has ultimately strengthened his ambition to replace Tony Blair as Prime Minister one day.[1]

HOW 'PRUDENT' IS GORDON BROWN?

Since 1997 the government has avoided any economic crisis comparable in the voters' minds to Black Wednesday, or those associated with previous Labour governments, and avoided any of the problems raised by union militancy. However, the Chancellor has introduced 66 stealth tax rises in order to fund a major increase in resources provided for public services. He has also increased the burden of bureaucracy on the private sector despite a commitment to supply-side economics, and overseen a massive rise in public sector employment. Indeed most of the 2 million jobs created since 1997 have been in the public sector (Toynbee and Walker 2005: 156).

In the light of a record increase in the level of spending on health and education, the current level of government borrowing and the Chancellor's habit of making over-optimistic growth forecasts, one must question the extent of Brown's alleged 'prudence'. Moreover, prudence has not always been the correct approach to the economy. Brown has also been criticised for being too cautious on the issue of the euro, for failing to provide sufficient incentives for industrial investment, and for his reluctance to cut taxes even though the economy might benefit from such a move.

Gordon Brown's management of the economy has also

---

[1] One could of course argue that Brown has simply been 'lucky', in that he inherited a golden legacy from the Conservatives, and due to the fact that Tory Chancellors took many tough decisions in the 1980s in the face of rising unemployment.

come under recent criticism for his manipulation of the golden rule. By changing the start time of the present economic cycle to 1997, Brown has effectively awarded himself an additional £12 billion to play with before breaking his own golden rule on borrowing (www.conservatives.com/tile.do? def=policy.topic.pageandtabID=1). This is not the first time the Chancellor has come under fire for his 'flexible' interpretation of the so-called golden rule. Gordon Brown has also been criticised by the European Commission for running a larger budget deficit than the Eurozone would allow.

THE GOVERNMENT'S ECONOMIC RECORD

Gordon Brown is one of our most successful Chancellors. Inflation is currently at its lowest level for 30 years, interest rates remain low and Britain currently enjoys the highest level of employment in its history. The UK's economic performance under Gordon Brown is particularly impressive when one contrasts it with our main competitors. Since 1997 the UK's output per worker has risen faster than France, Germany or the USA, and public sector debt is lower than either the USA or the Eurozone. Moreover, we are currently in the longest period of sustained economic growth for over 200 years (Toynbee and Walker 2005: 117–152).

However, there are several economic problems facing Britain today.

> ➢ Inflation now stands at 2% (*Economist*, 11/2/06: 108).
> ➢ Relatively low productivity.
> ➢ Economic growth is at its lowest level for 12 years (*Economist*, 1/10/05: 27).
> ➢ The trade gap has deteriorated significantly since Labour came to power.

173

➢ The continued decline of the manufacturing sector.
➢ 20% of all job vacancies are thought to go unfilled because of a skills shortage (Toynbee and Walker 2005: 118).
➢ The UK now ranks thirteenth in the competitiveness index compiled by the World Economic Forum, down from fourth place in 1997 (*Times*, 29/9/05: 48).
➢ The possibility of a slump in house prices.
➢ The poor performance of the stock market.
➢ Consumer debt to the tune of £1 trillion (http://news.bbc.co.uk/1/hi/business/3935671.stm).

TO WHAT EXTENT DOES A CONSENSUS EXIST AMONG THE MAIN PARTIES?

Consensus has been a feature of British politics for much of the post-war era. From 1945 to the late 1970s both main parties were committed to Keynesian economics. Those on the Left wished to expand the role of the state via nationalisation and a prices and incomes policy, a combined approach which came to characterise Old Labour governments. In contrast those on the Right supported a reduction in the role of the state, but until the economic problems of the 1970s the Conservatives accepted the broad thrust of Keynesian economic policy.

In the 1980s the parties moved sharply in different ideological directions. Under Mrs Thatcher and later John Major, the Conservative Party aimed to limit the role of the state by a vigorous policy of privatisation, monetarism and *laissez faire* economics. In contrast the Labour Party moved sharply to the left, while the SDP-Liberal Alliance offered a centrist alternative.

Since the mid-1990s, New Labour and the Conservatives have moved closer together in terms of economic policy.

174

Both main parties support an enabling role for the state, in which the government concentrates on supply-side measures rather than Keynesian demand management. The two main parties also recognise the impact of globalisation and accept the so-called 'Washington consensus' which consists of balanced budgets, low tax and monetary prudence. Britain now has a flexible labour force, low direct taxation (particularly for higher earners) and a Chancellor who has made a virtue of 'prudence with a purpose'. Since 1979 the free market ethic has been retained and there has been no return to the corporatist days of the 1960s and 1970s. Indeed, according to the Milken Institute, a think tank from California, Britain now has the best financial environment for entrepreneurs in the world (*Economist*, 5/11/05: 132).

The consensus between the two main parties has been forged during a period of relative economic prosperity, which has helped to underline the desirability of privatisation and supply-side economics. It is always more difficult for advocates of an alternative economic approach when the dominant economic theory appears to be delivering a relatively stable economy. Today, the differences between the two main parties consist of policy *details*, rather than ideological substance.

POLICIES OF THE MAJOR PARTIES

In the 2005 general election, the Labour Party pledged to:

> ➢ achieve full employment in every region;
> ➢ reform the tax and benefits system to guarantee decent family incomes;
> ➢ raise the productivity of the UK economy by investing in skills, science and innovation, building modern manufacturing strength and encouraging enterprise.

The broad direction of the New Labour manifesto was in favour of workers' rights and greater regulation of business activity. In contrast, the Tories advocated less state regulation, a lower rate for the minimum wage and to create a country in which 'the people are big and the state is small'. Their specific pledges included plans to:

> abolish 168 public bodies;
> cut the size of the Department for Trade and Industry;
> introduce a Deregulation Bill;
> guarantee independence for the Bank of England.

Only the Liberal Democrats wished to raise the level of tax to pay for better public services, with a top rate for income tax of 50% for those earning in excess of £100,000 a year. Yet even they are trying to shed their 'high tax' image due to demands from a group of young, ambitious MPs, known as the 'Orange Bookers'. As with other policy areas, the Liberal Democrats offer an alternative to the two main parties. In their 2005 manifesto, the Party pledged to:

> reallocate over £5 billion a year of low priority spending to pensions, policing, health and education;
> replace the Council Tax with a local income tax;
> lift over 400,000 home-buyers out of paying stamp duty.

WHAT HAVE BEEN THE EFFECTS OF CONSENSUS?

One of the disadvantages of consensus politics is that it can be undemocratic, as it restricts electoral choice, discourages radical change and leads to an entrenched centrist approach. There are vast swathes of the electorate who believe there is no real difference between the two main parties, and the degree of consensus over a wide range of policies may be one reason for voter apathy. To illustrate the point, the difference between the spending plans of the two main parties during the 2005 general election was less than 1% of GDP (*Economist*, 16/4/05: 31).

The shift from Old to New Labour in terms of economic policy has placed the Conservatives in a difficult position. Any further moves to the right, in terms of privatisation and tax cuts, may prove unpopular. The public appears to have lost its appetite for policies that proved popular during the 1980s and 1990s, and David Cameron faces great difficulty in winning back support for the Party. Thus far, the new Tory leader has been cautious over his plans for public expenditure, although he has said that the fruits of economic growth should be shared between lower taxes and strengthened public services.

THE EURO

A degree of consensus between the two main parties exists over the broad direction of economic policy. There is, however, one exception we have yet to consider: Britain's possible membership of the euro.

The Conservative Party is opposed to British membership of the euro over the lifetime of a Parliament, whereas the government's policy is in favour of entry 'once the economic conditions are right', and after a referendum by the people. As the most pro-European party, the Liberal Democrats want Britain to join the Eurozone. The nationalist parties are also in favour, but the UK Independence party (UKIP) wants Britain to withdraw completely from the EU.

During the 2005 general election the Labour Party found it easy to outmanoeuvre the Tories on the issue of the euro.

Labour's promise of a referendum before entry, and Gordon Brown's five economic tests, helped to neutralise an issue voters do not consider a high priority.

The five tests provide Brown with an effective veto over any decision to join the euro (Stephens 2004: 165), and for all the talk of economics the Chancellor will inevitably take the decision based on hard-headed politics. Gordon Brown may ultimately want to try and outmanoeuvre Blair on the issue, such is the rivalry between the two men (Naughtie 2003).

The majority of the tabloid and broadsheet press is hostile to Britain adopting the euro, as is the electorate. As such, there are real electoral risks for the government on this issue. However, public opinion has, in the past, proved changeable on European matters, as in the 1975 referendum. In the run up to that plebiscite, opinion polls suggested the public would vote against, but by a majority of two to one, the public supported continued membership of the EC. At the present time, membership of the euro is *not* on the government's agenda (*Financial Times*, 19/7/05: 6).

Opposition to the euro is as much emotional as rational. Many British people are reluctant to surrender such a clear and everyday example of British sovereignty as the pound. Despite such opposition, it is entirely plausible that Britain will eventually use the single currency. Furthermore, most of the public expect a single currency to be introduced in Britain at some point in the future (Leonard 2005: 286).

SHOULD BRITAIN JOIN THE EUROZONE?

Our possible membership of the euro holds massive political implications, and there are several arguments for and against Britain joining.

Arguments FOR

➢ Britain will join a major economic currency that may, in time, rival the American dollar.

➢ British industry will find it easier to do business with other European economies because of lower transaction costs, as firms will no longer need to convert national currencies.

➢ Britain's membership of the euro should encourage investment and trade, and create more jobs. The Treasury estimates that if Britain joined the single currency, our economic growth could increase by 0.25% a year (www. hm-treasury.gov.uk/documents/the_euro/assessment/ report/euro_assess03_repchap5.cfm).

➢ By adopting the same currency, we will pool sovereignty with other member states. British influence within the EU will therefore be strengthened.

➢ The single currency is simply the inevitable result of deeper European integration.

➢ Common currencies can, and do, work. After all, four countries in the UK use the pound sterling.

➢ Despite the relative stability of the economy in recent years, the UK economy is too small to go it alone in the long run.

➢ Sounder public finances due to the fiscal discipline imposed by the European Central Bank (ECB), which currently sets lower interest rates than those in the UK.

➢ A single currency strengthens people's identity with Europe. In several countries, the euro is promoted as 'Europe in your pocket'.

➢ Citizens can access the same bank account throughout the Eurozone.

➢ Greater competition and price transparency within the Eurozone means lower prices. Companies will have to keep prices low due to the wider choice available to consumers.

Arguments AGAINST

- ➤ Loss of national sovereignty. Monetary policy would be set by the ECB, and any possible economic gain could never compensate for the political cost inherent in losing sovereignty.
- ➤ It may prove virtually impossible to set an economic policy that will satisfy all member countries. Can one size really fit all?
- ➤ The ECB has failed to enforce its own rules against the two most powerful members (France and Germany), thus a question mark must be raised over the effectiveness of the Bank.
- ➤ Britain is doing well outside the euro, while the Eurozone is suffering economic problems. Unemployment is higher in the Eurozone than the UK, and Britain now has the highest GDP per head of the four largest EU countries (*Financial Times*, 15/7/05: 19).
- ➤ Initial short-term costs of switching from our national currency to the euro.
- ➤ Rather than reducing inflation, the euro is thought to have increased the cost of living in Germany and Italy.
- ➤ The wealthier countries, such as Britain, may have to provide even more resources to help the poorer countries (i.e. those in Central and Eastern Europe) adjust to the euro in the near future.
- ➤ The impact of joining is likely to be considerable due to our high proportion of home-owners, which makes Britain highly sensitive to a change in interest rates.
- ➤ The needs of the British economy would be sidelined for the greater European good. The ECB may have

to implement policies that work against the interests of the UK economy.

➤ Britain's economic cycle is not aligned to the Eurozone.
➤ The ECB is unelected and therefore unaccountable.
➤ The euro may face similar problems that the ERM experienced in the early 1990s.

THE EXCHANGE RATE MECHANISM (ERM)

In an attempt to reduce inflation and improve the competitiveness of UK goods and services, Britain joined the ERM in October 1990. By tying the pound to the economic success of the German economy it was hoped that Britain could maintain downward pressure on prices and ensure that wages remained in line with those of our European competitors. All the main political parties supported the Conservative government's decision to join.

The simple fact is that Britain joined at too high a rate. This led to recession, with the knock-on effect of higher unemployment. Throughout 1992, the Bank of England spent vast amounts of Britain's foreign exchange reserves in order to maintain the high value of the pound. By 16 September 1992 Britain finally crashed out of the ERM after the Chancellor Norman Lamont had raised interest rates to a crippling 15%.

Britain's membership of the ERM was a major economic and political disaster for the Conservatives, and the political fallout can still be felt today. It was the first time a Conservative government had been forced to devalue, and cost Britain £3.3 billion in foreign currency reserves (*Times*, 7/4/05: 7). In political terms, Black Wednesday effectively destroyed the Tories' image as the party that could best run the economy.

In common with the ERM, joining the euro involves major implications for national sovereignty and stringent constraints on what the Chancellor could do. Unlike the ERM, Britain would be locked into an economic system over which it would have *no* direct control over. The political stakes are therefore high, and rarely has a debate held such profound influence for Britain's national sovereignty and political future.

THE IMPACT OF THE EU ON UK ECONOMIC POLICY

In 1972 around a third of UK trade was with the EC (Leonard 2005: 289). Today, the figure is over 50% (*Independent*, 16/6/04: 1). In contrast, trading links with the White Commonwealth (such as Australia, Canada and New Zealand) have declined since we joined in 1973.

As well as trade, the political impact of EU membership on UK economic policymaking is of deep significance. Our national sovereignty is undermined when decisions in the Council of Ministers are made on the basis of qualified majority voting. The ERM crisis was another visible example of a loss of sovereignty, but in everyday terms the importance of EU membership to our standard of living is immense. While estimates vary, it is thought that 3 million jobs are dependent on EU membership (Geddes 2004: 139).

The main impact of UK membership of the EU is on micro- rather than macro-economic policy. The EU has a direct impact on the regulation of our economy in terms of health and safety laws, workers' rights deriving from the Social Chapter, and funding in the form of regional aid to the poorer parts of Britain. The EU's competition policy has arguably had the greatest effect, as it restricts the ability of companies to create a monopoly and prevents the government from providing subsidies to failing industries.

The impact of EU membership on macro-economic policy is of more limited significance. However when the Bank of

England formulates monetary policy, it must base its decisions on the value of the pound on the foreign exchange markets, which of course includes the euro. Our interest rates also have to take into account the state of the Eurozone economy as so much of our trade is dependent on demand from other European countries.

European integration has fundamentally changed UK economic policymaking, and nothing will affect this relationship more than Britain joining the Eurozone. *If* Britain eventually joins, our monetary policy will effectively be decided by the ECB. Fiscal policy (taxation and public expenditure) would still be in the hands of the government, but our ability to set tax rates and levels of public spending would be greatly influenced by the wider needs of the Eurozone. Added to the many arguments both for and against our possible membership of the euro, a political question must be raised over the ECB's democratic accountability.

9

European Cooperation and the UK

Objectives from the syllabus

* Students should gain a knowledge of the major stages in the process of European integration since 1945 and of the developing relationship between the UK and the EEC/EC/EU. However, the main focus will be on contemporary developments in the post-1979 period.
* Students will not be expected to have a detailed knowledge of the treaties, but should be aware of their general thrust and significance.

Internet websites

www.europa.eu.int
www.ue.eu.int/en/summ.htm
www.cer.org.uk
www.essex.ac.uk/ECPR/

Old exam questions

15 minutes

Distinguish between supranationalism and intergovernmentalism in the EU.   June 2004

How do member states' views on subsidiarity differ?   Spec

Outline the issues associated with the enlargement of the EU.   Spec

What are the main problems associated with the planned enlargement of the EU?   June 2002

Explain the main conditions which candidate countries have to meet in order to join the EU.   June 2004

45 minutes

Assess the impact of the enlargement of the European Union in and after 2004.   June 2005

45 minutes (synoptic)

In what ways, and to what extent, can member states of the EU preserve their national interests and sovereignty?
                                                          June 2003

Distinguish between intergovernmentalism and supranationalism and explain which of these terms better describes the European Union.   Spec

INTRODUCTION

To explain why European integration took place, we need to begin with the Second World War. Most European countries experienced a severe challenge to the nation state; either from German occupation, or, in the case of Italy and Germany, at the hands of the Allies. Almost all had suffered from the excesses of political extremism; either from a home-grown version, or one imposed on them. A new form of political cooperation was needed in order to establish peace within Europe. The need was particularly acute between France and Germany, who had fought three land wars in the space of

70 years. It was the desire to avoid another war that provided the inspiration for European integration.

The first concrete step along the path to European integration was the European Coal and Steel Community (ECSC) in 1952. The objective was to lock the coal and steel industries so closely together as to render another war between France and Germany 'materially impossible'. To remove the possibility of elected politicians appealing to their country's national interests, the ECSC was established as a supranational institution.

Supranational institutions

A supranational institution is one that exists *above* the nation state, and has the power to impose decisions on member states. Many of the EU's institutions are supranational, such as the Commission, the European Court of Justice (ECJ) and the European Central Bank (ECB). The key implication is that *any* decision made by a supranational body takes precedence over national law. It is also important to note that a supranational institution is independent of the member states. Member states voluntarily transfer sovereignty to a supranational institution, and do so in the hope of gaining political and economic benefits. In the case of the ECSC, it was the prevention of war. As coal and steel are vital raw materials in the production of a mass army, it was assumed that no member state would have either the ability, or the reason, to rebuild its war machine if those industries fell under the control of a supranational institution. It is not hard to see why the ECSC appealed to those countries devastated by war.

Since the creation of the ECSC national governments have surrendered or pooled sovereignty in order to gain various benefits. Furthermore, nation states can no longer achieve their aims, such as the prevention of terrorism and the protection of the environment, without some form of cooperation with other countries.

The success of the ECSC established a practical path for European integration, and in 1957 six countries (France, Germany, Belgium, Luxembourg, Holland and Italy) agreed to extend the principle of supranationalism. This led to the creation of two new communities: the European Atomic Energy Community (or Euratom), and the European Economic Community (EEC). Both of these were established by the 1957 Treaties of Rome, and were later merged under the more widely used title European Community, or EC.

The most important of the three communities was the EEC, which established a customs union among the six member states. A customs union exists where tariffs and quotas are eliminated between the member states, and an external tariff is imposed on goods and services entering any of the member states from outside. The customs union made trade easier between the six member states, and facilitated a rapid increase in economic growth.

Two other institutions were established in the immediate post-war period: the Western European Union (WEU) and the Council of Europe. The WEU covers military cooperation among its members, while the Council of Europe is best known for the European Convention of Human Rights (ECHR), a wide-ranging document covering several rights and freedoms. While neither institution is part of the EU, they are significant in the sense that both were based on intergovernmentalism.

> **Intergovernmentalism**
>
> Intergovernmentalism can be defined as cooperation between governments of EU member states, in which the national veto is retained. Intergovernmental organisations 'allow national states to cooperate on specific matters while maintaining their national sovereignty' (Budge *et al.* 2001: 87). The two main intergovernmental institutions within the EU are the European Council and the Council of Ministers. The UK has always favoured intergovernmentalism as opposed to supranationalism, regardless of the party in power. Even the relatively pro-European Tony Blair has gone on record opposing a federal superstate (Booker and North 2003: 414).

FEDERALISM VERSUS INTERGOVERNMENTALISM

The EU owes a huge debt to federalist thinkers such as Robert Schuman, Jean Monnet, Altiero Spinelli and Paul-Henri Spaak. The founding fathers of European integration shared a vision in which the people of Europe would live in peace, and nation states would be subsumed by a 'United States of Europe'. Decisions would be left to non-elected bureaucrats who would pursue the European interest, rather than elected politicians who tend to pursue their own national interests in the hope of electoral benefit. The principal focus for decision-making would be the Commission, acting as the engine of integration and seeking European-wide solutions to those issues facing the people of Europe.

The EU today has elements of a federal structure, although it is far from a United States of Europe. The EU's legislative branch is the European Parliament, the EU's judiciary is the

European Court of Justice, and the nearest thing the EU has to an executive is the Commission. Each of those EU institutions holds supranational powers to a greater or lesser extent. The EU also displays the symbols of a federal state such as a single currency, a flag, a common passport and an anthem (Beethoven's *Ode to Joy*).

We cannot discuss federalism without a consideration of neo-functionalism. One of the leading neo-functionalists was Jean Monnet, who argued that the process of closer integration would, in time, allow the people of Europe to appreciate the practical and economic benefits of closer integration. To take the example we began with, the ECSC locked together the industries of war in order to ensure peace throughout mainland Europe. Once people began to appreciate such benefits, they would become more supportive of further moves towards a federal Europe.

Neo-functionalism

Neo-functionalism states that the EU should proceed on the basis of incremental progress. It provides a practical method by which the goal of a United States of Europe could be achieved, and might therefore be described as 'federalism by stealth'.

According to the neo-functionalists, the process of integration would proceed on a gradual basis due to the effects of spillover. That is, once integration spills over from one area (e.g. coal and steel) to another, the process of integration gains its own momentum. The French Foreign Minister Robert Schuman argued that the ECSC would create pressure for a common energy policy, and eventually industrial and economic policy. To take a more recent case, the single market has spilled over into the creation of a single currency.

190

Each small step towards further integration would entail only a minor erosion of national sovereignty, and therefore none of those steps alone would be radical enough to result in a public backlash, or significant opposition from the member states. European integration would therefore proceed on a gradual, rather than sudden, basis.

WHAT ARE THE PROBLEMS WITH THE NEO-FUNCTIONALIST APPROACH?

- It is inherently undemocratic. Many EU institutions are unelected and unaccountable, such as the ECB. Even those that are accountable suffer from a so-called democratic deficit.
- Bureaucrats may not be the most appropriate people to deal with political issues, partly because they do not represent the interests of the people.
- It creates bureaucracy. Although the number of European civil servants is about the same as a medium-sized city council, some EU policy areas are prone to waste and excessive red tape.
- Removed from any electoral considerations, the Commission has faced allegations of corruption and fraud.

In a federal Europe, power would be shared between the EU, member states and local government. The EU would do what is appropriate for a central government, such as setting monetary policy and negotiating agreements with external actors, while national governments would retain power over policies such as education and health. The local level would deal with issues closest to the people, such as local transport.

191

WHAT WOULD BE THE PROBLEMS WITH A FEDERAL EUROPE?

- It would centralise power to Brussels. Critics say that a federal Europe would be little more than a bureaucratic superstate, dictating our lives from Brussels without any true accountability to the people.
- It would prove ineffective due to the huge diversity of national interests within an organisation of 25 member states.
- The loss of national sovereignty would be unacceptable to the member states.

Despite the hopes of the early federalists, the EU has not developed into a United States of Europe. This is due to four factors:

1 The influence of political leaders who have favoured intergovernmentalism, such as Mrs Thatcher and the former French President Charles De Gaulle.
2 National governments have on occasions proved reluctant to hand over powers to supranational bodies: from the French Parliament's rejection of a European Defence Community in 1954, to Mrs Thatcher's famous 'no, no, no' reply to Jacques Delors' aim to create a federal Europe.
3 Public opinion is not generally supportive of greater federalism – the turnout at each EP election has steadily declined, Danish voters refused to ratify the Maastricht Treaty, as did the Irish over the Nice Treaty, and in 2005 both the French and the Dutch voted against the EU Constitution.
4 In an organisation of 25 states, a United States of Europe would inevitably face difficulties due to the diverse range of national interests.

192

The fundamental aim of intergovernmentalism is to maintain national sovereignty. Intergovernmentalists are not opposed to European integration itself (even Mrs Thatcher was a keen advocate of the single European market), but they believe that the EU should *only* act and work together if the member states agree to it. Charles De Gaulle once declared that 'there is, and can be no Europe other than a Europe of the States', which stands in contrast to the federal goal of a United States of Europe.

WHAT ARE THE PROBLEMS WITH INTERGOVERNMENTALISM?

- Inevitably leads to agreement based on the lowest common denominator, which can mean the EU failing to agree on an effective position, such as during the Bosnian war.
- The pace of European integration is dictated by the slowest ship.
- In an organisation of 25 member states decision-making can prove cumbersome, particularly when unanimity is required.
- Member states may place their own national interests above the collective European interest.

According to intergovernmentalists, only the elected representatives of the member states should drive European integration forward. Intergovernmentalism could therefore claim to be more democratic than the supranational alternative, although it is arguably less efficient. The main inter-governmental institutions are the European Council and the Council of Ministers. In the European Council each Head of State/government meets to discuss issues of major importance, with decisions reached on the basis of unanimity.

193

In the Council of Ministers, most decisions are taken on the basis of qualified majority voting (QMV), while the most important areas are subject to national veto, such as the accession of new members.

QMV

In the Council of Ministers, member states have a set number of votes allocated on the basis of their population. Decisions are reached on a majority basis, rather than unanimity. QMV is controversial because the representatives of member states lose the right to veto and may therefore be forced to accept a decision they do not support.

As an organisation of 25 member states, it is somewhat inevitable that the EU has been influenced by both federalism and intergovernmentalism. The driving force behind a federal Europe has always been the Franco-German alliance, often with the support of the core states (Italy, Belgium, Holland and Luxembourg), the Club Med (Spain, Portugal and Greece) and Ireland. The British preference for intergovernmentalism has found allies in Sweden, Denmark and the new member states of Central and Eastern Europe. Naturally, alliances depend on the issue. For instance, in recent years Holland has taken a more sceptical view of the EU due to fears of mass immigration from the new member states, and the fact that the Dutch pay the most *per head* into the EU. Public opinion can also render such categories meaningless, as the dramatic rejection of the EU Constitution by the French and the Dutch demonstrated in 2005. However, such broad categories have often held true throughout the development of European integration.

Although they are less powerful than the member states,

the EU institutions have played a key role in the development of European integration. Both the European Parliament and the Commission favour greater federalism, and have on occasions actively campaigned to achieve that goal. For example, in a report entitled *Constructing a Political Europe* (2004), the then President of the European Commission Romano Prodi recommended 50 policies designed to deepen integration. As the study derived from the President of the Commission, it came as no surprise that such measures would have led to a more federal Europe.

Political ideology plays a less significant part in the process of European integration, although it deserves a mention. Centrist politicians tend to be the most supportive of European integration. In contrast, those on the left criticise the EU for serving the interests of big business, and for its attachment to neo-liberal economics. Those on the right dismiss the EU as a bureaucratic socialist institution, committed to redistributive policies (e.g. the Common Agricultural Policy and regional policy) that undermine economic growth. They are deeply reluctant to accept any further loss of national sovereignty and argue that 'Brussels' is too interventionist.

THE HISTORICAL DEVELOPMENT OF EUROPEAN INTEGRATION

The development of European integration could be characterised as a 'permanent tension' (Hutton 2002: 287) between supra-nationalism and intergovernmentalism. The debate between the federalists against those who wish to protect the national interests of the member states has shaped the process of European integration, and does so to this day. One might argue there have been several periods in the development of the European Community/Union, each one characterised by the dominance of either intergovernmentalism or federalism.

1945–1950: intergovernmentalism

The original supporters of a more united Europe drew together French idealists such as Monnet and Schuman, alongside British Conservatives such as Duncan-Sandys. The most notable endorsement of a federal Europe came from Sir Winston Churchill, who suggested that France should lead Germany into a United States of Europe (Pinder 1998: 4). Despite such support, the immediate post-war era was dominated by a cautious approach to what was a new and radical experiment. The European nations that emerged out of the carnage of war had little desire to completely abandon their hard-fought sovereignty to an all-embracing political federation. In addition, the fact that Nazi Germany had attempted to create their own Fascist version of a united Europe had somewhat discredited the goal of a United States of Europe.

The Organisation for European Economic Cooperation (OEEC) was based firmly upon cooperation between the states, which reflected the intergovernmental theme of the immediate post-war era. Two important non-EU institutions were also set up along intergovernmental lines: the Council of Europe and the North Atlantic Treaty Organisation (NATO). The European nations were simply not willing to accept a federal Europe at that time.

1950–1966: federalism

The 1950s and 1960s was the golden age of European integration. During a period of rapid economic growth and relative stability within Europe, the core European states of France, Germany, Italy, Belgium, Luxembourg and the Netherlands took steps towards deeper integration along a supranational path.

The importance of the ECSC can hardly be overstated.

196

Made up of technocrats and bureaucrats rather than politicians, it was a courageous and ultimately successful move that demonstrated the practical advantages of supranational institutions. It has since been disbanded, but its legacy can be found today in the legitimacy afforded to other unelected bodies within the EU, such as the ECB in Frankfurt.

The key event during this era was the creation of the European Community in 1957. The original six members formed a unique organisation committed to the federal aim of 'an ever closer union' (the preamble to the Treaty of Rome), and to securing four freedoms throughout the member states:

1 Movement of goods. Internal tariffs and quotas were finally abolished in 1968.
2 Movement of capital. Exchange controls were abolished during the mid 1980s, as the member states moved towards a single European market.
3 Movement of people. Despite all the EU's efforts since 1957, the goal of free movement of labour throughout Europe has not been achieved. While all EU citizens are entitled to work in another member state, only 0.4% actually do so (Crosbie 2004: 54). Part of the reason is that Europe is not like the USA. Whereas America shares a common language and history, and to some extent a shared set of values, Europeans retain their own national cultures rather than sharing a common European identity. Other barriers include different tax rules, the fact that some qualifications are not recognised in all the member states, and immigration restrictions on the citizens of the ten newest member states (Crosbie 2004: 54).
4 Movement of services. The Lisbon strategy (2000) aims to ensure the completion of an internal market in financial services. Providers of financial services can

197

now offer the full range of services throughout the member states (Cowles and Dinan 2004: 106). The UK government is strongly in favour of a single market in services, due to the economic gains it could bring to the City of London.

1966–1985: intergovernmentalism

The Luxembourg compromise of 1966 marked a turning point in the development of European integration. It came about due to the French President Charles De Gaulle's insistence that national sovereignty should not be threatened by European integration. The agreement that followed granted the power of veto to the member states on issues of vital national interest. It marked a clear victory for the inter-governmentalists.

During the 1970s and early 1980s, intergovernmentalism was the dominant approach. The creation of the European Council, the accession of the United Kingdom, the establishment of European political cooperation and prolonged negotiations resulting in the British rebate dogged any potential progress towards 'an ever closer union'. This was the era of Eurosclerosis, when the development of European integration slowed down considerably.

1985–present day: federalism and intergovernmentalism

Since the Rome Treaties were signed in 1957, the EU has instigated four treaties. To understand the significance of those treaties, we need to distinguish between widening and deepening in the context of European integration. The debate between widening and deepening reflects the tension between intergovernmentalists such as the UK on the one hand and federalists such as Germany, France and the Benelux countries on the other.

Widening versus deepening

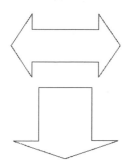

Widening consists of enlarging the EU. This has occurred five times, with ten new members joining on 1 May 2004.

Deepening consists of further integration among the existing member states. It entails a shift towards a federal Europe, and is more common than widening.

THE SINGLE EUROPEAN ACT

The Single European Act (SEA) marked the first comprehensive revision of the Treaties of Rome. The SEA was signed during a period of dynamism within the EC under the President of the Commission Jacques Delors. It placed a renewed emphasis on deeper integration and marked a shift towards a federal Europe.

The main policy of the SEA was the Single European Market (SEM). The aims of the SEM were to establish the world's biggest single market and ensure the free movement of goods, people, capital and services throughout the EC.

Although primarily concerned with the SEM, the SEA improved the decision-making process by strengthening the role of the supranational institutions. For example, the acceptance of new member states would now require the consent of the European Parliament, and QMV was introduced in the Council of Ministers. Although unanimity remained on issues of major importance, the ability of member states to veto proposals they disagreed with was removed. This was undoubtedly a milestone in the development of European integration.

The impetus behind the SEA was political *and* economic. The economic aim of the SEA was to limit inflation by member states working together towards a single currency. The political objective was to allow 12 member states to act in a more decisive manner, and as a way of binding Germany within Europe. The German Chancellor Helmut Kohl spoke for many federalists when he said that an economic union would only survive if it was based on a political union.

Mrs Thatcher signed the SEA because she firmly believed that it would lead to a deregulated free trade Europe. However, she was in the minority and became increasingly critical of the federalist direction of the EC after the SEA. The clash of ideas and personality between Thatcher and the Commission President Jacques Delors soured Britain's relationship with Europe during the late 1980s.

THE MAASTRICHT TREATY

During the early 1990s, Europe was radically transformed by the collapse of Communism and the reunification of Germany on 1 October 1990. The EU's response to this new Europe was the Maastricht Treaty (also known as the Treaty on European Union). Under the forceful influence of Jacques Delors, Maastricht was unmistakably federalist in scope and direction, although the 'f-word' was removed from the text on Britain's insistence. The UK Prime Minister John Major signed the Treaty after securing an opt-out from the Social Chapter.

The main elements of the Maastricht Treaty were:

➢ co-decision making between the Council of Ministers and the European Parliament;
➢ a common European citizenship was established;

➤ QMV was extended;
➤ following the establishment of a single European Market, Maastricht laid down a blueprint for economic and monetary union (EMU), namely the introduction of a single currency;
➤ renaming the EC as the EU, comprising three pillars (Economic and Monetary Union, the Common Foreign and Security Policy, and Justice and Home Affairs);
➤ the implementation of a Social Chapter to guarantee workers certain rights;
➤ a cohesion fund to help poorer states and regions, along with the Committee of the Regions. Both measures were designed to enhance the involvement of the regions in accordance with the principle of subsidiarity.

What is subsidiarity?

Subsidiarity can be defined as 'the principle that decisions should be made at the most appropriate level'. Article 3b of the Maastricht Treaty states that the EU can 'take action ... only if and insofar as the objective of the proposed action cannot be sufficiently achieved by the member states and can by reasons of its scale and effects be better achieved by the Community'. Therefore, decisions can be taken *below* the nation-state *or* by the member states *or* by the EU. The advantage of subsidiarity is that it appeals to both federalists and intergovernmentalists. John Major claimed that the concept ensured the dominance of national governments, whereas pro-Europeans claimed that subsidiarity meant more federalism. To an intergovernmentalist such as John Major, the most appropriate level is clearly the national government. To a federalist, subsidiairity means sharing power

> between the EU, the member states, and regional/ local government. Since the Maastricht Treaty was ratified, Sweden has used the concept of subsidiarity to promote the benefits of EU membership to its citizens, and for federal countries like Germany subsidiarity fits in well to existing political structures. For John Major, it represented 'game, set and match to Britain'.

The Maastricht Treaty set in motion a debate over European integration that divided the Conservative Party during the 1990s. After the 1992 general election, John Major was dependent on cross-party support to defeat a sizeable number of Eurosceptics within his own party. He even had to threaten the dissolution of Parliament in order to persuade enough backbench MPs to toe the Party line. The Maastricht Treaty was eventually ratified by the UK Parliament on 24 July 1993, after a large-scale rebellion from Tory backbenchers.

THE TREATY OF AMSTERDAM

Political support for European integration declined between 1992 and 1997. Referendums held in Denmark, France and Ireland highlighted considerable public opposition to the Maastricht Treaty. In economic terms, no less than five currencies in the ERM were forced to devalue, with two (including the UK) actually leaving the scheme. Added to the diplomatic row over BSE in British beef, progress towards an 'ever closer union' appeared to slow down.

Due to the public's less than wholehearted endorsement of the federalist direction of Maastricht, the Treaty of Amsterdam (TOA) was merely a 'tidying up exercise' that consisted of the following measures:

- after the election of a new Labour government, Britain opted into the Social Chapter;
- a new supranational institution, Europol, was established;
- the member states agreed to coordinate a common immigration and asylum policy;
- Article 13 extended anti-discrimination measures;
- enhanced cooperation was introduced, which allows groups of states to use EU institutions in order to promote closer cooperation among themselves;
- the rules governing EMU were finalised under the title Stability and Growth Pact.

The TOA failed to resolve the problematic issue of a common defence policy, due primarily to opposition from the neutral states, who blocked an attempt to merge the Western European Union (WEU) into the EU. As a compromise, it was agreed that NATO would remain the security guarantor of the EU member states. More importantly, the cumbersome process of institutional reform in order to accommodate the proposed enlargement of the EU was shelved. The member states could only agree on a series of proposals called Agenda 2000, raising issues for discussion that were due to be resolved at the Nice Summit of December 2000.

THE TREATY OF NICE

After lengthy negotiations and a second Irish referendum, the Nice Treaty was finally ratified in October 2002. The key focus of the Nice Treaty was institutional reform to accommodate enlargement towards Central and Eastern Europe. There were three main changes:

203

1   The size of the Commission would be limited to one
    member from each country.
2   The number of MEPs was increased to 732.
3   QMV was extended in 23 new areas, although Britain
    did succeed in getting a proposal for QMV over tax
    and social security dropped.

The only other item of note was the establishment of the
Charter of Fundamental Rights.

SUMMARY

The EU is neither wholly intergovernmental nor wholly
federal. While it contains federal-like institutions, one could
argue the most important institutions are intergovernmental.
The EU could even be described as a confederation, in which
sovereign states have voluntarily (as opposed to being coerced
by a foreign power) surrendered or pooled sovereignty in
several policy areas. Under this system power is ultimately
held by the member states, and the EU derives authority
from the states (McCormick 2004: 7). In fact, any country
could withdraw from the EU. Thus far, the only country to
have left the EU is Greenland, soon after they gained
independence from Denmark in 1984.

The EU is currently in a 'pause for reflection' after the
rejection of the EU constitution by Dutch and French voters.
Deeper integration appears unlikely in the foreseeable future,
although the pro-federalist states remain in favour. The more
likely path is to widen the EU from 25 to 28 members.
Bulgaria and Romania are due to join in 2008, and Turkey
should join by 2015.

ENLARGEMENT

The final issue to consider in the historical development of European integration is enlargement. The Rome Treaties invite 'any European state' to apply for membership. Since then, the EC/EU has been enlarged five times:

1 1973 – UK, Ireland and Denmark
2 1981 – Greece
3 1986 – Spain and Portugal
4 1995 – Austria, Finland and Sweden
5 2004 – Malta, Cyprus, Czech Republic, Slovakia, Slovenia, Hungary, Poland, Latvia, Lithuania and Estonia.[1]

To become a member of the EU, an applicant state must first satisfy the Copenhagen criteria (1993). In political terms, an applicant state must be able to guarantee democracy, respect human rights, sign and abide by the existing EU treaties and pledge to protect minorities. In economic terms, they would have to make progress towards the creation of a market economy, ensure that they could cope with the single European market and implement the four freedoms of the EU, and fully accept the goal of EMU.

WHY WOULD COUNTRIES WISH TO JOIN THE EU?

There are two economic reasons why a country would wish to join the EU. One is to gain access to the world's biggest single market, the other is to obtain resources from the Common Agricultural Policy and the EU's regional policy.

---

[1] 13 countries currently hold applicant status.

205

Politically, EU membership provides states with a greater influence on world affairs, strengthens their national security and often helps to ensure domestic political stability. From the perspective of individuals in those countries, freedom of movement throughout the EU is an attractive proposition.

WHAT PROBLEMS HAVE BEEN CAUSED BY THE ENLARGEMENT OF THE EU IN 2004?

➤ The new member states are relatively poor, so they are a drain on the EU's finances, particularly the Common Agricultural Policy and regional aid.

➤ Decision-making in an expanded organisation has become more cumbersome. For instance, it is now more difficult for the Commission to put forward the EU's collective position in negotiations with external actors.

➤ Enlargement has weakened a whole range of common policies, such as the Common Foreign and Security Policy.

➤ Linked to the above argument is the practical issue of how to apportion voting rights in the Council of Ministers. The crucial question is not 'how many votes should a state have?', but the effect of those votes when combined with others. The EU Constitution proposes a 'double majority', so that EU laws could only be passed when 55% of the members, representing at least 65% of the EU's combined population, voted in favour.

➤ Some of the new member states may experience political instability in the future, which could ultimately affect the rest of the EU. This is a particular concern for Germany due to their close proximity to the new member states of Central and Eastern Europe.

- There is unease among the EU-15 over the economic and political impact of migration from the new states. It is equally true that investment and jobs may be transferred from Western Europe towards the East, as multinational companies tend to be attracted by cheap labour and low taxation.
- There is growing evidence from some member states of a 'clash of civilisations' between Islam and a western, secular ideology. Although it was not a major concern in the recent enlargement of the EU, this argument is crucial to the whole question of Turkish membership.
- The new members must comply with 80,000 pages of *acquis communautaire* (the rules of the Community), implement the four freedoms and accommodate the existing EU treaties. Inevitably, they will face some problems in doing so.
- Enlargement may make EU relations with Russia more complex due to Moscow's traditional influence within Eastern Europe.
- Enlargement has increased the level of bureaucracy in the EU.
- Enlargement of the EU to Central and Eastern Europe may lead to a multispeed Europe, which would be to the detriment of the federalists. Equally, enlargement has resulted in a greater use of QMV in the Council of Ministers, unwelcome news for the intergovernmentalists.

WHAT ARE THE ARGUMENTS IN FAVOUR OF ENLARGEMENT?

- Enlargement has consolidated peace and stability in a continent in which 40 million people died during wars fought in the twentieth century.

- It strengthens what is already the world's largest single market.
- It helps to spread democratic values within the new member states, as it did to the former dictatorships of Greece, Spain and Portugal during the 1980s.
- Enlargement will increase the standard of living in the new member states, and bolster the GDP of the existing member states. In 2002 the Commission estimated that enlargement would increase the GDP growth of the new members by 1.3% to 2.1% each year, and will add 0.7% a year to the existing members' growth rates (M. Leonard 2005: 81). In practice, the economic growth of the Central European countries that joined in 2004 is already above 5% (*Economist*, 16/7/05: 38).
- It should prove easier to deal with cross-border problems such as illegal immigration, asylum and drug trafficking. One could equally say the opposite is true, as the freedom of movement within the EU may make such problems more widespread.
- Widening the EU will, in all probability, benefit Britain in the long term. Thus far, the new member states have been allies to the British cause on issues ranging from the Iraq war to the Lisbon agenda. However, during the UK's presidency of the EU in the latter half of 2005, the Blair government won few friends with its proposal to cut the level of regional aid.
- It is both desirable and inevitable to continue the expansion of the EU. The possible membership of Turkey could, however, challenge this assumption.

WILL TURKEY BE ALLOWED TO JOIN THE EU?

Turkey presents controversial questions that go to the very heart of the debate over enlargement. The barriers to Turkish

208

membership are primarily, but not exclusively, political. There are three problems one must consider:

> the Turkish government has a lengthy history of human rights violations against its Kurdish minority;
> its troops currently occupy Northern Cyprus;
> Turkey is a Muslim country, whereas the EU is a predominately Christian organisation.

There are also economic obstacles to Turkish membership. GDP per person is less than a third of the EU's current average, and its economy is heavily dependent on agriculture (*Economist*, 'The world in 2005': 47–48). Turkey would therefore prove a massive drain on the EU's regional policy and the Common Agricultural Policy. One must also consider geography, as 95% of Turkey's population is outside Europe (http://news.bbc.co.uk/2/low/europe/2420697.stm). Turkish membership would, inevitably, raise the long-term question of admitting more Muslim members, principally from North Africa. The issue of Turkish membership is, therefore, a hugely significant one for the future direction of the EU.

WHAT HAS TURKEY DONE TO SATISFY THE COPENHAGEN CRITERIA?

Under the leadership of Recep Tayyip Erdogan, Turkey has taken massive strides towards meeting the Copenhagen criteria. It recently abolished the death penalty, watered down its stance on Cyprus, reduced the political role of the military and granted wider freedoms to Kurdish minorities. It also has a long tradition as a secular, western-orientated country. For example, it joined the Council of Europe in 1949, NATO in 1952, has been party to an Association Agreement with the EU since 1963, holds associate status in the WEU and signed a customs union with the EU back in 1995.

WHERE DO THE MEMBER STATES STAND ON THE ISSUE OF TURKISH MEMBERSHIP?

Britain and the USA are the main supporters of Turkey's application to join the EU, principally for security reasons. As events such as 11 September 2001 and the Iraq war have shown, Turkish membership of the EU might go some way towards reconciling what the American political scientist Samuel Huntington (2002) called 'the clash of civilizations' between Christianity and Islam. From a British perspective, the membership of Turkey would weaken the federalist cause and the Franco-German alliance.

Britain faces opposition from Catholic countries such as Italy and Poland, who are reluctant to accept Turkey's 70 million people, most of whom are Muslim, into what is a predominately Christian club. Germany is also sceptical of Turkish membership due to the difficulties they have faced in assimilating 3 million Turkish immigrants. Concerns over assimilation are also shared by the Dutch, but the main opposition to Turkish membership is the French, who are set to hold a referendum on new members after Bulgaria and Romania join the EU. Austria will also hold a referendum, and neither of those countries seem likely to produce a yes vote (*Economist*, 16/7/05: 38).[2]

The biggest problem of all is the Turkish occupation of Northern Cyprus. While Greece is no longer opposed to Turkish membership in principle, it is vital that Turkey

---

[2] Due to concerns among some of the member states, a compromise may have to be reached. One possibility is 'privileged partnership' between Turkey and the EU, a position favoured by Austria and the German Chancellor Angela Merkel.

recognises the democratically elected government in southern Cyprus *before* it has any realistic chance of joining the EU. One must also acknowledge that Turkey would immediately become the largest country, something that the EU would find difficult to accommodate.

Despite such obstacles, and last-minute opposition from Austria, talks between the EU and the Turkish government began on 3 October 2005. EU membership is expected by 2015 but, reflecting concerns among the existing member states, Turkey faces two stipulations. An emergency brake procedure is in place if Turkish democratic reforms stall, and there is a safeguard measure designed to restrict the right of Turks to work in the more affluent western Europe if there is a mass influx of immigrants. An existing member state can also veto any of the 35 different 'chapters' of negotiations.

10

Political Systems of the EU

Objectives from the syllabus

* A knowledge of the key EU institutions and of the balance of policymaking power between them.
* A knowledge of the role of transnational political groupings and pressure groups and of their policy impact.
* A knowledge of debates about the political effectiveness and democratic accountability of EU institutions, and of proposals for political reform within the EU.

Internet websites

www.europarl.eu.int   European Parliament
www.curia.eu.int/index.htm   European Court of Justice
www.cec.org.uk   European Commission

Old exam questions

15 minutes

To what extent is there a democratic deficit at the heart of the European Union?   Spec

What criticisms have been levelled against the EU Commission?   June 2002

What are the functions and importance of the President of
the European Commission?   June 2003

In what ways has the European Central Bank become a
significant institution?   June 2004

45 minutes

Analyse the various proposals which have been made to
correct the 'democratic deficit' in the EU.   June 2004

Why does the European Parliament remain so weak?
                                                         June 2002

'The European Parliament remains merely a talking shop.'
Discuss.   June 2003

THE DEMOCRATIC DEFICIT

In a chapter on the EU institutions, one must begin with a
description of the democratic deficit. The democratic deficit
is a significant problem for the EU. It damages the image
of the EU among the public and gives ammunition for
Eurosceptics in several member states, particularly the UK.
One academic has even claimed that if the EU applied to
join itself, it would be refused entry because it is not
democratic enough (Giddens 1998: 142)!

There are four elements to the democratic deficit:

1 Lack of accountability among the EU's institutions.
2 The weak legitimacy of the European Parliament.
3 A lack of openness over how the EU operates.
4 Fraud.

Lack of accountability

Most EU institutions lack a sufficient degree of accountability. Supranational institutions such as the ECB and European Court of Justice (ECJ) are unelected and therefore unaccountable, and while the Commission is accountable to the European Parliament, the level of scrutiny has failed to prevent misconduct from individual Commissioners.

While representatives within the intergovernmental institutions are answerable to their national legislatures and public opinion, the extent to which they are held to account is weak. For instance, decisions taken in the Council of Ministers are made in secret.

The European Parliament is the *only* directly elected body in the EU, but it too lacks sufficient accountability. There are several reasons for this. There are no European-wide political parties, nor is there a clear distinction between a governing and opposition party within the Parliament. Parties do not gain a clear mandate from the European public either, because political parties focus on national issues rather than campaigning on a European-wide manifesto. Moreover there is no equivalent of *Question Time*, in which the governing party could be scrutinised and held to account by a government-in-waiting.

The unwieldy nature of the Parliament is another factor to consider. With over 200 national parties contesting elections, and constituencies made up of approximately 600,000 voters, it is highly unlikely that people know the views of their MEP. Indeed, many people do not even know who their MEP is!

The EP's weak legitimacy

Turnout for European elections has declined at each election since 1979, which has inevitably raised a question mark over the level of legitimacy the European Parliament can claim from the European public. In 2004 turnout was 45.3%; lower than the 2005 UK general election and the US Presidental elections in 2000. Turnout among the new member states was particularly low, with Slovakia recording just 17%.

Lack of openness

The Council of Ministers is one of the few, if not the only, lawmaking bodies in the democratic world that takes its main decisions behind closed doors (Bomberg and Stubb 2003: 52). There is no public record of how the representatives of the member states voted, which is clearly a major part of the EU's democratic deficit. Similar criticisms have been made concerning the ECB.

Fraud

Removed from electoral considerations and any direct accountability to the European public, the degree to which EU officials have committed fraudulent actions is of concern to many. Here are some examples:

> The Commission has faced several criticisms over fraud and corruption among its members, particularly under the Presidency of Jacques Santer (1994–1999). Despite an increase in the level of scrutiny from the European Parliament, the Commission was recently involved in another major scandal, this time over Eurostat, the EU's agency for statistics (Booker and North 2003: 420–421).

> In the early 1990s, a British economist called Bernard Connolly (1995) exposed some of the 'dodgy things' he claimed were being done in order to make the ERM work.

➤ Paul van Buiten (now an MEP, but at that stage, an EU official) was suspended after 'whistleblowing' about accountancy fraud.

➤ In August 2004, the British official Robert McCoy was removed from his post as auditor of the Committee of the Regions after informing his superiors of fraud.

➤ A whistleblower who remained in his job was the German MEP Hans Peter Martin. He used a concealed minicam to film other MEPs making use of the generous perks and expenses provided. His main target was the widespread practice of signing in on a Friday morning for a full day's work, collecting the €262 allowance and then taking an early flight home (*Economist*, 5/6/04: 36).

➤ According to the UK's Public Accounts Committee, the level of fraud in the EU totalled £630 million in 2003 (*Telegraph*, 4/4/05: 12).

WHAT HAS BEEN DONE TO DEAL WITH THE DEMOCRATIC DEFICIT?

During negotiations at Maastricht, the member states agreed to introduce the concept of subsidiarity to the EU. Subsidiarity provides citizens and politicians of the member states with the right to scrutinise decisions made by the EU, and in theory helps to ensure that those decisions are taken at the most appropriate level. In recent years, the creation of a European ombudsman could be seen as another positive step.

One of the aims of the EU Constitution was to bring Europe 'closer to its citizens'. It proposed that the Council of Ministers should meet in public when agreeing to legislation, a new President of the Council should be elected, and there should be a greater flow of information from the Commission.

Further measures could include:

217

➤ electing all supranational bodies, including the ECB and the Commission;
➤ strengthening the role of the European Parliament in order to hold the Council of Ministers to account;
➤ replacing the Council of Ministers with a second chamber of Parliament. This proposal is strongly favoured by those who wish to establish a federal Europe;
➤ the creation of pan-European parties, campaigning on a common manifesto, and seeking a true mandate from the people;
➤ greater use of referendums;
➤ a system of checks and balances comparable to the Constitution of the USA;
➤ More openness in the activities of the EU;
➤ greater powers for the Court of Auditors to deal with the problem of fraud.

AN OVERVIEW OF THE EU INSTITUTIONS

Before taking a more detailed look at the EU institutions, it might be helpful to consider a few preliminary points:

- The institutions of the EU are not based on the institutions of the member states. Even the European Parliament does not compare easily to a national Parliament. Thus to understand how the institutions operate, one has to recognise them as unique bodies.
- The power to make decisions is shared by many institutions, as is the ability to implement those decisions.
- Policymaking in the EU is dominated by the European Council, the Council of Ministers, the Commission and the European Parliament.
- In an organisation of 25 members and several institutions,

218

decision-making will inevitably be the result of lengthy and often complex bargaining.

- The Council of Ministers and the European Council are the main intergovernmental bodies, whereas the Commission, the ECJ, the ECB and the European Parliament are supranational.

THE EUROPEAN COUNCIL

The European Council consists of 25 heads of state/government, who meet approximately four times a year. They take high profile decisions, such as agreeing to the Copenhagen criteria for EU membership, and try to resolve major issues, such as the diplomatic row over British beef.

Meetings of the European Council are sometimes referred to as summits, and are chaired by the rotating presidency. Each member state takes on the presidency for six months, during which they host Council meetings. Britain held the chair during the latter half of 2005.[1]

The Council provides 'political leadership for the entire EU' (Bomberg and Stubb 2003: 55), although most of its work is spent endorsing decisions already taken by the Council of Ministers. As one of the most powerful of the EU institutions, it has the ability to set the EU's agenda and to drive major EU projects, such as the Rapid Reaction Force, and attracts by far the most media attention.

Reaching agreement among 25 member states is often a difficult and lengthy process. During Council meetings or summits, a great deal of bargaining and compromise occurs before a common position is reached. As such the Council has been criticised for taking decisions based on the lowest

---

[1] The Constitution proposed replacing the rotating presidency with a President elected by the member states for a period of two and a half years.

common denominator, particularly when faced with controversial issues, such as the Bosnian conflict.

The European Council is the most democratic of all the EU's institutions. The heads of state and government are held accountable to their national parliaments, and to some extent their own electorate. As the leaders of a country, they have to be seen as defending or pursuing the national interest.

THE COUNCIL OF MINISTERS

The Council of Ministers (also known as the Council of the European Union) is *not* one body, but several. It is a term used to describe meetings at ministerial level concerning EU policy areas (see Chapter 12) such as agriculture, the environment, trade, foreign affairs etc. There are over a hundred meetings annually (McNaughton 2003: 226), although this will depend on the Council in question. For example, the agricultural, economic and finance (EcoFin) ministers usually meet just once a month (Bomberg and Stubb 2003: 51).

The Council of Ministers has five functions:

1   To pass European law (a role shared with the European Parliament).
2   To approve the EU's budget (with agreement from the European Parliament).
3   To debate EU policies.
4   To develop the Common Foreign and Security Policy.
5   To coordinate the third pillar of the EU (Justice and Home Affairs).

Although the Council of Ministers is the EU's main decision-making body, most of the routine ministerial decisions are taken by the Committee of Permanent Representatives

220

(COREPER). The ministers are only concerned with issues that have *not* been resolved by COREPER.

COREPER

COREPER consists of civil servants from each of the member states who aim to reach agreement where possible. If the civil servants in COREPER cannot put aside the national interests of their own governments, then the issue will go to the Council of Ministers. COREPER is a branch of the EU's Civil Service, the other being the Commission. Although COREPER gains little attention, it is responsible for 90% of EU legislation (M. Leonard 2005: 24), and remains an important institution.

In the Council of Ministers, each state has a set number of votes that broadly corresponds with the size of their population. The UK has 29 votes, whereas the smallest of the member states (Malta) has just 3 votes. The voting system is biased in favour of the smaller states, thus preventing the domination of the larger and more powerful countries.

For a proposal from the Commission to become EU law, the Council of Ministers must at some stage agree to it. The ministers can either reject a proposal, refer it back to the Commission for further amendment, or accept it outright. Whatever the course of action taken, decisions are made on the basis of unanimity (where member states have a veto) or QMV. The former includes sensitive issues such as tax harmonisation, whereas the latter is now more commonplace.

The Council of Ministers is an intergovernmental institution, but since the introduction of QMV, member states have lost their national veto in many areas. They could therefore be forced to accept decisions they may not agree with.

Approximately four-fifths of all EU legislation is decided on the basis of QMV.

Most EU legislation is subject to co-decision, in which the Council of Ministers and the European Parliament share decision-making powers. The use of co-decision has increased significantly, and currently applies to two-thirds of all legislation. If the Council of Ministers and the Parliament are in disagreement, the proposal goes to a special committee in order to reach a compromise position acceptable to both bodies. The co-decision procedure would have been extended to *all* EU policy areas by the EU Constitution, and renamed the 'legislative procedure'.

As it is made up of elected representatives from the member states, the Council of Ministers is one of the most democratic of the EU bodies. Even when QMV applies, the winning side must gather a higher threshold of support than any other parliament system in the world (M. Leonard 2005: 88). However, this level of democratic legitimacy does not of course apply to COREPER, which makes a great deal of the routine decisions that would normally be the concern of the national ministers. Moreover meetings within the Council of Ministers are held in secret without any parliamentarian or member of the public in attendance, with no record of how the ministers voted. This allows ministers to blame 'Europe' for imposing decisions on them, even though they may have agreed to it in the Council of Ministers. Another way of ensuring favourable press coverage back home is to leak information, placing the best possible spin on it.

As with several other institutions, the Council of Ministers has in recent years faced demands for reform in order to accommodate enlargement to Central and Eastern Europe. The EU Constitution proposed a 'double majority' so that EU laws could only be passed if 55% of the members, representing at least 65% of the EU's combined population, vote in favour. The Constitution also proposed greater openness over the work of the Council of Ministers.

Another area of potential reform concerns the degree to which QMV should be used. What issues should require unanimity and what areas should be subject to QMV is a highly controversial topic. This issue has become more salient since enlargement to Central and Eastern Europe.

The power of the Council of Ministers has declined in recent years, principally due to the co-decision procedure, yet it remains 'the most powerful of the Community's organs' (D. Leonard 2005: 54), and 'its primary decision-making body' (Bomberg and Stubb 2003: 49).

THE COMMISSION

The Commission could best be described as somewhere between an executive and a Civil Service. It is the nearest thing the EU has to an executive, but it also acts as an administrative body. Thus it was the Commission that drove forward the SEM in a role similar to an executive, while taking on the administrative roles that derived from the SEM project.

The founding fathers wanted the Commission to be the engine of integration, placing great faith in the ability of technocrats to drive the process of European integration forward. As such the Commission pursues the European interest and remains a major force within the EU's institutional system.

The Commission has four roles:

1 To propose legislation.
2 To implement EU policies, although this is limited to only a few areas.
3 To enforce EU law (jointly with the ECJ).
4 To represent the EU on the international stage.

Twenty-five Commissioners are appointed by the member states. They meet once a week and hold various roles, much like the British Cabinet. The composition of the Commission is decided by the EU President. The Commissioner from Britain is currently Peter Mandelson, who holds the trade portfolio.

Since its heyday under Jacques Delors, the influence of the Commission has declined. Power has been lost to the European Parliament, which can now scrutinise the Commission. In terms of its ability to set the EU's agenda, the Commission has also lost out to the European Council. The demise in the power of the Commission was primarily due to criticisms following widespread corruption and fraud under the Santer presidency. Indeed, it is no exaggeration to say that the Commission is the most discredited of all the EU institutions.

Why has the Commission been discredited by fraud and corruption?

Part of the reason is the character of the Commission. It contains a group of politicians selected or appointed by national governments, which led the then Conservative Cabinet Minister Nicholas Ridley to describe it as a group of 'unelected reject politicians with no accountability to anybody' (Sampson 2004: 361).

While the Commission is not directly accountable to the public, it is accountable to the European Parliament in several ways. For instance, a committee of MEPs scrutinises all the Commission's financial agreements. MEPs can also form inspection teams with the right to see official papers, and submit oral and written questions to the Commissioners. More importantly, the European Parliament can remove the whole of the Commission, as it did in 1999.

The controversy surrounding the appointment of the arch-

Catholic Rocco Buttiglione in October 2004 once again placed the Commission at the centre of political controversy. Buttiglione labelled single mothers as bad, said that homosexuality was a sin and described AIDS as a divine punishment. Liberal and Socialist MEPs argued that such views made him unfit to hold the post of Commissioner for Justice and Home Affairs. In order to get his new Commission accepted by the Parliament, the Commission President José Manuel Barroso was forced to replace Buttiglione with a less controversial candidate. The Latvian Commissioner also had to be withdrawn after pressure from the Parliament.

The Commission is often seen as bureaucratic and inefficient, and as failing to take sufficient account of the needs and circumstances of different member states, particularly when implementing EU directives. The Commission has also been criticised for its inability to ensure that member states implement EU law. For example, it failed to enforce the raising of the ban on British beef in 1999, which led to complaints from British farmers of double standards. At the very least, it highlighted the ineffectiveness of the Commission in the face of a real political crisis.

The Commission is also seen as weak because it lacks sufficient resources and finds policies difficult to monitor due to the high number of agencies used. Those who implement Commission proposals may follow their own agenda (George and Bache 2001: 239), which has proved a particular problem for the EU's environmental policy.

Most EU institutions have been reformed in some way to accommodate enlargement to Central and Eastern Europe. At the Nice summit in 2000, the member states agreed to limit the number of Commissioners to one from each state, and in the EU Constitution it was proposed that the number of Commissioners would drop to 15 by the year 2009. This was to prevent the EU becoming too cumbersome, although it could also be perceived as a reflection of recent criticisms.

The President of the Commission

A separate mention must go to the President of the Commission José Manuel Barroso. He is the nearest thing the EU has to a head of state. He holds a range of responsibilities including:

> developing the long-term strategic direction of the EU;
> taking the lead in settling major disputes;
> representing the EU on the international stage;
> coordinating the work of the other Commissioners;
> playing a key role during treaty negotiations;
> holding a major role in the admission of new members;
> driving major projects forward.

The last of these is potentially the most important, as a President with a clear vision and enthusiasm can play a forceful role in the development of European integration. Jacques Delors (1985–1994) pursued the goal of a SEM with considerable vigour, whereas José Barroso is primarily concerned with the Lisbon agenda (see page 249).

THE EUROPEAN PARLIAMENT

The European Parliament consists of 732 MEPs elected on the basis of proportional representation from the 25 member states. As its members are the only representatives in the EU directly elected by the people, the purpose of the Parliament is to provide democratic legitimacy to the EU. However, the Parliament fails to fulfil this worthy goal for several reasons.[2]

It has gained a great deal of power since direct elections

---

[2] Due to the prospect of future enlargement, the maximum number of MEPs is now set at 750.

226

were first held in 1979, yet electoral turnout has decreased. This inverse relationship may reflect a lack of support from the public for the European Parliament. It is perceived as a remote body with little direct relevance to the lives of voters. With one MEP to approximately 600,000 voters, the link between constituent and elected representative is hardly a meaningful one, and absenteeism among its members is widespread. One might also criticise the Parliament for being too costly due to having three locations, each in a different member state, and for awarding generous travel expenses to its members.

Other factors that could explain low turnout in European parliamentary elections include:

➤ the knowledge deficit, as few voters actually know what the Parliament does. As one academic notes, '[m]ost people in Britain know little and care less about the role and powers of the European Parliament and its members' (Denver 2004: 17);
➤ there is no change of government at stake;
➤ the European Parliament has little or no impact on those policies considered important by voters such as health, education and taxation;
➤ wider concerns over a loss of sovereignty to Brussels;
➤ of less direct relevance than national/local elections;
➤ the media takes little interest in European elections, especially in the UK;
➤ Euroscepticism among voters.

The newly-enlarged Parliament has various powers. It can:

➤ amend EU legislation;
➤ reject the EU budget;
➤ block the accession of potential member states;
➤ scrutinise the Commission, and to some extent the Council of Ministers;

227

> share co-decision powers with the Council of Ministers;
> refer proposals back to the Commission;
> debate EU policy areas.

Despite these powers, the effectiveness of the Parliament is limited in several ways. The most significant problem is its inability to initiate legislation. It can only respond to initiatives from the Commission, in stark contrast to national parliaments that can initiate legislation (although it is done primarily through the government/executive). Other weaknesses include:

> the inability to develop policy;
> limited opportunities to hold the Commission and Council of Ministers to account;
> ineffective control over the EU's budget;
> lack of political direction;
> MEPs are divided along national and political lines;
> individual MEPs are less powerful than national parliamentarians;
> the Commission controls the implementation of EU legislation.

The EU constitution proposed a major reform of the Parliament. Reflecting the trend of recent times, the Parliament would have gained greater powers to influence and reject legislation. For example, the areas in which co-legislative powers apply would have increased from 34 to 70. The Parliament would also have the final say over the EU's budget, and be able to amend expenditure on the biggest single item, the Common Agricultural Policy.

Federalists want to strengthen the Parliament in order to address the EU's democratic deficit. Germany is a strong advocate of a more powerful Parliament that could, in time, perform many of the activities one would associate with a national legislature. Yet the Parliament is unlikely to become the equivalent of a national parliament because a relatively weak Parliament suits the interests of most member states. One reason why the European Parliament remains weak is that it does not hold the same level of legitimacy as national legislatures, as shown when comparing electoral turnout. Across the EU, the gap between national and European elections is around 22% (*Economist*, 12/6/04: 45). Moreover the smaller states have always prefered to work through the Commission and the Council of Ministers. As for the British, successive governments have tried to prevent the Parliament emerging as a rival to Westminster.

Although it is not currently on the agenda, another potential route for reform would be to establish the European Parliament as a parliamentary system, with the Commission dependent on majority support in the Parliament. Alternatively, it could adopt a presidential system in which the Commission President would be directly elected and held to account by MEPs.

THE EUROPEAN COURT OF JUSTICE

The European Court of Justice (ECJ) is a supranational body consisting of 25 judges, one from each of the member states. The judges are appointed by the member states for a term of six years. No judge can be removed on the basis of decisions reached, and to counter any possible charge of bias a judge cannot attend a case involving their own country.

The primary role of the ECJ is to interpret EU law. Disputes between the member states, or local and national governments, may also be heard in the Court. In 1993, Lancashire County Council successfully prosecuted the UK government for its failure to clean up bathing beaches in the county. The ECJ is the only body that can resolve disputes over the meaning of EU treaties, or the meaning and operation of a regulation or directive.

Judgements of the Court are made on a majority basis, and pronounced at a public hearing. Dissenting opinions are not expressed, which could be seen as an element of the EU's democratic deficit. Furthermore its members are unelected, and unrepresentative of society.

The ECJ is the last court of appeal in the member states, and has passed a number of important judgements ranging from pension rights to the prosecution of suspected terrorists. Perhaps the most well-known case was the Bosman ruling, which allows footballers the right to move freely from one club to another, once their contract expires.

The ECJ is one of the most respected of all the EU institutions, and perhaps for this reason reform is not on the EU's agenda. There has, however, been one minor change made in recent years. Due to enlargement, it is now possible for the Court to sit as a Grand Chamber of just 11 judges, rather than as a plenary session of all 25. The burden of work in the ECJ is shared by the Court of First Instance, a little-known EU institution.

THE EUROPEAN CENTRAL BANK

The objective of the European Central Bank (ECB) is price stability, and its primary role is to set monetary policy throughout the Eurozone economy. This consists of a single interest rate applicable to all 12 members, and control of the money supply. To ensure the smooth running of the single currency, the member states are obliged to follow the Stability and Growth Pact (since renamed the Growth and Jobs Strategy).

The ECB is a supranational institution that consists of three decision-making bodies: the Executive Board, the Governing Council and the General Council. Decisions are based on consultation with the European System of Central Banks (ESCB), a body that represents all 25 of the EU's member states. As the Eurozone applies to 306 million people in 12 member states, and the euro is one of the main rivals to the predominance of the US dollar on the foreign exchange markets, the ECB is a powerful institution.

The President of the ECB is Jean Claude Trichet, who was appointed for a fixed term by the Council of Ministers. France and Germany managed to suspend the sanctions mechanism of the Stability and Growth Pact in 2004, fuelling suspicion that Trichet was appointed because he would be more favourable to his native France. This also raised a question mark over the supposed 'independence' of the ECB.

Some have argued that the ECB has done a creditable job (Cowles and Dinan 2004: 97; Reid 2004: 285; *Economist*, 16/7/05: 13), while others have criticised the workings of the ECB. The most serious criticism of the ECB concerns a failure to apply its own rules. This is a major embarrassment and has lowered the value of the euro on the foreign exchange markets. The rules and targets of the Pact have also been described as wholly arbitrary, and the commitment to low inflation may be at the expense of other economic goals, such as high economic growth and full employment. One might also argue the inflation target of 2% is both unrealistic (because it has rarely been achieved) and inflexible, or that a single interest rate cannot take into account the diverging needs of the countries and regions involved. There is, however, some flexibility within the Pact. Exceptions can be made under the Excessive Deficit Procedure, such as a severe recession, and in March 2005, the Pact was amended to include a number of 'get-out clauses' for some of the countries involved (*Independent*, 23/3/05: 38).

The members of the ECB are unelected and their meetings are held in secret. The ECB therefore has no democratic accountability to any institution. For example, in June 2001, the Economic and Monetary Affairs Committee of the European Parliament *recommended* the ECB rethink its policies, but that was all the elected representatives could do.

At the time of writing, the Eurozone members are unwilling to reform the ECB. In December 2002, the ECB submitted a proposal to reform the voting rules, under which the Governing Council would consist of six Executive Board members, and a maximum of 15 national central bank governors (Cowles and Dinan 2004: 96). It remains to be seen if the ECB goes down this route, but reform is more likely if, and when, more members join.

THE COURT OF AUDITORS

The Court of Auditors is an independent body that consists of 25 members. It could be described as the 'financial conscience of the Union', and has two key functions. One is to consider the efficiency of the EU's policies and institutions by carrying out on-the-spot checks on any item of EU income and expenditure. Its secondary function is to investigate cases of corruption within the EU, and recommend action where appropriate.

Whereas the Commission represents the European interest, and the European Council/Council of Ministers put forward national interests, the objective of the Court of Auditors is to protect the interests of the European taxpayer.

The salience of the Court has increased due to high-profile cases of corruption and fraud within the EU. The Court of Auditors essentially takes on the role a committee in the European Parliament might have, and could best be compared to the UK's Public Accounts Committee, a well-respected select committee that investigates public expenditure.

The Court of Auditors is an independent institution free

to decide how to schedule its auditing activities, how and when to present its observations, and what publicity to give to its reports and opinions. However, it lacks sufficient resources and has no legal powers of its own. EU auditors can only pass on information about fraud or financial irregularities to the EU bodies responsible so they can take the appropriate action, which they rarely do. Without the necessary powers, the EU has done little to address the fact that the accounts have not been signed off for the past eleven years (*Times*, 16/11/05: 19).

There are at present no proposals to reform the Court of Auditors. The only limited change in recent years has occurred due to enlargement. The Court can now set up chambers with only a few members each, in order to adopt certain types of report or opinion.

THE COMMITTEE OF THE REGIONS

The Committee of the Regions was established after ratification of the Maastricht Treaty. It reflects the concept of a 'Europe of the regions', which appeals to both federalists and intergovernmentalists. Federal states such as Spain, Belgium and Germany support the concept as it reflects their domestic structure and strong sense of regional government. In contrast, intergovernmentalists claim that a Europe of the regions weakens the power of supranational bodies in the EU. Nationalist parties in Scotland, Wales and Northern Ireland also support the concept of a Europe of the regions, as it strengthens their own claims to national autonomy.

The Committee of the Regions is made up of 317 members nominated from regional bodies, and appointed on a five-year basis by the European Council. Members put forward local and regional points of view in order to ensure the regions are fully represented. As with the Court of Auditors, the Committee takes on a role that might otherwise be the responsibility of the Parliament. Members of the Committee of the Regions are accountable to their own national parliaments.

The Committee ensures that regional funding is distributed fairly, and takes a major role in promoting the interests of poorer regions such as Northern Ireland and South-West England. It is for this reason that the Committee has been praised for bringing direct benefits to the public, imperative in Eurosceptic countries such as the UK.

The Commission, the Council of Ministers and the European Parliament are required to consult with the Committee of the Regions in case there are regional implications of any new proposal. As such the Committee holds partial influence within the EU, but it is limited by internal divisions, and has yet to exert the influence its supporters originally intended (Bomberg and Stubb 2003: 63).

ECONOMIC AND SOCIAL COMMITTEE

The Economic and Social Committee (ESC) [also known as the European Economic and Social Committee (EESC)] runs in parallel to the Committee of the Regions. It is of the same size and composition, the only difference being that the ESC represents a variety of pressure groups. The second point to note is that the ESC is of less importance than the Committee of the Regions.

The main decision-making bodies in the EU are obliged to consult the ESC on issues ranging from consumer protection to the free movement of labour. As with the Committee of the Regions, the main role of the ESC is a consultative one.

The ESC reflects the pluralist character of the EU, and could therefore be seen as a comparatively democratic body.

234

Yet some of the national governments see it as challenging their role as representatives of the national interest, and as such it is unlikely to be strengthened in the near future.

11

European Integration and Economic Policy

Objectives from the syllabus

- A knowledge of how and why the process of European integration accelerated from the 1980s onwards and of the major developments through which this occurred, e.g. the single market, monetary union, growing use of QMV, the enlargement debate etc.

Internet websites

www.euro.ecb.into/
www.euro.gov.uk/home.asp

Old exam questions

15 minutes

What difficulties have arisen from the introduction of EMU?
Spec

Why has there been pressure for tax harmonisation among members of the EU? June 2002

45 minutes

Why was a single currency introduced, and how successful has it been so far? June 2002

What have been the main effects of the introduction of the single European currency? June 2003

To what extent has a Single European Market been achieved? June 2004

WHAT IS THE SINGLE EUROPEAN MARKET (SEM)?

The centrepiece of the Rome Treaties is the declaratory goal of a single market in which goods, services, capital and people can move without restriction across national borders (Cowles and Dinan 2004: 100). Although vague as to what a single market might entail, the Rome Treaties do make reference to 'the coordination of member states' monetary policy (e.g. exchange rates, money supply, targets to combat inflation etc.), and Title II calls for 'progressively approximating the economic policies of member states' (Geddes 2004: 144).

The development of the SEM

The first landmark along the road towards the SEM was the creation of a customs union in 1968. A customs union exists where trade among the member states is not subject to tariffs or quotas. Trade between the six member states was therefore free from restrictions placed by national governments. As trade became easier, the EC experienced a period of rapid economic growth. Between 1958 and 1972 the growth rates of the EC economies exceeded that of the USA (Crosbie 2004: 9), but further progress towards a single market was hampered by non-tariff barriers, such as subsidies and state monopolies.

During the 1970s economic growth in Europe slowed down considerably, with the world economy suffering high inflation and rising unemployment. At a time when member states were reluctant to open up their economies to greater competition, two attempts to introduce cooperation among national currencies failed.

European Monetary System

Agreement among 8 of the member states was finally reached in March 1979 with the launch of the European Monetary System (EMS). It consisted of two elements:[1]

1　The European Currency Unit, or ECU. It was the forerunner to the single currency, or euro, which is now used in 12 member states.
2　The ERM, which aimed to ensure low and stable inflation via the cooperation of national governments on the foreign exchange markets.

At least until the end of the 1980s, the EMS was considered a success. All the member states experienced a large and sustained fall in their rate of inflation. In contrast the inflation rate in the UK, which had stayed out of the EMS, reached 10% by the end of the decade.

After considerable pressure from Europhile Cabinet heavyweights such as Nigel Lawson and Geoffrey Howe, Britain eventually joined the ERM on 6 October 1990 under Mrs Thatcher. The value of the pound was set at 2.95 Deutschmarks, subject to a 6% deviation either way.

Most commentators agree that Britain joined at too high a rate, which led to high interest rates in order to maintain the value of the pound. This contributed to a damaging recession, a significant rise in unemployment and a loss of foreign currency reserves. After a vain attempt to maintain

---

[1] The UK government of James Callaghan declined to join the EMS.

the value of the pound on the foreign exchange markets, Britain left the ERM on 16 September 1992. The so-called Black Wednesday debacle was humiliating for the UK, yet the long-term effects of our withdrawal from the ERM have been largely positive. Some commentators now describe it as White Wednesday (Lyons 1999: 78; *Observer* business section, 13/2/05: 11).

Britain was not the only country to face problems. By the mid-1990s, four other currencies had been forced to devalue or leave the ERM altogether. At that point the whole ERM was in danger of collapse, but it gradually gained stability with the readmission of the Italian lira in 1996, and the membership of Finland, Austria and Greece. With a successful and stable currency system once again in place, the EU was ready to progress towards the next stage of a single market: economic and monetary union (EMU).

Economic and Monetary Union (EMU)

EMU owes a great deal to the shared vision of French President Francois Mitterand, the German Chancellor Helmut Kohl, and the President of the Commission Jacques Delors. All had a desire to reinvigorate the Community after years of Eurosclerosis, with Delors giving his name to the plan to create EMU.

The Delors Plan

In 1985 the Commission published a White Paper outlining how the EC could complete the internal market. Jacques Delors set a deadline for the implementation of around 300 measures by 31 December 1992. The Council enacted most of the measures, with a limited role for the Commission.

Four years later, the President of the Commission published the Delors Plan, which aimed to transform the European monetary system into a European Monetary Union (EMU). The wording is significant, as a 'Union' implies deeper integration and a shift towards a federal Europe. As a neo-functionalist, Delors believed that EMU could be achieved on a gradual basis. As such he specified three stages, with Stage 2 initiated on 1 January 1994, and Stage 3 completed on 1 January 1999. As a socialist, Delors wanted to add a 'social dimension' to the single market. This was achieved via the Social Chapter.

Supporters of EMU argued that by removing trade barriers such as the cost of foreign currency transactions, and by getting rid of divergences in domestic law throughout the member states, economic growth would increase. EMU would also make progress towards two of the original goals of the Rome Treaties, namely 'the free movement of labour' and 'the free movement of capital'.

If barriers to trade between the member states were to be removed, the level of trade would inevitably increase. This would improve economic efficiency and encourage greater specialisation, and as a result all countries would benefit from the growth in trade. Secondly, if the member states could work together to reduce trade barriers between them, they would have a greater impact on the global economy. On their own, the economies of the member states are too small to make much of a difference to the global economy, but together they would be part of the biggest single market in the world. In time, the euro would rival the US dollar as the world's leading currency.

The UK's reaction to the Delors Plan

Mrs Thatcher was firmly committed to the economics of EMU, as it matched her commitment to free trade. Yet EMU clearly held a political dimension which did not match her view of Britain's relationship with Europe. She opposed the federalist ambitions of Delors, and for good measure stood firm against the Social Chapter, which she considered as little more than an attempt to introduce socialism by the back door. She later said 'we have not successfully rolled back the frontiers of the state in Britain only to see them reimposed at a European level with a European superstate exercising a new dominance from Brussels' (www//news.bbc.co.uk/2/hi/ uk_politics/653550.stm).

Her attitude both frustrated and confused our European partners. Based on the Continental preference for a 'social Europe' to rival the Anglo-Saxon approach, the Social Chapter was entirely consistent with EMU. This was certainly not the view of Mrs Thatcher or the Conservative Party, and it took until 1997 and the election of a Labour government before Britain signed up to the Social Chapter.

THE SINGLE CURRENCY

The single currency, or euro, became legal tender on 1 January 1999, when foreign exchange markets between the Eurozone (or Euroland) members ceased to exist. On 1 January 2002, the euro replaced all the national currencies of the Eurozone members. It was the biggest currency conversion in history, and was achieved without a hitch. The launch of the euro made the EMS obsolete, replacing both the ECU and the ERM.

The single currency is now used by 306 million people in 12 member states (France, Germany, Belgium, Luxembourg, Italy, Holland, Spain, Portugal, Greece, Austria, Finland and Ireland). Britain, Sweden, Denmark and the ten new member states remain outside the Eurozone.

For all the talk about economics, the single European market is unquestionably political. To quote the then German foreign minister Joschka Fischer, the creation of the euro was 'a profoundly political act' (McCormick 2004: 167). Moreover, this view is widely accepted among the governments of the Eurozone members. Only in the UK has EMU been presented to the public as primarily economic in intent (Leach 2004: 72).

How does a member state qualify to join the single currency?

In order for a member state to adopt the single currency, their national economy has to meet the convergence criteria agreed at Maastricht. The goal of the criteria is to ensure low and stable inflation. There are three aspects:

1 Public debt no higher than 60% of GDP.
2 Budget deficit no greater than 3% of GDP.
3 Inflation within 1.5%, and interest rates within 2% of the three best performing economies within the EU. Applicants also need to ensure exchange rate stability, usually via membership of the ERM, although this is not part of the convergence criteria.

Once a country adopts the euro, it transfers sovereignty over monetary policy to the ECB, a supranational institution based in Frankfurt. Among its many roles (i.e. controlling the money supply, setting a common interest rate), the ECB aims to ensure that all national governments abide by the Stability and Growth Pact (since renamed the Growth and Jobs Strategy).

The Growth and Jobs Strategy

Germany wished to replicate the success of the Bundesbank in maintaining low inflation at a wider European level. They argued that low inflation was crucial to the strength of the euro, and the wider needs of the Eurozone economy. Although the French government managed to water down some of the German proposals so as not to exacerbate unemployment, the Stability and Growth Pact was unquestionably a German idea.

If a country fails to abide by the Pact, they face penalties set by the ECB. According to the rules of the ECB, a member state in breach of the Stability and Growth Pact should hand over 0.2% of its GDP to the EU. If the conditions of the Pact are not met within two years, the deposit becomes a fine. In February 2001, Ireland became the first country to be told to amend its budget plans by the ECB.

Since the euro was introduced the ECB's rules have been flouted by Portugal, Holland, Italy and Greece; yet by far the most serious divergers from the rules of the Pact have undoubtedly, and ironically considering whose idea the Pact was in the first place, been France and Germany. As the two most powerful states, they managed to force the suspension of the sanctions mechanism contained in the Pact in 2004. However, problems had occurred before the euro was even launched, with the convergence criteria fudged in order to accommodate Italy, Belgium and Greece.

In 2004 the Commission took the European Council to court to challenge the decision to suspend the penalty. The fact that EU institutions were in a legal dispute made something of a mockery of the whole scheme, and even the most ardent pro-Europeans have accepted that the Pact has not worked in the way that it should. The former President of the Commission Romano Prodi once described the Pact as 'stupid' (Geddes 2004: 146), and left-wing critics argue that the ECB prioritises the needs of big business and neo-classical economics, which has resulted in high unemployment and the erosion of a 'social Europe'.

Among supporters of the single currency, the assumption that the euro would stimulate economic growth within the

Eurozone has not materialised. Growth rates currently stand at 1.6% compared to 3.1% in the USA. Even the achievement of low inflation has not been without considerable cost to people's lives. Unemployment is almost double the rate of the UK (*Economist*, 11/2/06: 108) and the adoption of the euro has caused problems for poorer regions, who find it difficult to compete with more efficient producers. This creates greater inequality within the EU, although that it partially offset by the EU's regional policy.

At the present time, the position of the Eurozone economy is clearly not what the architects of the single currency would have wished for. While the trade balance is in surplus and interest rates are lower than those of the UK, Jacques Delors spoke for many Euro enthusiasts when he recently admitted that the euro was not working in the way that it should. However, the long-term effects of the single currency are likely to result in lower prices for the consumer. The euro should also increase trade, enhance economic stability, result in further harmonisation throughout the EU and create a gradual convergence in the economic cycles of the member states.

The UK's position on the single currency

If it was simply a question of economics Britain might have already joined the Eurozone, but due to political reasons we have yet to adopt the single currency. On 7 June 2003 Gordon Brown announced that Britain was not yet ready to join, as only one of the five tests (see page 171) had been met. Critics point out that the implicit (and unspoken) sixth test is the most important, and that is, 'can the government win the referendum?' After 'no' votes in Demark (2000) and Sweden (2003), and with opinion polls suggesting the public is opposed to the euro, the government has yet to set a date for the referendum.

There are various pressure groups contesting the issue of Britain's membership of the euro, such as the European

Movement and the Campaign Against Euro Federalism. The CBI, the TUC and most multi-national companies are in favour. Naturally, their reasons differ. Business groups believe that more trade within the world's largest single market will hold economic benefits, while trade unions are keen to adopt similar levels of workers' rights as those of the Eurozone economy. However, this is not a uniform picture. Some union leaders and CBI members are against Britain joining the euro, as is the pressure group No Euro.

Public debate over Britain's possible membership of the euro reflects a wider debate between the two views of sovereignty. Those who believe that the concept of sovereignty can be pooled have little objection to the UK joining the euro, whereas those who consider sovereignty to be fixed and absolute tend to oppose Britain joining.

It is highly debatable whether joining the Eurozone is desirable or not. It would of course represent an irreversible step for the future of this country, and is undoubtedly the biggest decision facing Britain and its relationship with the rest of Europe.

Tony Blair wants Britain to adopt the single currency, partly because it would form part of his legacy as Prime Minister. While the Prime Minister has admitted that joining the euro not on the agenda at the present time (*Financial Times*, 19/7/05: 6), the government has set up 12 Euro Preparations Units throughout the country, and launched a website (www.euro.gov.uk) in the expectation of Britain joining at some stage. His probable successor, Gordon Brown, is thought to be more sceptical.

How has the single currency performed?

The performance of the euro has been determined by two factors: the role of the ECB and the value of the euro on the foreign exchange markets.

246

The ECB is responsible for maintaining low inflation throughout the Eurozone. Its strategy for achieving price stability consists of setting monetary policy to ensure the cost of living stays within the target range of below 2%. In its determination to meet the target, the ECB has adopted a more rigorous interest rate stance than the Monetary Policy Committee (MPC) of the Bank of England. Despite such fiscal discipline, inflation has often been *above* 2% since the launch of the euro.

All the ingredients for a strong euro are there, such as a focus on low inflation, no monetary financing of debts and deficits and a high exchange rate in terms of other currencies (Cowles and Dinan 2004: 90), but the performance of the single currency has undoubtedly been damaged by the failure of the ECB to enforce its own rules. Foreign currency investors cannot hold full confidence in the single currency when the member states ignore the Pact. This has inevitably undermined the value of the euro.

When the single currency was launched in January 1999, one euro stood at £0.70. Against the US dollar, the figure was $1.18. The euro fell consistently in value, reaching its lowest point in October 2000. The currency's initial weakness was a reflection of the sluggish performance of the Eurozone economy, and the institutional weakness of the ECB. Since then the euro's fortunes have turned around with the euro gaining in value, and by the end of 2005 one euro stood at $1.18 again (*Economist*, 3/12/05: 115). To some extent, the rise in the euro has been due to concerns over the US economy, and one effect of the euro's appreciation in value has been a decline in the competitiveness of exporters based in the Eurozone.

The politics of the euro

The aim of Economic and monetary union was to ensure a single market throughout the EU. In order to achieve this, members of the Eurozone have relinquished their ability to set monetary policy to the ECB. Member states also have to adhere to the convergence criteria agreed at Maastricht, and their fiscal policy is heavily influenced by the ECB. All these political implications must be considered if Britain is to join the Eurozone.

In the case of the 12 Eurozone countries, their participation in the ERM provided a transparent basis for deciding if exchange rate stability had been achieved. For the UK this is more difficult because the government refuses to join ERM2, a scheme that allows currencies to float at a rate of 15% either side of the euro. Only Denmark is a member, though the new member states of Central and Eastern European countries may join in the near future.

With the ERM2 operating at a generous 15% band, it would be relatively unproblematic for the UK to take the same path as Denmark. Gordon Brown claims that such a step would be unnecessary, as Britain can just as easily demonstrate exchange rate stability outside the ERM2. Part of the reason for the government's reluctance is a fear of repeating Black Wednesday, and a possible loss of electoral support.

In reaching a judgement about whether it would be in the UK's interests to join the single currency, the exchange rate at which sterling becomes fixed to the euro is of absolutely vital importance. Joining at the wrong rate, either too low or too high, would do lasting damage to the UK economy. Ideally, the rate of entry should be one acceptable to British exporters, while satisfying other Eurozone members. In a study commissioned by the UK government in 2003, the appropriate rate for entry was judged to be in the range of £0.74 to £0.85 per euro. It is interesting to note that this matter is not dealt with explicitly in any of the Chancellor's five tests, thus awarding the government maximum flexibility on this crucial question.

The Lisbon strategy

At the Lisbon summit in 2000, the member states pledged to create 'the most competitive and dynamic knowledge-based economy in the world, capable of sustainable economic growth with more and better jobs; by 2015'. In order to achieve this somewhat ambitious goal, they promised major reform along the lines of supply-side economics. The Lisbon strategy is therefore consistent with attempts to create a single market. The Lisbon agenda has led to 'a discernible, if reluctant shift in Europe toward a more market-orientated economic policy' (Stephens 2004: 160). For example, the German government has instigated the Hartz reforms in order to create a more flexible labour force, the French Parliament voted to end the statutory 35-hour week and the French Prime Minister Dominique de Villepin is attempting to reduce the top rate of income tax from 48% to 40% (*Economist*, 24/9/05: 51). The President of the Commission José Manuel Barroso is known to have free trade sympathies, and the ten member states in Central and Eastern Europe are all broadly in favour of lower tax and a more flexible labour force.

The extent of reform along the lines agreed at Lisbon differs from one country to another. Britain, Spain, Holland and the Scandinavian countries have implemented the Lisbon strategy with some enthusiasm, whereas France and Germany have dragged their feet due to the unpopularity of such reforms at a time of high unemployment. Progress has therefore been slow. The key reason for such reluctance is that most of the national governments support a 'social Europe' and do not endorse the Anglo-Saxon model of supply-side economics.

The most recent Lisbon-related initiative was the Bolkestein directive, which aimed to remove trade barriers in the tertiary sector. Its leading supporters were the British government, who claimed it could create 600,000 jobs. However, France managed to get the directive dropped. The French government fear that the whole direction of the Lisbon strategy is turning the EU into a neo-liberal economic organisation committed to the Anglo-Saxon model, with the French President Jacques Chirac going so far as to claim that 'ultra-liberalism is the new Communism of our age' (*Independent*, 23/3/05: 23).

TO WHAT EXTENT DOES THE EU HAVE A SINGLE EUROPEAN MARKET?

There are several criteria the EU has to meet before it can claim to have a fully functioning single market. They include:

> ➤ applying the four freedoms of the Rome Treaties (the free movement of goods, people, capital and services) throughout the EU;
> ➤ there should be no trading costs (e.g. different exchange rates) between one member state and another;
> ➤ the same labour laws, health and safety legislation etc. should apply throughout the EU;
> ➤ trade between companies from different member states should operate on the same basis as trading between one company and another in the same country;
> ➤ a single currency should be in use throughout the EU, as should a common monetary and fiscal policy.

Considerable progress has been made towards fulfilling the four freedoms of the Rome Treaties. Trade barriers such as internal tariffs and quotas have been largely eradicated, exchange controls were abolished back in the mid-1980s and capital controls were removed in the mid-1990s. However, the freedom of movement has proved elusive due to differences in language and culture. Other problems include countries opting out of the Schengen Agreement, and restrictions placed on citizens from the new member states.

In order for a SEM to exist there should be a level playing field throughout the EU, but this is clearly not the case in practice. Although the EU has taken some steps towards harmonisation, the single market is distorted because the laws of one member state differ markedly from another.

While the ECB sets the monetary policy of 12 countries, fiscal policy remains the sole responsibility of national governments. Neither tax nor social security have been harmonised and although many countries do use the same currency, the majority of the member states do not.

A single European market would, in effect, operate as a single economy. It should therefore be clear that the EU does not have a SEM, and thus the single market could best be described as 'an uncompleted process' (Leach 2004: 191). The enlargement of the EU in May 2004 makes the goal of a single market even more unrealistic, as the economies of the new member states are far less developed than those in the West.

Harmonisation can be defined as 'attempts to create common product standards and a level playing field throughout the EU in the interests of the SEM'. Examples include health and safety measures and agreed standards for the labelling and selling of food and drink. Harmonisation has been welcomed by pro-federalist states as an inevitable step towards a SEM, yet the EU has not yet achieved a true single market because many areas of social and fiscal policy do not apply throughout the EU.

WHAT HAVE BEEN THE EFFECTS OF HARMONISATION ON THE UK?

Harmonisation has been controversial in Britain. In the mid-1990s, the Commission requested that British chocolate makers change the name of their produce to vegelate, because British firms make chocolate differently from the rest of Europe (a compromise was finally reached in 1999). A more dramatic case occurred in April 2001, when a market trader from Sunderland called Steve Thorburn (the so-called 'metric martyr') was prosecuted under EU laws designed to harmonise labelling. His crime was to serve bananas by the imperial, rather than the metric, system.

The UK government has traditionally been supportive of the SEM, but this does not extend to losing/pooling sovereignty in controversial areas. During negotiations leading up to the EU Constitution, the UK laid down several 'red liners' over key areas of criminal procedural law, social security, the method by which member states' contributions are decided on, and tax.

WHY IS THE GOVERNMENT OPPOSED TO HARMONISATION IN CERTAIN POLICY AREAS?

The government believes that our national interests would be threatened by harmonisation in several areas. Thus if fiscal policy were to be harmonised, it is highly likely that the level of taxation in the UK would rise to a figure closer to the European average. The Chancellor wants to retain our relatively lower level of tax, and the government did not want further regulation from the EU during the run-up to the 2005 general election.

TAX HARMONISATION

The EU has moved some way down the road to tax harmonisation. Since the Nice Treaty was ratified, the scope of the British government to decide what goods and services are exempt from VAT has diminished, and corporate tax fraud and evasion are now subject to European, rather than domestic, law. For example, in April 2005 a senior judge in the ECJ ruled that the Inland Revenue should pay back billions of pounds to businesses in a decision that undermined the UK's sovereignty over taxes (*Times*, 14/9/05: 4). Due to the steady erosion of national sovereignty on such a sensitive matter, some have predicted that retained savings tax, excise duties, corporate taxation and national insurance contributions could be harmonised in the near future. Yet even the slightest development in this area would face considerable opposition from Britain and the new member states.

One of the arguments in favour of the UK's position is the beneficial effect of tax competition. As 25 member states set different tax levels, there is inherent competition within the EU to offer the lowest possible level of taxation. The assumption here is that low tax is desirable for economic growth. This has been borne out by the experience of Britain, which has achieved a higher growth rate than the Eurozone in recent years. One might add that the USA operates well with different rates of sales tax, so why not the EU?

It was the German finance minister Oscar Lafontaine who first suggested that VAT and corporation tax should be harmonised throughout Europe. His proposal was supported by France. Both countries wished to harmonise fiscal policy in order to ensure a level playing field, arguing that such a move would be consistent with the SEM. For all the high-minded talk from France and Germany of a level playing field throughout Europe, national interests are at work here. High-tax countries fear losing out to what they consider as harmful competition from the lower-tax countries. This view has become more prevalent since the enlargement of the EU.

12

EU Policy

Objectives from the syllabus

- A knowledge of the general development of EU policy in areas such as agriculture, fishing, the environment, the regions and anti-discriminatory legislation.
- Students will not be expected to have a knowledge of all EU policies, but only those that have been important or newsworthy in the UK during the three years preceding the date of the examination.

Internet websites

www.europe.eu.int/pol/financ/index_en.htm
www.europe.eu.int/pol/agr/index_en.htm
www.europe.eu.int/pol/fish/index_en.htm
www.europe.eu.int/pol/cfsp/index_en.htm
www.europe.eu.int/pol/justice/index_en.htm
www.europe.eu.int/pol/rights/index_en.htm

Old exam questions

15 minutes

Why has it been so difficult to reform the Common Agricultural Policy?   June 2005

Why has EU agricultural policy proved to be controversial?

Spec

Outline the main problems associated with the Common Agricultural Policy.

June 2004

Why is it difficult for the European Union to develop a common defence policy?

June 2002

Why is the establishment of the EU rapid reaction force contentious?

June 2003

How does regional policy operate within the EU?

June 2003

What is the significance of the Social Chapter of the Treaty of European Union?

June 2003

45 minutes

Why has it proved so difficult to reform the Common Agricultural Policy?

June 2002

What have been the main difficulties in developing common defence, foreign and security policies for the European Union?

June 2005

THE EU'S BUDGET

The size of the EU's budget is relatively small. In 2004 it totalled €100 billion (*Economist*, 18/6/05: 39), just over 1% of the combined gross national income of the member states (*Independent*, 13/6/05: 6). That works out at less than what the UK government spends on health and education per year.

There are two reasons for the relatively small size of the budget. Many policy areas (e.g. education, law and order) are decided at the national, rather than European, level. Secondly, the cost of EU policies tends to fall on the member states and/or the private sector, rather than the EU itself.

How does the EU raise its revenue?

1 Tariffs on imports entering the EU.
2 Levies placed on agriculture.
3 A percentage of revenue from VAT.
4 Member states' contributions, which are by far the most important source. The contribution made by each country is based on a proportion of their total GDP. Britain is the second largest contributor, but gains a unique rebate worth around £3 billion a year (http://news.bbc.co.uk/2/hi/uk_news/politics/4084594.stm) due to the disproportionate impact of the Common Agricultural Policy (CAP) on our economy.

How is agreement reached on the budget?

The budget is set for a fixed length of time, usually six or seven years. It is drawn up by the Commission and approved by representatives of the member states. It is then scrutinised by the European Parliament. The European Parliament can either accept the budget as it is, suggest amendments, or reject the budget altogether. If they chose the latter, the whole process begins again until a budget is approved.

How does the EU spend its budget?

- 43% CAP;
- 36% regional policy;
- 8% research, energy, industry and transport;
- 7% external activities and pre-accession;

- 5% administration;
- 1% miscellaneous (D. Leonard 2005: 98).

How the EU 'gets and spends' its money has often been controversial. In the early 1980s the member states experienced protracted negotiations with Mrs Thatcher over the British rebate. Today, there are three issues on the agenda:

1   How to accommodate the 2004 enlargement of the EU towards Central and Eastern Europe.
2   Reform of the CAP.
3   The UK rebate.

In 2005 the Budget Commissioner Dalia Grybauskaité called for each member state to contribute a little more, around 1.14%, of its GDP (*Times*, 14/1/05: 4). This is near to the maximum figure the EU can ask for; currently set at 1.27% (Crosbie 2004: 25). Her request was opposed by Britain, France and Germany, all of whom want to cap the contribution level to 1% of gross national income. The other net contributors (Sweden, Italy, Denmark, Austria, Finland, Holland and Cyprus) also wish to limit, or even reduce, the EU budget.

Only the CAP and regional policy take up a significant share of the EU budget, and both policies could be said to redistribute resources from the wealthy to those in greater need. It therefore seems appropriate to begin with the largest item on the EU's budget.

THE CAP

The objectives of the CAP are to:

➢   increase agricultural productivity;
➢   achieve a reasonable standard of living for farmers;

258

> ➢ stabilise markets in agricultural products;
> ➢ ensure supplies to consumers at reasonable prices;
> ➢ provide adequate supplies of food.

Why was the CAP created?

During negotiations at Rome in 1957, the French government were worried that the proposed customs union would benefit the more efficient Germans. As a compromise France insisted on special consideration for agriculture, due in part to the political importance of the farming lobby. Although the other member states also wished to offer some protection to their farmers, the CAP is commonly attributed to the French.

How does the CAP work?

The Council of (agricultural) Ministers sets a target price regarded as the most appropriate to meet the objectives of the CAP. Whenever the world market price falls below the target price the EU makes up the difference and gives it to the farming industry. Farmers are therefore guaranteed a high price, and a consumer, for their output.

What has been the impact of the CAP on Britain?

We joined the EC in 1973 when the rules governing many of the EC's policies had already been set. This undoubtedly worked to our disadvantage, and nowhere is the cost of EU membership clearer than with the CAP.

The CAP is meant to benefit farmers, yet British farmers have gained little from the CAP as our agricultural sector is more efficient than the European norm. For consumers, the CAP costs the average British household £1,000 a year (Leach 2004: xviii).

The CAP has also imposed political costs on Britain. Since

1973, we have sacrificed many of our trading links with the Commonwealth and North America. Agriculture has also proved a flashpoint between Britain and its EU partners. After cases of BSE in British beef, the EU imposed an export ban in 1996. The decision was against both the rules and the spirit of the SEM. The UK government claimed the ban on British beef was illegal under the Treaty of Rome, and in retaliation the UK blocked EU business for almost a month. After lengthy bargaining and a high-profile diplomatic row with France, the EU finally lifted the ban. In a less controversial measure, the movement of British produce within the EU was restricted during the foot and mouth crisis in 2001.

Reform of the CAP

Before the CAP was reformed in the mid-1980s, the policy accounted for three-quarters of the EU's budget. Today, the CAP takes up just under half of the money spent by the EU, with expenditure capped until 2013. The reduction was agreed by the EU-15 in order to prepare for the impact of EU enlargement to Central and Eastern Europe. However, the policy still faces considerable criticism.

One of the most common criticisms of the CAP is its uneven application. A quarter of the CAP goes to just 2% of the wealthiest farmers (*Guardian*, 24/12/04: 5), with the Duke of Westminster's estate receiving just under half a million pounds between 2003 and 2004 (*Independent*, 23/3/05: 16). The CAP has also led to cases of corruption and disproportionately favours France and Germany.

Agriculture accounts for just 3% of the EU's total GDP, and less than 5% of its total employment (*Independent*, 23/6/05: 4). Comparable figures are even lower for the UK, thus the level of resources allocated to agriculture is way out of proportion to its importance to the European (and

British) economy. The CAP also consists of a 'double whammy' for consumers in that it means both higher prices and higher taxes.

Both sides of the political spectrum have cause to criticise the CAP. The Left argue that the CAP discriminates against farmers from outside the EU, many of whom are in desperate need of fair access to the world's largest single market. Critics point out that the annual income from a European dairy cow exceeds that of half the world's human population (*Independent*, 13/6/05: 25). The fact that the EU then dumps its agricultural surplus on developing countries is another problem.

Those on the Right argue that this misguided policy of protectionism has led to a massive surplus of food and drink. During the early 1980s, the so-called butter mountain actually weighed more than the population of Austria (Coyle 2002: 39). Excessive surpluses of food and drink are far less of a problem now because the link between subsidy and high production has been broken, yet one could argue that surplus production is still a waste of taxpayers' money.

Why has the CAP led to a huge surplus of food and drink?

Farmers are guaranteed a buyer for their output at a price *above* the market level, and therefore have an incentive to overproduce rather than meeting the demands of the market. The target price is always above the market price because farming unions exert pressure on agricultural ministers to set a high target price.

Recent reforms

The CAP was reformed in 2003 in order to:

> ➢ reduce the overall cost;

➤ protect the environment;
➤ increase competition and efficiency;
➤ prevent the production of surplus food.

In order to achieve these aims, it was agreed that the level of prices for several products would be reduced, and subsidies going to large farms would diminish. The system of payment was changed to a single lump sum payable to each farm according to its size. Farmers also receive subsidies for protecting the environment and for diversifying production.

At the June 2005 summit France, Germany, Luxembourg and some of the new member states called for an end to Britain's rebate. In reply, Britain said it would consider a reduction in the rebate provided it was linked to reform of the CAP. As this option held out the possibility of reducing the EU budget, the UK's position was backed by Sweden, Finland and Holland. In reply, France and Germany refused to reopen negotiations on the 2003 reforms. Progress on this complex issue therefore looks unlikely in the short term, and will probably not occur until a change of leadership occurs in France and Britain.

A review of the CAP is due in 2008, at which time a number of options would be available. One is quotas, a path attempted on a limited basis since the late 1970s. Another is to offer direct support to the very poorest farmers or dismantle export subsidies. A more radical solution would be to scrap the CAP altogether and leave member states to decide on their own level of subsidy, although this is highly unlikely due to vested interests.

Why has it proved so difficult to reform the CAP?

Reform of the CAP has consistently faced opposition from the French, who are deeply committed to the CAP for several reasons. Economically, France receives a significant amount

262

of resources from the policy. Secondly, it has a well-organised and highly effective farming lobby. The CAP also holds a wider cultural significance within France, conjuring images of gastronomic excellence and an idyllic rural lifestyle. The Italians, the Irish, the Club Med states and the Germans are also broadly in favour of the CAP, principally due to the electoral impact of the farming industry.

Agricultural ministers in the Council of Ministers are strong supporters of the CAP because farming unions are a powerful pressure group in many of the member states. Some of their actions have even been militant, such as French farmers burning sheep transported on British lorries entering Calais. Even the modest measures contained in Agenda 2000 led to 40,000 farmers protesting on the streets of Brussels (MacDonald and Bowden 2005: 147). Farmers are also perceived to be an integral element to the way of life in Greece, Ireland, Spain, Portugal and Germany and thus have a wider cultural significance that makes any reform of the CAP problematic. The European Parliament and the Commission also defend the policy.

The two groups in favour of reform are consumers and taxpayers. Unlike the farmers, neither group is well organised, thus the possibility of fundamental change appears remote. While finance ministers have expressed concern over the rising costs of the CAP, and have succeeded in capping resources, the policy looks set to remain unchanged in the near future.[1]

THE COMMON FISHERIES POLICY (CFP)

As with the CAP, the CFP could hardly be said to cover an area of major economic concern. The fishing industry employs just 0.2% of the EU's total workforce (McCormick 2004:

---

[1] Although the UK government recently placed the issue of CAP reform high on the agenda, the British Presidency of the EU failed to achieve a breakthrough.

183). Despite this, the CFP has been an important policy area for the EU, and thus one we cannot ignore.

WHY WAS THE CFP CREATED?

In the 1960s the six member states were low on fish stocks, while the first wave of applicant countries (the UK, Ireland, Denmark and Norway) had plentiful supplies. In order to benefit all consumers and reflect the wider spirit of the EC, the CFP was established. From a British perspective, we once again paid the price for joining a club in which the rules had already been set.

The then Prime Minister Edward Heath did at least manage to gain a temporary waiver from the CFP in order to protect British coastal fishing by setting an exclusion zone of 12 miles. When the derogation agreement expired in 1982 Mrs Thatcher gained a better deal for British fishermen, in which they were permitted to access just over a third of the EC's total fish stocks. Yet at the time, two-thirds of all the fish available to the fishing industry of the member states derived from UK waters (Leach 2004: 35).

When Spain and Portugal joined in 1986, the number of EC fishing fleets increased substantially. Due to concerns about over-fishing, it was agreed that the integration of Spain and Portugal into the CFP would be delayed until 2002. From the perspective of Spanish and Portugese fishermen the decision was highly unfair, and after the 1992 review of the CFP, their governments took an opportunity to address the situation. Spain and Portugal threatened to veto the enlargement of the EU to Austria, Finland and Sweden unless their fleets gained accelerated integration into the CFP. After bargaining between the member states a compromise was reached in 1996 over Spanish and Portugese access to the Irish Sea, which of course affects Britain and Ireland.

How does the CFP work?

The CFP sets quotas on the fishing industries of the member states. This is to ensure the preservation of fish stocks and protection of the environment. However, the problem of quota-hopping has never been successfully tackled, because the CFP is such a difficult policy to monitor.

As with the CAP, the CFP has been criticised as wasteful. In 2003 the policy was reformed in the light of those criticisms (D. Leonard 2005: 212), but there are currently no plans to reform the CFP at the present time.

What have been the effects of the CFP on Britain?

When Spanish fishermen were thought to be quota-hopping in the late 1980s, the UK Parliament passed the Merchant Shipping Act. The legislation contravened EU law, and was later overturned by the ECJ in the Factortame case. The CFP has also been controversial in the UK because quotas directly affect the livelihood of fishing communities in Scotland and the South West.

As with the CAP, the CFP is highly unpopular in Britain. Some have even claimed that it has destroyed much of our fishing industry (Black 2004: 182; Leach 2004: xviii; MacDonald and Bowden 2005: 149), yet this may have more to do with a lack of interest shown by successive governments, who have consistently failed to defend fishing communities. This is in contrast to the position of those member states that enjoy special consideration within the CFP. As for the biggest shipping fleet in the EU, the Spanish have managed to successfully defend their national interests on several occasions. For instance, in 1996 the UK government was sued for compensation over an allegation that the Spanish fishing fleet had shipped illegally in Canadian waters. The final bill to the British taxpayer, over an issue that could have been easily avoided by the government, exceeded £100 million (Booker and North 2003: 326). One might also add that Iceland and Norway view the CFP as a threat to their fishing industries, which might partly explain why they have decided to stay out of the EU.

THE ENVIRONMENT

Environmental problems do not respect national borders. Member states therefore share a common interest in pooling sovereignty to tackle cross-border issues, and it is unsurprising to find that the environment is one of the most wide-ranging of all the EU's policy areas.

History of the EU's environmental policy

The EU's environment policy dates back to 1972. As with other policy areas, progress was slow during the Eurosclerosis era of the 1970s and early 1980s, but since the Single European Act was ratified the Commission has issued a vast number of directives on a range of environmental issues (e.g. banning the use of CFCs). The Commission also set up the European Environmental Agency to collate scientific research from the member states on environmental issues.

In the early 1990s, the Maastricht Treaty specified the objectives of EU environmental policy. They are:

> to preserve, protect and improve the environment;
> to protect natural resources;
> to increase international cooperation in order to deal with environmental problems.

The Treaty of Amsterdam (TOA) further developed the EU's environmental policy. Since Maastricht, the EU has been

266

required to incorporate 'the protection of the environment' into all relevant legislation. The TOA also enshrined the principle of sustainable development and extended co-decision powers to the European Parliament over some environmental issues.

How does the EU's environmental policy work?

Member states must meet environmental targets set by the Commission, and implement decisions made by the European Parliament. If they fail to do so, they can face prosecution from the European Court of Justice (ECJ). The EU's environment policy does not usually involve EU funds, as the costs are met by the member states.

Criticisms of the EU's environmental policy

The EU's record on the environment has been criticised for a lack of financial and technical resources, organisational problems within the EU and the difficulties faced in enforcing such policies. As the EU relies on the member states to provide the money to implement decisions, some countries have been reluctant to stump up the cash, especially when they disagree with the EU's position. Moreover, environmental issues hold less priority in Central and Eastern Europe, and coupled with a lack of resources the new member states have found it difficult to meet targets set by the Commission.

Where do the member states stand?

There is strong support for environmental protection from Holland, Austria, Germany and the Scandinavian countries. Along with 42 Green MEPs, influential pressure groups and a deep commitment to such issues within the Commission, there is a significant Green lobby within the EU.

Impact on the UK

Around 90% of the UK's environmental policy originates from the EU (www.rspb.org.uk/international/policy/prioritise.asp), thus the impact of the EU in this area has been considerable. The effect of the EU on UK environmental policy ranges from land use planning, which is relatively unaffected, to water quality, which is extensively Europeanised.

Britain has been dubbed 'the dirty man of Europe' due to its poor environmental record. The UK has been criticised by the Commission for sub-standard water, dirty beaches and the environmental effects of building new roads such as the M3 in Twyford Down. It was because of the EU that the UK government set up a National Rivers Authority. Moreover, Britain would face prosecution from the ECJ if it failed to preserve designated heritage sites such as Epping Forest and the Chilterns.

One might therefore suggest that the EU's environmental policy is a highly visible example of Britain's loss of sovereignty, yet one could argue that the EU's role over the environment transcends the sovereignty of the nation state, and is ultimately a good thing for everyone. It is certainly the case that Britain has pursued a greener approach since 1973 due to membership of the EU, and one can see evidence of that in several areas. To take one example, over 70% of England's beaches now meet the EU's highest quality standard. Back in the early 1990s, it was less than a third (*Times*, 9/11/05: 31).

SOCIAL POLICY

The 1957 Rome Treaties commit the EU to:

> ensure the free movement of labour;
> improve working conditions and living standards;

> ensure equal pay for men and women;
> provide social security for migrant workers;
> establish a European social fund to retrain workers who have lost their jobs.

Since then the EU's social policy has grown considerably. The most significant development in this area was the Social Chapter in 1989. It was the brainchild of the former Commission President Jacques Delors, who wished to extend the notion of a 'social Europe' to all the member states. Following the election of a Labour government in 1997, all member states were pledged to implement the Social Chapter.

The Social Chapter contains several workers' rights including:

> a minimum wage;
> limits on working hours;
> improvements in working conditions;
> measures to combat social exclusion;
> employer-employee discussion forums (for example, due to the Social Chapter, every company in Europe with more than 2,000 workers must now 'inform and consult' with its workforce and form a works council).

What has been the impact on the UK?

When the UK joined in 1973, the EC's social policy was broadly consistent with our own corporatist approach to economic management. Since 1979, we have gradually diverged from the rest of Europe over macro-economic policy.

The Social Chapter stands against everything the New Right advocates, such as flexible labour markets and limiting the role of the state. It was firmly opposed by Mrs Thatcher, who dismissed it as 'Marxist' (George and Bache 2001: 123), whereas the Labour Party warmly welcomed it. The Labour Party's attitude to the EC was transformed in the late 1980s due to the notion of a 'social Europe'. It also gave trade unions an opportunity to regain some of the influence they had lost under Mrs Thatcher.

During negotiations over the Maastricht Treaty, John Major gained an opt-out for the UK. As promised in their 1997 election manifesto, the Labour government opted into the Social Chapter. Today, the Conservative Party remains opposed to the Social Chapter, and pledged to negotiate another opt-out in the 2005 general election campaign. Arguments for and against the Social Chapter are shown in Table 12.1.

Why does the EU's approach to social policy differ from the UK's?

The main reason is a difference in work culture. The British work longer hours than anyone else in the EU (Crosbie 2004:

Table 12.1 Arguments for and against the Social Chapter

Arguments for	Arguments against
Protects workers rights.	Reduces the international competitiveness of the Eurozone economy. Although high labour costs might be one reason for this, there are other factors to consider such as labour rigidity and relatively low economic growth.
Ensures a level playing field throughout the whole of Europe.	Might increase unemployment due to higher labour costs.
Supports the notion of a 'social Europe'.	Contributes to a 'fortress Europe' where cheap foreign labour is discouraged from migrating to EU countries.
Avoids the exploitation of workers.	Contributes to the negative effects of corporatism (e.g. trade union militancy, over-regulation). According to the New Right, corporatism damaged the British economy during the post-war era.

114), a trend that has actually increased in recent years. More Britons now work beyond the Working Time Directive of 48 hours a week than when the legislation was first passed in 1993.[2]

The second reason is due to the impact of the New Right. Governments of both parties have applied supply-side economics to the labour market since 1979. It is a clear measure of the difference between Britain and its European partners that a Labour government has refused to award any special favours to the trade unions, whereas union militancy has led to disruption in France, and Austria. Many of the Continental countries have a greater level of workers' rights, and union consultation, than the British.

The UK's preference for supply-side economics stands in direct contrast to the Rhineland model of generous worker protection, and this divergence surfaced during the bad-tempered Luxembourg summit of June 2005. It was partly concerns over the 'liberal' direction of the EU that led to the French rejecting the EU Constitution, whereas Tony Blair can contrast our relative economic success against the sluggish performance of the Eurozone.

REGIONAL POLICY

The EU's regional policy aims to ensure that regional problems are taken into consideration in all EU policy areas. The EU also attempts to coordinate the regional policies of the member states and provides financial support for the development of the EU's poorer regions. There are three sources of regional policy:

---

[2] In 2005 the European Parliament tried (unsuccessfully) to remove Britain's right to opt out of the EU's Working Time Directive

> the European Social Fund (ESF), which dates back to 1957;
> the European Regional Development Fund (ERDF), created in 1975;
> the Cohesion Fund (1987).[3]

How does regional policy work?

There are three categories of regional policy. Objective One consists of areas where the GDP per head is less than 75% of the EU average, such as Cornwall. Around 70% of the budget allocated to regional policy goes on Objective One. Objective Two consists of grants to small businesses, with the aim of job creation. The third objective is a mix of education programmes and job training. A small amount of the budget also goes on new projects to see if they might work on a larger scale. If they are successful, more resources will follow at a later date.

The two institutions who decide on the EU's regional policy are the Commission and the Committee of the Regions. Both are involved in the negotiation process, and once agreement has been reached resources are then distributed.

History of regional policy

Regional policy began with the ESF, although the level of resources allocated to it was small. It was added to the Treaty of Rome by Italy, as their economy was the weakest of the original six member states.

The membership of the UK in 1973 gave added impetus to regional policy. The Prime Minister Edward Heath campaigned for a Regional Development Fund to provide

---

[3] One might add the EAGGF (Agricultural guidance and financial instrument on fisheries) to the list, although it is relatively insignificant.

assistance to poorer areas. He gained the support of Ireland and Italy, but could not convince the wealthier states to provide sufficient funds. Against the background of the economic problems of the 1970s, the amount of money provided was, once again, modest.

During negotiations leading up to the Single European Act (SEA), the member states expressed concern over the impact of the Single European Market (SEM) on disadvantaged areas. They wished to increase resources awarded to regional policy and to improve the economic performance of poorer areas by redistributing money towards them. A Cohesion Fund was therefore established.

The Cohesion Fund was designed to promote economic growth and address the problem of poverty. It was consistent with the Maastricht Treaty's commitment to a Europe of the regions, and might also be considered as part of the EU's wider commitment to a 'social dimension' (alongside social policy).

In response to successive enlargements, the money allocated to regional policy has grown in order to accommodate the membership of poorer countries such as Spain, Portugal and the new member states of Central and Eastern Europe. Thus between 1988 and 1993 resources doubled, and from 1994 to 1999 doubled once again (Pinder 1998: 133–134).

The position of the member states

The main beneficiaries of regional policy, led by the Spanish government, are keen to maintain the amount of resources they receive. In contrast the wealthier countries wish to reduce their contributions to the budget, with regional policy being a key area for cutting back. Germany is the most forceful advocate for a reduction in the EU's regional policy budget, due to the massive ongoing cost of German unification since 1990.

273

As the UK is one of the largest contributors to the EU budget, the Chancellor believes our national interests are best served by limiting the amount allocated to regional policy. He also wants the richer EU countries to accept responsibility for their own regional policy, but he is unlikely to persuade the others on this point.

Reform of the EU's regional policy

Traditionally, reform of regional policy has led to an increase in resources. The first reform occurred in the period 1989 to 1993, at which time regional policy accounted for 20% of the total budget. From 1993 to 1999 the share allocated to regional policy increased to 30%, and in the current period regional policy totals €37 billion a year. After the budget deal agreed at the end of 2005, regional aid will be reduced by €16 billion (*Economist*, 24/12/05: 43). Further reform is now unlikely, and it remains unclear as to what direction it might take. Both Sweden and Britain wish to reclaim sovereignty over regional policy. In contrast, the Commission and the Committee of the Regions want extra resources in return for simplifying procedures. Regional policy might even prioritise economic growth over cohesion in the near future.

What has been the impact on the UK?

As one of the wealthiest economies in the EU, the UK is hardly likely to benefit greatly from regional policy. However, some regions of Britain do benefit from regional policy, such as Northern Ireland, Scotland, Wales, parts of Northern England and the South West. Initiatives funded by the EU include helping small businesses, retraining workers who have lost their jobs, rebuilding urban infrastructure and restructuring industry. An example of the impact of regional policy is the effect on regional development in North West England.

EUROPEAN FOREIGN POLICY

The first attempt to establish a European foreign policy was rejected by the French Assembly in 1954, with Britain (the most important military power in western Europe at the time) stating that it would not join anyway. The alternative British proposal, the Western European Union (WEU), was adapted outside of the EC. As the British were the driving force behind its creation, it is hardly surprising that the WEU is an intergovernmental institution.[4]

The original six member states wished to strengthen the EC's voice in world affairs, and at the 1969 Hague summit they established the first step towards a European foreign policy. It was called European Political Cooperation, or EPC, but it was little more than an informal arrangement designed to coordinate member states' foreign policies. A year later, the Luxembourg Report pledged to intensify political cooperation and harmonise views on international affairs.

The EC's activity in foreign affairs was limited to a largely diplomatic role throughout the 1970s and 1980s, as national governments were reluctant to transfer or pool sovereignty over such a sensitive area. Although EPC gained legal status in the Single European Act, it was not until the Maastricht Treaty that the member states made any significant progress.

The Common Foreign and Security Policy (CFSP)

At Maastricht, EPC was replaced by the CFSP. It combines political cooperation with a defence and security dimension founded on the WEU, and is the second pillar of the EU.

CFSP policymaking is primarily intergovernmental, although the Commission is fully associated within the

---

[4] In recent years cooperation between the WEU and the EU has been strengthened, although the WEU remains *outside* the EU.

decision-making process. The two main areas of the CFSP are common positions and joint actions. The former are declaratory statements, while joint actions are more important. As some member states are neutral, CFSP allows for a type of opt-out called constructive abstention whereby a member state can abstain from the vote in the Council of Ministers without blocking an otherwise unanimous decision.

In the Treaty of Amsterdam a High Representative for the EU was established. He or she is the nearest the EU has to a European Foreign Minister, although the EU does not have a single foreign policy. In practice, the EU often fails to establish a common foreign policy at all.

Why does the EU find it difficult to adopt a common foreign policy?

The reason for the EU's failure to establish a common foreign policy is the sheer divergence in the national interests of the member states. Some are neutral, the Germans are reluctant to deploy their troops abroad and the smaller member states have few resources anyway. In contrast France and Britain hold a wide global influence due to their possession of nuclear weapons, and their status on the UN Security Council. As such they rarely gain from adopting a common European position. One might also add that the UK has a special relationship with the USA, and some member states only hold observer status within the WEU.

The difficulty in reaching a common position tends to increase in proportion to the seriousness of the action considered. Reaching a vague statement of intent (i.e. 'We support the international community's efforts to achieve peace in Iraq') is relatively easy. Reaching an agreement to take action in Iraq is considerably more problematic, and nowhere is the task of establishing a common policy more difficult than in the realm of defence.

DEFENCE

The EU's abject failure to resolve the Bosnian war in the 1990s instigated a prolonged search for a common defence policy. The first landmark along this path was the 1998 St Malo Declaration by France and Britain, which outlined the terms of a European Security and Defence Policy. It marked the first firm commitment to the establishment of a military role for the EU.

In 2002 the European Security and Defence Policy was finally established, with troops from the member states pledged to act together in the name of the EU. Their activities are strictly limited to 'humanitarian operations, peacekeeping and crisis management'. In March 2003 the EU launched its first military mission, sending 400 peacekeeping troops from 13 member states to Macedonia. It was the first Allied military mission in Europe since 1945 that did not include the Americans (Reid 2004: 178).

Soon after the mission to Macedonia, the EU committed its first troops outside Europe, dispatching 1,400 soldiers to the Congo (Rifkin 2004: 314). EU troops are currently stationed in Bosnia and Afghanistan, but on a strictly peacekeeping basis.

Beyond peacekeeping? The Rapid Reaction Force

At the 1999 Helsinki Council the member states agreed to create a Rapid Reaction Force (RRF) of 50–60,000 EU troops. The RRF would be ready to operate anywhere in and around Europe. Three hundred combat aircraft, and 100 warships would also be made available to the RRF by the member states (Reid 2004: 182).

One of the arguments in favour of the RRF is related to economies of scale, whereby the burden of defence expenditure on the member states is reduced considerably. Despite the advantages of pooling sovereignty in this area progress towards the creation of the RRF has been 'slow' (Buller 2004: 200), and we have yet to see how it will fare in action.

Taking military action with the RRF is a wholly different matter from sending troops on a peacekeeping exercise. The neutral states would certainly object, the practical issues of cost and command need to be addressed, as do the finer points of the decision-making process, such as how to ensure accountability. One must also take into account the ever-present debate over supranationalism, or intergovernmentalism. The former view would lead to a fully-fledged European army, a proposal firmly opposed by the UK.

Prospects for reform

The most likely area of reform is a possible merger of the WEU into the EU. The French argue that it would bolster European military influence in the world and establish the EU as a military rival to the USA. The EU could then take responsibility for its own security, rather than depending on the USA, and 'speak with one voice' on the world stage. However, divisions between the member states are so great that the EU is likely to offer a whispering voice at best.

The proposal to merge the WEU into the EU is firmly opposed by the UK, which prefers a strong role for NATO as it assures American involvement in the security of Europe. The USA and the Atlanticist states (Italy, Holland and most of the new member states) also support the predominance of NATO.

The EU Constitution proposed the creation of a European Foreign Minister, bringing together the current High Representative and the Commissioner for External Relations into one post. Article 40 (6) would have also allowed for structured cooperation in areas relating to the implementation of the CFSP and defence policy, with member states retaining the right to opt-out of the policies decided on by the EU's Foreign Minister. It is unlikely these proposals will be removed from the EU's agenda, thus the member states may implement such changes in the near future.

HOW IMPORTANT IS EUROPEAN FOREIGN POLICY?

The war in Iraq demonstrated how divisions between the national interests of the member states can cause major problems for European foreign policy, with 'new' Europe (led by Britain and consisting of Italy, Denmark, Holland, Spain and Poland) supporting America and 'old' Europe (a derogatory term used by Donald Rumsfeld of the Bush administration) firmly against. The Iraq war once again raised the question that has always dogged the EU: 'How can a European foreign policy work when national interests are so diverse?'

For all the problems facing European foreign policy, the EU does hold significant diplomatic power throughout the world, and may in time rival the USA as a major player in international relations. The EU has stood united on issues such as the international treaty banning anti-personnel land mines, the establishment of an International Criminal Court and the Kyoto Protocol (Reid 2004: 193). The EU also has the ability to take a different stance from the USA in several areas of international relations. For example, the EU supports a two-state solution to the long-standing conflict between Palestinians and Israelis, and in 2005 removed its arms embargo on China despite opposition from George Bush. The EU has also cooperated with the USA in the Middle East to coordinate the 'road map' to peace.

It is undoubtedly the case that the EU is stronger diplomatically than militarily, and has justifiably been described as 'an economic giant but a political pygmy' (Leach 2004: 96). While the EU is no match for the military might of the USA it does provide more aid, has more votes in international forums, and accounts for more trade than its transatlantic partner (Reid 2004: 1). The visit of George Bush to Brussels in February 2005, the first American President to do so, does to some extent underline the importance of European foreign policy within international relations. Whether the EU should, or could, take a stronger foreign policy role is, of course, an open question.

Impact on the UK

The UK has often proved reluctant to pool sovereignty in the realm of foreign policy due to three factors:

1   Britain's global influence within world affairs.
2   Our status as a nuclear power.
3   The special relationship with the USA.

The last point has proved particularly relevant since 1997. Tony Blair has sent British troops into conflict on several occasions, often in alliance with the USA in the face of European obduracy. In part this reflects the UK's traditional preference for the Atlantic alliance, as opposed to working together with our European partners. It also reflects a deep cultural and political affiliation with the USA, which sets Britain apart from Continental Europe.

JUSTICE AND HOME AFFAIRS

Justice and Home Affairs (JHA) was established by the Maastricht Treaty, and is the third pillar of the EU. As with the CFSP, JHA is based firmly on intergovernmentalism. It covers a wide range of issues such as asylum, border control, immigration and terrorism. JHA was developed further in the TOA (1997), in which immigration and asylum policy were integrated into the competency of the EU.[5]

How does JHA work?

The Commission initiates numerous proposals on issues relating to JHA, but it is the Council of Ministers that takes the final decision, usually (but not solely) on the basis of unanimity. The Council of Ministers holds regular meetings on JHA (D. Leonard 2005: 219), and the European Parliament has a minor role.

Asylum

In 2005 the EU leaders agreed to remove the right of veto on all asylum and illegal immigration matters in the Council of Ministers. The justification for a common asylum policy is to combat the problem of so-called 'asylum shoppers', whereby an asylum seeker applies to more than one country for refugee status. As a result of the common policy, asylum shoppers are now deported to the first EU country they entered.

Border control

Few issues are as sensitive to national sovereignty as border

---

[5] Europol was created after ratification of the Maastricht Treaty, and is responsible for the collation, analysis and exchange of information between national police forces. Since 2002 Europol has supported investigations into a wide range of crimes, with its powers having grown steadily since then. Eurojust does a similar job, bringing together member states' magistrates, prosecutors and police officers to cooperate in the fight against crime. JHA, Europol and Eurojust could collectively be described as the EU's criminal justice system.

control. To address public concern over the related issues of asylum and immigration, many of the member states have signed up to the Schengen Agreement, which dates back to 1985, but did not come into force until ten years later. It has gone some way towards the creation of a borderless Europe, a goal consistent with the desire to establish freedom of movement throughout the EU, and currently applies to most of the EU member states.

In practice the Schengen Agreement has failed to control the number of illegal immigrants and bogus asylum seekers entering participant countries, and this has undermined public confidence in the agreement. The Belgian government even suspended its Schengen obligations to restore its own border controls, and Italy and Greece took years to meet Schengen standards (Guiraudon 2004: 174). France also reintroduced passport checks in the mid-1990s.

Britain and Ireland remain outside the Schengen Agreement, but have adopted Schengen rules. Their shared experience of combating terrorism in Northern Ireland, and a long history of free movement between the two countries explain why the UK and Ireland have not yet signed up to the Schengen Agreement. The electoral salience of issues such as illegal immigration and bogus asylum seekers might also be considered.

Immigration and terrorism

At the 1999 JHA summit in Tampere, the EU leaders agreed to develop a comprehensive immigration policy, and since the 11 September terrorist attacks on the USA, EU leaders have linked the fight against terrorism to the issue of illegal immigration. They have also sought to reinforce border controls by enforcing a firmer visa policy. A European-wide arrest warrant, a fingerprint database for asylum seekers and a greater role for Europol have all been established since 2001.

How has the issue of immigration shaped JHA in recent years?

Each year around one and a half million legal immigrants arrive in the EU, with the total number of illegal immigrants likely to be much higher (Guiraudon 2004: 161–162). With the growing popularity of anti-immigration parties in Holland, Austria, France and Denmark, EU leaders are highly sensitive to the importance of this issue among the voters. As such, the broad aim of JHA has been to prevent 'undesirable migrants from reaching the EU' (Guiraudon 2004: 176).

To achieve this aim, the EU has placed three quarters of non-EU countries on a 'blacklist'. Anyone from those countries entering the EU must first secure visas for a maximum of three months, and European airlines currently prevent around 5,000 people from boarding each year because they lack the required visa (Guiraudon 2004: 177). EU foreign ministers have also discussed national quotas for legal immigrants, which has led to accusations that the EU is becoming little more than a 'fortress Europe'.

As well as acting 'tough' on immigration, the EU has used some of its considerable economic and diplomatic resources to establish 'an area of freedom, security and justice' around its borders. For instance, in June 2003 the Commission pledged €250 million in aid over five years to those countries that sign readmission agreements with the EU, and in February that year, the EU established a small group of border guards (Guiraudon 2004: 178–179).

European efforts to combat terrorism are headed by Gijs de Vries, dubbed the EU's 'Terrorism Czar'. His role is to coordinate the activities of the EU institutions on terrorism and persuade member states to implement EU anti-terrorist legislation (D. Leonard 2005: 224). The Schengen information system has also been improved due to more effective cooperation with Europol and Eurojust.

Despite considerable attention paid to immigration and terrorism, the unanimity rule in the Council of Ministers has slowed down the harmonisation of immigration policy. Instead, the member states have found it easier to establish informal cooperation, working together where common interests can be found.

Possible reform of JHA

The salience of JHA has undoubtedly grown since the Madrid bombings in March 2004 and the terrorist attacks in London during July 2005 but progress on the implementation of JHA has been slow. To some extent JHA suffers from the same problem as the CFSP, in that national governments are reluctant to transfer sovereignty of an area that has traditionally been a core function of the nation state.

It remains to be seen how the implementation of JHA could be changed in the near future. If elements of the Constitution survive in some form, then the EU may go ahead with plans to develop a common immigration policy. On the plus side, it might ensure a fairer allocation of immigrants among the member states. However, that could result in a country being ordered by the EU to take in more immigrants. Clearly this would be an explosive political move, and would probably cause a public backlash against the EU (Lawes 2005: 138).

Any other possible areas for reform are more difficult to anticipate. One proposal is to pool sovereignty and form a fully operational police force throughout the EU. Germany is very much in favour, but the UK is less enthusiastic. However, the main stumbling block remains the French, who do not wish to lose control over their national police force.

Another possible area for reform is to bring JHA within the competence of the Commission, which would then deal more effectively with the issues of asylum, illegal immigration and terrorism. This would transform JHA from an intergovernmental to a supranational format. As such issues could best be dealt with at the EU level, the member states (even the UK) may in time welcome this bold step.

Under recent proposals put forward by the Commission, the member states could collate and share information in the fight against terrorism. This may consist of a register of all EU travel documents and a European DNA database (*Times*, 25/11/05: 28). However, the proposal failed to gain a consensus among the member states, although plans may resurface in the future.

Harmonisation of law and order

The maintenance of law and order is central to the sovereignty of a nation state. Therefore any erosion of national sovereignty in such a sensitive area would prove difficult, but not impossible, as the case of foreign and defence policy shows.

The advantage of harmonising law and order policies throughout the EU is to deal more effectively with cross-border problems such as the drugs trade, terrorism and organised crime. However, several obstacles stand in the way of a common law and order policy for the EU.

The main obstacle is cultural and legal differences between the UK and the rest of Europe. Only the UK has a common law tradition and an uncodified constitution. Britain would therefore have to radically overhaul its legal traditions in order to adapt to a common European judiciary system. Secondly, the national governments see little need to transfer sovereignty to the EU, and finally, would an EU police force ever acquire popular legitimacy?

The position of the UK

Both main parties in the UK have supported the inter-governmental approach to JHA. Michael Howard blocked the involvement of the supranational ECJ over Europol while he was Home Secretary, and it was under a Labour government that TREVI (the forerunner to JHA) was set up in 1976 along intergovernmental lines.

Despite its traditional reluctance regarding European integration, the UK government is campaigning for the introduction of QMV over the area of immigration policy. The government claims that such a move would help combat the number of illegal immigrants entering the country, which is a major electoral issue. In 2005 the Home Secretary Charles Clarke attempted to harmonise EU policy in the fight against terrorism. He wished to standardise the recording of phone messages among the member states. Only Spain supported his proposal, and the measure was defeated.

The government's main initiative at the present time is the introduction of ID cards, which partly reflects a trend towards harmonisation throughout Europe. The terrorist attacks on London on 7 July 2005 have added political impetus to the government's desire to implement ID cards, which will be introduced in 2006.

RIGHTS AND CITIZENSHIP

The idea of everyone in the EU holding citizenship status was first put forward in 1984, but it was not until the early 1990s that EU citizenship finally gained legal recognition. Article 8 of the Maastricht Treaty reads 'every person holding the nationality of a member state shall be a citizen of the Union'. As such, we are *all* citizens of the EU. The TOA (1997) added that 'citizenship of the Union shall complement and not replace national citizenship', and that 'the question whether an individual possesses the nationality of a Member State shall be settled solely by reference to the national law of the Member State concerned'. Therefore it is the

286

responsibility of national governments to define who is legally entitled to citizenship. In the UK, only British subjects with the right of abode qualify (Leach 2004: 26).

What rights derive from the EU?

There is a strong 'rights culture' in the EU, and that has led to several EU-wide measures designed to strengthen people's rights. Examples include the Social Chapter, anti-discrimination laws and the four freedoms of the Rome Treaties. It is also possible to vote and stand for office in an election to the European Parliament held in another member state, as the British-born James Goldsmith (the founder of the now defunct Referendum Party) did when he stood for election as an MEP in France. However, it is not possible to vote in a national election held in another EU country.

As with other EU policy areas, one cannot ignore the impact of enlargement. Some of the new member states do not share the same legal and cultural traditions concerning human rights and the rule of law as the EU-15. Thus as a last resort, a country guilty of persistent human rights offences could be deprived of some of its voting rights in the Council of Ministers.

The second area for concern relates to the effects of cheap labour migrating from Central and Eastern Europe. In response to this problem, the EU-15 have placed several restrictions on the free movement of labour. From the perspective of the new member states, the wealthier countries appear to be treating them as 'second-class citizens'.

Does EU citizenship strengthen intergovernmentalism, or does it imply more federalism?

Citizenship is traditionally linked to the relationship between the state and the citizen, thus the concept of EU citizenship would suggest an incremental shift towards federalism. One might also argue that EU citizenship offers no more than a modest addition to the rights already enjoyed by many Europeans as citizens of their own countries, and that the TOA reaffirms the importance of national governments in this area. So while federalists see the creation of EU citizenship as another step towards a United States of Europe, inter-governmentalists view such changes as merely symbolic. Moreover, there is still no concept of a European citizen. Unlike the USA, the EU does not have a constitution or a codified set of rights. The nearest the EU has to a US-style Bill of Rights is the Charter of Fundamental Rights.

The Charter of Fundamental Rights

The EU's Charter of Fundamental Rights was drawn up in parallel to the Nice Intergovernmental Conference (IGC), but was not included in the Treaty and therefore has no binding legal force. As such, it does not create law-making powers for the EU, but may do so in the future. The Charter is divided into six chapters, ranging from citizens' rights to justice. Under the Charter, citizens have the right to invite the Commission to submit a proposal to the European Parliament if 1 million signatures are collected in a significant number of member states. Due to the difficulty faced in achieving such a target, the practicality of this measure is highly questionable. The most controversial item in the Charter of Fundamental Rights is Article II–28, which could be used to justify secondary picketing (currently illegal under UK law). The UK government refused to allow the Charter to become legally enforceable, as it would have strengthened the right to strike, and due to the fact that it stood in contrast to Britain's preference for a flexible labour market.

13

Institutions and Policy-making

Objectives from the syllabus

- A knowledge of the ways in which political parties, pressure groups, elections and referendums help to set the policy agenda, and of how policies are formulated and decided through the legislative and executive processes of government within the context of EU membership. The focus will be on key economic, social and European policies addressed in Units 4A and 5A.
- Although a general understanding of the policy process is helpful, no knowledge of the theory of policy analysis or of technical matters related to the policy process, such as the role of policy networks, is required. Note that although the emphasis of this unit is on recent policy developments, a knowledge of general developments in the post-1945 period will be helpful for students. However, the main focus of the unit will be on contemporary developments in the post-1979 period.

Internet websites

www.labour.org.uk
www.conservatives.com
www.libdems.org.uk
www.snp.org
www.plaidcymru.org

www.independenceuk.org.uk/
www.britainineurope.org.uk
www.no-euro.com
www.poptel.org.uk/against-eurofederalism
www.cbi.org.uk
www.tuc.org.uk

Old exam questions

15 minutes

Why do some pressure groups target the institutions of the EU?   Spec

45 minutes (synoptic)

'In the context of the European Union, UK pressure groups are a more effective vehicle for representations than UK political parties.' Discuss.   June 2005

Analyse how EU membership has affected the political parties in the UK.   Spec

Discuss the attitude of UK political parties towards increased European integration since 1979.   June 2004

To what extent have the activities of pressure groups been affected by the UK's membership of the EU?   June 2002

What has been the impact of membership of the EU on UK political parties and pressure groups?   June 2003

POLITICAL PARTIES AND THE EU

Political parties are a coalition of various interests, whose members group together under a common label and policy programme. Disagreement within such a broad church is inevitable, particularly for catch-all parties such as the Conservatives and the Labour Party. In one sense, discussion is a healthy sign of democracy within a political party. Yet when internal divisions become too great, it can deeply damage a party's electoral chances. This was the case with Labour in 1983 and the Conservatives in 1997 and 2001.

No other issue has the ability to divide political parties as much as Europe. Membership of the EC split the Labour Party from the late 1970s to the early 1980s, and during the late 1980s and 1990s the Conservative Party was divided over closer European integration. In historical terms, the ability of Europe to divide political parties is comparable to the Corn Laws and Home Rule for Ireland.

THE CONSERVATIVE PARTY AND EUROPEAN INTEGRATION

Throughout the 1960s and 1970s, the Conservatives were a pro-European party. While Labour dismissed the EC as little more than a capitalist club, the Tories supported the EC's attempt to increase trade and stimulate economic growth via a customs union. The then Conservative government took Britain into the EC in 1973. Although there were some dissenting voices on the Right of the party, such as Enoch Powell, the Prime Minister Edward Heath managed to persuade his party that joining the EC was in Britain's economic interests.

By the late 1980s, the position of the main parties had changed. Although Mrs Thatcher was keen on the economic advantages of the single market, she was deeply hostile to any transfer of political sovereignty to Brussels. She wanted a free trade Europe without political union, and most certainly without the Social Chapter. Most Tories agreed with her, but several pro-European Cabinet members could not accept her increasingly Eurosceptic tone.

The issue of European integration proved deeply damaging to the Conservative Party, leading to the resignation of pro-European Cabinet members such as Michael Heseltine, Leon Brittan, Geoffrey Howe and Nigel Lawson. European integration was also a factor in the downfall of Mrs Thatcher herself.

John Major pledged to restore Britain's position at 'the heart of Europe', but he was unable to play a constructive role within the EU due to splits within the Party between Europhiles and Eurosceptics. His own position became more tenuous due to growing opposition from Eurosceptics within the party, many of whom had gained in confidence after Britain's exit from the ERM in 1992. He was forced to call a vote of confidence in his own government just 15 months after the general election, and in 1995 he faced a leadership challenge in which a third of the party failed to support him. Major also withdrew the Party whip from eight rebel backbench MPs, and had to contend with Eurosceptics in the Cabinet such as Norman Lamont and Michael Portillo, with the latter calling for Britain to 'stop the rot from Brussels' at the Party Conference.

After their landslide defeat in 1997 the rift between pro-Europeans and Eurosceptics was laid bare by the party's leadership campaign, in which the pro-European Kenneth Clarke lost out to the Eurosceptic candidate William Hague. Defections to the UK Independence Party (UKIP) further exposed the lack of unity within the Tory party, as did the decision taken by some pro-European Tory MPs to stand down at the 1997 general election.

Since the demise of Mrs Thatcher, all Tory leaders have tried to appease an increasingly Eurosceptic party. For instance, during William Hague's first speech as leader, he admitted that British membership of the ERM had been a mistake and publicly apologised on behalf of the Party for taking Britain into the scheme. Under Hague's leadership, the Party ruled out membership of the EMU for ten years, but this caused the resignation of two Shadow Cabinet members, and the defection of Peter Temple Morris to the Labour Party.

When Iain Duncan Smith became leader in 2001, he went one stage further than Hague by stating that Britain would never adopt the euro under a Conservative government (www.guardian.co.uk/print/0,3858,4679787–103685,00.html). His replacement, Michael Howard, campaigned for a more flexible Europe, in which those who wish to move towards a closer union would be able to do so, while other countries took a back seat. He also pledged to cut EU regulations by a quarter, restore national control over fisheries and aid, repeal EU legislation if five states or more agreed to it, and limit the powers of the Commission (*Times*, 30/4/04: 10).

The current policy of the Conservative Party is to be 'in Europe, not run by Europe'. It is opposed to any further loss of sovereignty and wants to renegotiate existing treaties. Unlike UKIP, the Conservative Party does not want to leave the EU. While some Tory MPs would prefer associate status, in which Britain would retain its national sovereignty, they hold only marginal influence within the Party.

In the 2001 general election campaign, the Party's pledge to 'keep the pound' found little favour with the electorate, partly because the issue of Europe ranked only eleventh among voter concerns (P. Lynch 2004: 19). The slogan may have also reminded voters of previous divisions within the Party. In the 2005 general election the Party did much better, securing a 3% swing from Labour. However, the Tories failed to persuade enough voters that they were a united party ready for government, and one of the causes was the issue of Europe.

It is undoubtedly the case that European integration has caused major damage to one of the most successful democratic parties in the world. However, the Conservatives are now more united on the issue of Europe, primarily due to a rapid decline in the influence of pro-Europeans within the Party. The Tory leader David Cameron should find it easier to deal with the issue of Europe than his recent predecessors.

LABOUR AND EUROPEAN INTEGRATION

Since the 1980s Labour has transformed itself from a party wishing to take Britain out of the EC, to a broadly pro-European party that favours adopting the single currency once the five economic tests have been met.

During the 1960s and 1970s, the Labour Party was split between pro-Europeans such as Roy Jenkins, and Eurosceptics from the Left of the Party. Due to divisions within the Party, the Prime Minister Harold Wilson called a nationwide referendum in 1975. He believed that allowing each side to present its case to the public would allow dissenting voices to be heard, and in doing so resolve a damaging and divisive issue for the Party.

After their election defeat in 1979, Labour moved sharply to the left. The 1980 Party Conference voted to withdraw Britain from the EC, which led to some Labour MPs leaving the Party to form the short-lived Social Democratic Party.

By the late 1980s, the position of the Party began to change in response to the presidency of Jacques Delors, a French socialist deeply committed to a 'social Europe'. The former 'capitalist club' had become far more sympathetic to workers' rights, an agenda clearly in tune with the Labour Party. Labour's change of policy was also tactical in that it exploited Tory divisions and recognised the need to become more like a European-style social democratic party in order to win back power.

Since Tony Blair became leader in 1994, Labour has remained relatively united on the issue of Europe. Although Labour does have Eurosceptic backbenchers, the government's policies have rarely caused internal controversy. Measures such as opting into the Social Chapter, signing the Amsterdam and Nice treaties and incorporating the European Convention of Human Rights into UK law have all been relatively unproblematic.

The only issue that has caused division within the Labour Party is the single currency. The euro is one of the many issues fuelling the rivalry between Blairites and Brownites. A number of Labour backbench MPs have formed a group called Labour Against a Superstate, and it is estimated that 50 or more left-wing Labour MPs will vote against Britain joining the euro when the time comes (P. Lynch 2004: 18). Such a large group of Eurosceptics could prove highly troublesome for Blair, who now governs on a much reduced majority.

THE OTHER PARTIES

Unlike the two main parties, the Liberal Democrats have always been united on the issue of Europe. They firmly support a 'Europe of the regions', whereby decision-making power is located at the regional level, and the principle of subsidiarity. They also favour Britain adopting the single currency.

From the opposite end of the political spectrum, UKIP wants Britain to withdraw from the EU. UKIP gained its first electoral seat in the 1999 European parliamentary elections, and surprised many political analysts by coming third in 2004. However, the future of the Party is uncertain after the loss of financial support from the businessman Paul Sykes, and the defection of Robert Kilroy Silk MEP. In the 2005 general election the Party failed to win a single seat, and its impact on British politics appears to be on the wane.

Both the Scottish and Welsh Nationalists have been strong

supporters of closer integration, as have the Northern Ireland parties. Generous regional aid to such areas, and the fact that subsidiarity strengthens the position of the regions explains why those parties support European integration.

To sum up, attitudes towards European integration among the two main parties have changed significantly over time. The Tories have become more Eurosceptic since the late 1980s, whereas Labour is now a broadly pro-European party. This represents a complete reversal in the position of the main parties during the 1970s and early 1980s. The Liberal Democrats remain unchallenged as the most pro-federal party, closely followed by Plaid Cymru, the Scottish Nationalists and the Northern Ireland parties. UKIP stand alone as a party that wants to take Britain out of the EU.

All three main parties believe there are political and economic benefits to membership, but the Tories do not want Britain to lose any more sovereignty, and are concerned at a possible loss of national identity within a more integrated Europe. The Labour Party is more sympathetic to the EU's social dimension, and may eventually take Britain into the eurozone. The position of the main parties could therefore be described as 'Tory scepticism, Labour cautiousness and ... Liberal Democrat enthusiasm' (Cowles and Dinan 2004: 56), and while the minor parties offer the voters greater choice, they have little political impact.

THE 2004 EUROPEAN PARLIAMENTARY ELECTIONS

Britain was the only country to use First Past the Post (FPTP) to elect MEPs, but since 1999 the election of 72 MEPs to multimember constituencies has been based on a closed party list system. As with *all* forms of proportional representation the Party list system favours the smaller parties. Both the

296

Greens and UKIP gained electoral representation for the first time in 1999, and managed to win a number of seats in 2004. In contrast, the position of the two main parties has been weakened since the adoption of proportional representation.

European Election Results (UK) June 2004

	%age	Change since 1999	Seats
Conservative	27.4	−10.1	25
Labour	22.3	− 5.7	17
UKIP	16.8	+ 9.3	12
Liberal Democrats	15.1	+ 2.1	11
Green	6.2	− 0.1	2
Plaid Cymru	1.1	− 1	1

1999 turnout 24% (lowest in Europe), 2004 turnout 37.6%

Rather than campaigning on European issues, the two main parties focused on domestic and foreign policy matters, principally Iraq and the whole question of trust in Tony Blair.

For Labour and the Conservatives, the election result was disappointing. The Labour Party recorded its worst result in a nationwide election since the Second World War, and whereas the Conservatives won, they only gained around a quarter of the vote. With the government's unpopularity over Iraq, the Tories expected to gain considerably more support.

The main event of the night was the success of UKIP, who quadrupled their number of seats to take third place, just ahead of the Liberal Democrats. UKIP took votes away from the Conservatives, while traditional Labour voters registered a protest vote for the Liberal Democrats or the Greens, both of whom opposed the war in Iraq.

Across Europe the centre-right parties (the equivalent of the British Conservatives) won 268 seats, with the Socialists (including Labour) coming second with 202, and the Liberal group third with 88. Eurosceptic parties did better than expected across Europe, particularly in the new member states of Central and Eastern Europe. Around 10 to 15% of all MEPs could now be described as Eurosceptic, such as the Greens and UKIP. However, Eurosceptic parties are an ineffective political grouping in the European Parliament because cooperation between them is highly unlikely due to their diverse range of ideologies and policies.

HOW DO UK POLITICAL PARTIES DIFFER FROM THOSE IN THE REST OF THE EU?

There are three aspects to British political parties that differentiate them from their European counterparts.

1   Regional and linguistic differences are not as great as say in Belgium or Spain. In comparison to many European states, Britain is a relatively cohesive country united by a common language and history. However, there is a separatist party that contests UK elections (Sinn Féin). Their activities could be compared to Basque separatists in Spain, who operate as the political wing of a terrorist organisation (ETA). While the Scottish Nationalists and Plaid Cymru are nationalist parties who favour independence for Scotland and Wales, they do not advocate political violence.

2   Britain retains FPTP at the national level, thus the opportunity for minority parties to establish themselves in Westminster is negligible. This has undoubtedly worked against the interests of the extreme right, and the BNP have failed to make the same breakthrough

as other comparable parties in Holland, France, Denmark and Austria.

3   In terms of political ideology and policy positions, the two main parties have moved closer in recent years over many policy issues. Yet British politics, at least at Westminster, remains adversarial rather than consensual. We are far from establishing the same degree of consensus politics common in Germany, Austria and Scandinavia.[1]

PARTY SYSTEMS

The UK party system has also been influenced by EU membership, although the effects have been more obvious since Labour came to power, instigated in part by a Prime Minister keen to establish his European credentials.

In 1997 New Labour was elected on a programme of radical constitutional reform. It is debatable whether or not the Labour Government intended to bring the UK into line with the rest of the EU, but that has undoubtedly been the effect of devolution and proportional representation.

Devolution has changed the UK's party system in three ways. The first is the use of proportional representation in the devolved assemblies, and the second is the formation of coalitions in Scotland and Wales. Devolution has also led to a more diverse party system, challenging the traditional two-party dominance that has characterised British politics.

The closed party list system was introduced for elections to the European Parliament in 1999, thus bringing the UK into line with the rest of Europe. This has undoubtedly benefited the smaller parties. Local mayors standing as independents have also done well under proportional representation.

---

[1] The consequence of our adversarial culture may well work to our disadvantage, as the EU tends to operate on the basis of a lengthy bargaining process common to coalition governments.

COALITIONS

A coalition is a group of two or more parties who work together to form the executive. Once described as 'unBritish' by the former Conservative leader Benjamin Disraeli, coalitions are not altogether unknown in Britain. For example, during the twentieth century, Britain was governed by some form of coalition for almost 20 years. Since 1997, coalitions have become more common as a result of proportional representation. The Labour Party and the Liberal Democrats currently share power in Scotland, and have worked together as a coalition in Wales.

Coalitions have to some extent changed the character of the UK's party system. So while Labour and the Liberal Democrats oppose each other at the despatch box in Westminster, they work together in Scotland. This has also encouraged greater policy divergence within the UK (e.g. tuition fees do not apply in Scotland, and school league tables do not apply in Northern Ireland), and has worked to the disadvantage of the Conservatives, who are unlikely to form a coalition with the Liberal Democrats in the devolved assemblies. Compared to the Labour Party, the Tories have less in common with the Liberal Democrats, although David Cameron has been described as a 'liberal conservative'.

The Northern Ireland Assembly is, of course, a unique case in point. It was created on a power-sharing basis to ensure both communities were adequately represented. Between 1999 and 2002 power was shared among the parties who supported the Good Friday Agreement. Although it was closed down by the Secretary of State for Northern Ireland in 2002, elections to the Northern Ireland Assembly continue.

PRESSURE GROUPS IN THE EU

A pressure group seeks to influence policymakers, but does not stand for elected office. There are several categories applicable to pressure groups, such as cause/sectional and ad hoc/permanent, but one of the most useful distinctions is between insider and outsider pressure groups.

An insider pressure group has regular contact with decision-makers, such as the National Farmers Union (NFU) with the UK's Ministry of Agriculture. In the European context, the influence of the NFU can affect the position taken by the UK government in the Council of (agricultural) Ministers. In the EU, insider pressure groups tend to derive from the trade unions and farming interests.

Outsider pressure groups have little or no contact with decision-makers. In order to exert influence, an outsider pressure group will often take direct action. For example, the anti-globalisation movement sent letter bombs to Italian MEPs in 2004 at the time of the G8 summit in Genoa.

Whatever the type of pressure group, all of them need to lobby those in power. Pressure groups simply cannot afford to ignore the EU if they wish to influence policy decisions and protect the interests of their members. In several cases, the policies and decisions that affect their members are made by EU institutions rather than by national governments. This is particularly true for agricultural and business pressure groups. For instance, during the late 1990s, the NFU lobbied the Council of Ministers and the European Court of Justice in an attempt to overturn the EU's decision to ban British beef. Environmental groups tend to operate at both levels, whereas law and order campaigners concentrate their efforts at the national level.

Pressure groups are represented by lobbyists who are also known as consultants or public affairs practitioners. Lobbying can be defined as 'an attempt to influence policymakers to adopt a course of action advantageous ... to a particular group or interest' (Bomberg and Stubb 2003: 90), and is of major importance within the EU. There are approximately 15,000 lobbyists, which equates to almost one lobbyist for every two people employed in the EU. Over 5,000 have a one-year pass, which amounts to more than seven lobbyists for each MEP (www.corporateeurope.org/consumerpolicy review.pdf#search='number%20of%20lobbyists%20in%20the %20european%20union').

The number of pressure groups lobbying EU institutions has grown considerably due to two main factors: the expansion in the legislative functions of the EU and the ever-widening range of EU policy areas. The gradual increase of the EU's budget has been another factor, as pressure groups have been keen to ensure they receive their share of Union funds. For example, the Merseyside local authority gained Objective One funding from the EU's regional policy as a result of direct lobbying in Brussels. Non-governmental organisations (NGOs) have also been keen to forge a close relationship with the Commission which funds many external projects ranging from developmental cooperation to the protection of human rights.

The impact of pressure groups

The substantial impact of pressure groups within the EU is partly due to the character of the EU itself. The pluralist nature of the EU offers numerous points of access in which pressure groups can influence decision-making. Many of the EU institutions are highly accessible to pressure groups, chiefly the European Parliament, the Commission, the ESC and the ECJ. Moreover, the trend in recent years has been more open to lobbying, particularly since the launch of the SEM.

Secondly, the scope for pressure group activity is consider-

302

able because political parties are relatively marginal actors in the EU decision-making process (Grant 2000: 124). Many commentators have argued that pressure groups are *more* important than political parties in terms of EU policymaking. This may be considered a beneficial situation, as the range of pressure group activity and involvement inevitably strengthens democracy within the EU. Critics say that pressure groups often lengthen the consultative process and insider groups can exert undue influence over decision-makers. Direct action taken by outsider pressure groups could also be described as undemocratic.

The tactics employed by pressure groups

If a decision is to be made by a supranational institution, a pressure group will lobby that particular institution. However, if a decision is being made by an intergovernmental institution, a pressure group will tend to lobby a representative of the national government.

The principal target of pressure groups operating in the EU is the Commission. This is due to its importance as a decision-maker and its receptiveness towards pressure groups. It has also been argued that the Commission derives democratic legitimacy from the endorsements given by pressure groups (Grant 2000: 112).

The European Court of Justice is another popular target, whereby pressure groups sponsor a test case in order to highlight an issue of interest to its members. Pressure groups are also likely to lobby MEPs directly rather than national governments. Naturally, MEPs from certain parties will be more sympathetic than others, such as Green MEPs towards environmental pressure groups, Liberal MEPs towards civil liberties groups and Socialist MEPs towards trade unions.

About 90% of decisions made by the Council of Ministers are taken before ministers actually get involved, thus contacts between pressure groups and civil servants in COREPER can prove a mutually rewarding channel of influence, in which pressure groups can influence decisions and EU civil servants can gain valuable information.

What types of pressure group operate in the EU?

There are three main types of pressure group active in Brussels: multinational companies, non-profit making organisations and local/regional government. Multinationals usually have their own representation in Brussels in addition to being a member of their relevant Eurogroup. For example, British Petroleum have their own representatives in Brussels, as well as being members of the Union of Industrial and Employers Confederations of Europe. Other notable Eurogroups include the European Trade Union Confederation and the Committee of Agricultural Organisations.[2]

Despite their relatively limited resources, NGOs such as the World Wildlife Fund can often influence policymakers in Brussels. Part of the reason may be that EU institutions wish to avoid the 'bad press' that would arise from ignoring the demands of such groups. In the case of the euro, the design of the new coin was changed to include special tactile marks because of pressure from the European Blind Union (www.news.bbc.co.uk/1/low/world/europe/1535238.stm).

Local and regional government have also been keen to pursue their interests at the EU level. Some local authorities such as Birmingham have even set up permanent liaison departments in order to maximise the benefits of EU membership. Issues that tend to affect local authorities include

---

[2] An understanding of pressure groups vis-à-vis the EU should not, of course, be limited to Eurogroups. Any pressure group that can mobilise enough support for its cause has a chance of influencing EU decision-makers. For instance, in 2005 the EU doubled its overseas aid budget in response to the Make Poverty History campaign (*Independent*, 4/7/05: 26).

transport, the environment and regional funds. Since the Maastricht Treaty, the influence of local/regional government has grown due to the principle of subsidiarity and the Committee of the Regions.

What determines the success of pressure groups in the EU?

The success of a pressure group depends on the level of resources in terms of finances and membership, the receptiveness of Brussels to their demands and the skill of their lobbyists. It is also the case that the most successful pressure groups have adopted an approach that reflects the federal structure in that both national and regional views need to be represented at the most appropriate EU institution.

Another factor to consider is the relative unity of a pressure group. In an EU of 25 countries, it is inevitable that some issues are of greater importance in one country than another. Reaching a common position can, therefore, be problematic, and the influence of a pressure group will, to some extent, depend on its level of cohesion. One must also consider the existence and importance of EU policy areas. For example, the main reason for the significance of environmental pressure groups in the EU is the Common Agricultural Policy (CAP), which accounts for just under half of the EU's total budget.

14

Impact of EU Membership on Institutions and the Policy Process

Objectives from the syllabus

* A knowledge of ways in which EU policymaking, policies and institutions have influenced the policy process in the UK and altered the distribution of policymaking power.
* A particular knowledge of how EU membership has impacted on UK political parties and pressure groups and altered the constitutional and political structure of UK government (including the relationship between and among institutions). Note that this goes beyond a narrow concern with the sovereignty debate and addresses issues such as the impact of EU membership on devolution, and therefore the unity of the UK, and the implications of EU membership for citizenship.

Internet websites

www.news.bbc.co.uk/1/hi/world/europe/2950276.stm
www.europa.eu.int/constitution/index_en.htm

Old exam questions (all 45 minutes)

The EU section

What impact has Europe had on the process of constitutional reform in the UK? Spec

In what ways has membership of the EU affected the working of the UK constitution? June 2003

Assess the case for and the case against the idea of a European 'superstate'. June 2004

Both UK and EU

Compare and contrast the role and importance of the European Parliament and the Westminster Parliament. June 2004

Compare and contrast the relationship between the legislature and the executive in the EU with that of the UK.
June 2005

How has the UK's membership of the EU affected domestic economic policymaking? June 2002

Why have Prime Ministers since 1979 been more involved with some domestic political issues than with others?
June 2005

THE EU CONSTITUTION

A constitution for the EU was first proposed by Altiero Spinelli back in the 1940s, yet the development of a written constitution for Europe is a relatively recent phenomenon.

In 2002/3, during 18 months of negotiations, the Convention on the Future of Europe tried to devise a constitution that would make the EU more understandable to European voters, and would streamline the decision-making process. The draft treaty establishing a Constitution for Europe was finally presented in December 2003.

The EU Constitution incorporates all the separate treaties

into one single legal text, and aims to bring the EU 'closer to its citizens' by making the institutions more accountable and more efficient.

More accountable

It was proposed that the Council of Ministers would meet in public, the President of the Council would be elected and improvements would be made to the flow of information from proposals made by the Commission. These rather limited measures must raise a question mark over the willingness of the Convention to address the full extent of the EU's democratic deficit. Gisela Stuart, the British representative at the Convention, revealed that 'not once ... did representatives question whether deeper integration is what the people of Europe want', which is surely what any democratic body must be concerned with.

More efficient

Due to the enlargement of the EU in May 2004, institutional reform was high on the Convention's agenda. The clear winner was the European Parliament, which gained more power to influence and reject legislation. For instance, the areas subject to co-legislation would increase to 70. The European Parliament would also have the final say on the EU's budget, be able to amend the Common Agricultural Policy (CAP), and approve or reject the member states' choice of the Commission President.

The Constitution also planned to give the European Court of Justice greater powers, namely the ability to interpret the new Constitution in a role similar to that of the US Supreme Court. The main loser among the institutions was the much-criticised Commission, which would have been reduced to 15 members by 2009. The Commission would also have to reconsider a proposal if a third of the member states objected to it. Other efficiency measures included the creation of a new EU Foreign Minister, which would have brought together the current High Representative and the Commissioner for External Relations into one post.

The Constitution also addressed the problematic issue of voting rights in the Council of Ministers. Under current rules, voting rights are way out of proportion to population size, with Germany holding the same number of votes as the Benelux countries (Belgium, Luxembourg and Holland) despite having three times their combined population. Secondly, the voting system can expose tensions between the core and periphery member states, as well as the bigger and smaller countries. To combat these problems, the Constitution proposed a 'double majority', so that EU laws could only be passed when 55% of the members, representing at least 65% of the EU's combined population, voted for them.

IS THE EU CONSTITUTION FEDERALIST?

There is ample evidence to support the view that the Constitution does 'represent a shift towards a federal Europe' (Lawes 2005: 137). Four clauses are worth highlighting:

1 Article 24 (4), the so-called Passerelle clause, would allow the EU to create new powers for itself, with the national parliaments having no say over those new powers.
2 The flexibility clause (Article 17) would provide the Commission with the power to act where there is no specific treaty basis. With this in mind, the Constitution actually lists areas where the EU may take decisions *if* the member states have not already done so. These include public health, industry and education.

310

3 Further harmonisation would of course aid the federalist cause, and Article III–62 (2) is phrased in a way that may lead to harmonisation in a range of areas considered 'red liners' by member governments, such as tax and social security.
4 The Charter of Fundamental Rights would be legally binding.

There are several other federalist areas of the Constitution, such as Article III–168, which states that the 'Union shall develop a common immigration policy'. The Constitution also marks the first formal statement of the primacy of EU law over national law (although that is already the case in practice) and would enable the EU to sign international agreements.

The new Constitution would also curtail the powers of member states in three areas:

1 Once transferred to the EU, power could not be returned to the member states.
2 No new national opt-outs would be allowed.
3 The modality clause may mean member states losing their ability to veto budgetary contributions, or in the case of Britain, its rebate. National governments would also lose their power of veto over criminal justice issues and social security measures for migrant workers.

European integration develops along the lines of a lengthy process of compromise between federalists and those who wish to preserve national sovereignty, and as such, there *is* something for the intergovernmentalists. Article 43 clarifies the system of enhanced cooperation, which allows a group of member states to use EU institutions without involving all the other members. In addition, Article 40 (6) enables structured cooperation in areas relating to the implementation of the Common Foreign and Security Policy (CFSP) and defence policy. Thus the draft Constitution facilitates a multispeed Europe, and is therefore consistent with a Europe of the States.

Three other areas of the Constitution could be said to be intergovernmental in their content. To ensure subsidiarity, it proposed to strengthen the role of national parliaments. For instance, if a sufficient number of parliaments in the member states believe the Commission is encroaching on national sovereignty, they could request that the proposal be amended or withdrawn. Secondly, Article 9 is designed to ensure proportionality by limiting the EU's powers to 'not go beyond what is necessary to achieve [its] objectives'. Of perhaps more significance, the national veto remained over sensitive areas such as defence and tax.

POSITION OF THE MEMBER STATES

During a speech delivered in November 2004, the British Prime Minister Tony Blair claimed that the Constitution was 'an expression of Europe as a union of nation states [and] the rejection of Europe as a federal superstate'. In total contrast, the Head of the Convention Giscard d'Estaing suggested that the EU could be renamed the 'United States of Europe' (Reid 2004: 56). There can be no clearer statement of d'Estaing's federalist intentions than that, even though the 'f-word' is not in the Constitution.

Most member states have said yes, but two (France and Holland) have said no. Originally, the EU stipulated that the Constitution must be ratified by each member state within two years, but during the Luxembourg presidency in June 2005 that timetable was aborted.

The future of the Constitution is unclear. The German Chancellor Angela Merkel has said that the 'Constitution has

312

so many positive elements that we must not abandon it' (*Economist*, 7/1/06: 39). The Austrian government is also keen to press ahead with the EU Constitution. However, Britain has declined to set a referendum, and at the time of writing, it seems that the Constitution is 'dead, but not yet buried'.

BRITISH ENTRY INTO THE EC

Although the UK did send a representative to the negotiations that led to the Treaty of Rome (1957), the British government decided *not* to join the EC. Our refusal to become a member from the outset has been criticised by pro-Europeans for failing to influence the rules of the organisation, with the Prime Minister Tony Blair once describing our policy on Europe as 'the greatest miscalculation of the post-war era'. For instance, it is most unlikely the Common Agricultural Policy would have survived in its original form if Britain had joined at the start. Yet there were, perhaps, some good reasons for our initial reluctance.

One has to recognise that Britain's experience during the Second World War was very different from the original six members of the EC. It had emerged victorious without suffering external occupation, and Britain was still a major, albeit diminishing, global power based on its Empire. While there were those in favour of European integration, such as Winston Churchill, the British adopted an aloof attitude to European integration.

Reflecting a preference for all things intergovernmental, the British government set up their own alternative to the EC called the European Free Trade Agreement (EFTA). Created in January 1960 as a loose organisation of seven European countries, EFTA was dominated by the UK.

During the early 1960s, the Conservative government led

313

by Harold Macmillan was forced to reassess Britain's stance on European integration due to economic and political reasons. The economic growth of the EC states far exceeded the UK's at a time when Britain suffered from a 'stop-go' economic policy. In political terms, Macmillan had to recognise Britain's relative decline on the world stage, due primarily to a loss of Empire, and the Suez crisis.

The UK applied to join the EC under Conservative (1963) and Labour (1967) governments. On both occasions, British membership was blocked by the French President Charles de Gaulle. After his removal from power at the end of the 1960s, British entry became a real possibility, and under the Tory government of Edward Heath Britain finally joined the EC in 1973 along with Ireland, and Denmark.

Britain joined the Community at a time when its economy faced serious problems, and it is no exaggeration to say that the UK joined primarily for economic reasons. The government hoped that increased trade and greater competition would stimulate the flagging British economy. Certainly the growth rates achieved by the original six members had been impressive, even surpassing the growth rate of the US economy (Crosbie 2004: 9).

On the controversial political issue of sovereignty, the Prime Minister Edward Heath assured the British people that membership was no threat to sovereignty. Some academics have claimed that the government misled the nation over EC membership (Black 2004: 182; Geddes 2004: 73) because it does entail a loss of sovereignty, if one accepts the more common understanding of the concept of sovereignty.

The British public never wholeheartedly signed up to the European idea. Policymakers sold membership on the basis of economic benefits (at that time the EC was widely called 'the Common Market') without clarity from our political leaders over the inherently federalist goal of the Rome Treaties. Since then, Britain has been described, with some justification, as the 'awkward partner' (George 1998).

British governments have traditionally favoured an inter-governmental approach, keen on the idea of retaining national sovereignty. For many policymakers and the majority of the press in this country, federalism is the 'f-word' of British politics. Due to the opposition it provokes in this country, both John Major and Tony Blair have removed the word federal from EU treaties.

In Britain, federalism has gained a significance way out of proportion to its actual meaning. One possible reason for this reluctance to accept a more federal Europe is our political culture. Whereas many European countries are federal, Britain is a unitary state. Therefore, federalism is inherently 'foreign' to our political culture. Eurosceptics have found it easy to link the term 'federal Europe' with the unpopular idea of a United States of Europe, when in reality federalism would not necessarily entail a 'superstate' based in Brussels.

THE TWO VIEWS OF SOVEREIGNTY

Sovereignty is a contested concept. The two views of sovereignty mirror the wider debate at the heart of European integration, namely federalists against those who advocate a Europe of the States.

In the UK, the most common understanding of sovereignty is in zero-sum terms. In short, a state either has ultimate decision-making authority or it does not. On this basis, we have lost sovereignty by being a member of the EU.

This view predominates in the UK because parliamentary sovereignty is fundamental to the UK constitution. Defined as 'the power of Parliament to make or repeal any law it wishes' (Budge *et al.* 2001: 110), parliamentary sovereignty has been undermined since we joined the EC, as the British Parliament cannot pass a law where Community legislation already exists, or where national law would be inconsistent with Community law.

The UK has also lost sovereignty in three specific areas. Supranational institutions such as the Commission and the European Court of Justice can impose decisions on Britain. EU law supersedes national law, and EU rulings must be implemented. Secondly, the aim of the Treaties of Rome is to make progress towards 'an ever closer union'. In pursuit of this goal, the range of EU policies (see Chapter 12) has grown considerably. Policies that were formerly the preserve of the national governments, such as foreign policy and environmental law, are now largely decided upon on an EU-wide basis. Finally, Britain has long since relinquished the right of veto in most policy areas. QMV now applies to four-fifths of Community legislation.

The contrasting view is that sovereignty can be pooled or shared by the member states. This is the position associated with pro-Europeans, who believe that EU membership provides Britain with considerable political and economic advantages. By being a member of the EU, our sovereignty is actually protected and even strengthened. As sovereignty is linked to power, pro-Europeans argue Britain can do *more* because it is a member of the EU.

Pooled sovereignty

Rather than being an immutable concept, sovereignty can actually be shared with the other member states. In simple terms, 25 can do more than 1. If we take the case of the environment, Britain can best ensure its own national interests if it works with other countries. Thus Britain has gained greater sovereignty due to EU membership. Being a member of the EU also gives Britain more influence on the world stage and

---

reflects the globalised world we inhabit (P. Lynch 2004: 17). There are several illustrations from outside the EU that clearly demonstrate how sovereignty can be pooled. For instance, Britain has always been committed to NATO membership, recognising that the UK cannot ensure its military objectives, or maintain its national security, simply by acting alone.

The British public tend to take the view that sovereignty is absolute, rather than something that can be pooled (Geddes 2004: 40). This may explain why the UK is one of the most Eurosceptic of the member states. In contrast, successive governments have taken a more pragmatic view, accepting further integration when it is judged to be in the national interest. Even Mrs Thatcher endorsed the single European market and acquiesced to the introduction of QMV.

The issue of sovereignty should not be seen solely in terms of the EU. In an increasingly interdependent world, Britain has lost/pooled sovereignty to a number of non-EU bodies, thus the concept of sovereignty holds wider implications than membership of the EU.

THE CONSTITUTIONAL IMPACT OF THE EU ON THE UK

Membership of the EU has affected the UK's uncodified constitution in six areas:

1 Parliamentary sovereignty.
2 Devolution and the unitary state.
3 The growing use of referendums.
4 Individual and collective ministerial responsibility.
5 The extent to which the constitution is written.
6 Constitutional reform.

Parliamentary sovereignty

The impact of EU membership was always going to be greater on the UK than any other member state due to parliamentary sovereignty. In a strictly legal sense, parliamentary sovereignty allows Parliament to make or unmake any law it wishes, with no external body capable of overruling Westminster. Parliament could even decide that Britain should leave the EU, although the political and financial costs involved would be immense.

In practice, there have always been political limitations on parliamentary sovereignty. For instance, when Britain applied for an International Monetary Fund (IMF) loan in 1976, the government had to accept monetarist policies imposed by the World Bank. The IMF loan represented a greater loss of sovereignty than anything associated with European integration. Other political limitations on parliamentary sovereignty include Britain's membership of NATO and its wider obligations within the international community (e.g. accepting asylum seekers, abiding by the UN Convention on Human Rights etc.). One could even argue that our 'special relationship' with the USA is the biggest political limitation of all.

While it is true that parliamentary sovereignty is central to the UK constitution, one must be careful not to overstate its significance, as the power of the executive can render the whole notion of parliamentary sovereignty something of an anachronism. What Lord Hailsham once described as the 'elected dictatorship' can get legislation through Parliament with little difficulty, provided the government's majority is significant. This has certainly been the case since 1997, even when the government has introduced controversial legislation on top-up fees and ID cards. However, with the government's much reduced majority since May 2005, and the reduction in Blair's authority, the executive now finds it more difficult to impose its will on Parliament.

318

It is undoubtedly the case that EU membership has undermined parliamentary sovereignty. UK law can be overturned by the EU, regardless of the views of the British Parliament. There was no clearer illustration than the Factortame case, when legislation passed by Westminster was overturned by the EU.

The use of qualified majority voting in the Council of Ministers also represents a loss of national sovereignty, as have judgements made by the European Court of Justice. British employers must now ensure equal pay between men and women, and the UK government must grant free prescriptions to all men and women over the age of 60. Both these cases were the result of decisions taken by European courts rather than the national courts. We also have to abide by EU policies, some of which work against our national interests (e.g. the CAP).

The two views of sovereignty

Those on the Right of the political spectrum argue that sovereignty cannot be shared, and therefore we have lost sovereignty because an outside body can now overrule Parliament. From the Left, Old Labour politicians such as Tony Benn have argued that parliamentary sovereignty has been transferred to a capitalist club that enshrines *laissez faire* economics. In contrast, pro-Europeans tend to see sovereignty as something that can be shared or pooled. One's view of parliamentary sovereignty is, ultimately, affected by which view of sovereignty is applied.

Devolution and the unitary state

The existence of devolved assemblies in Scotland, Wales and Northern Ireland brings us closer to the European norm

319

without adopting the federal structure of countries such as Spain, Germany and Belgium. To some extent devolution in the UK has been indirectly influenced by EU membership via the principle of subsidiarity and the existence of strong regional government in many EU states.

Devolution is of course very different from federalism, and is a direct consequence of Britain's status as a unitary, rather than a federal, state. In practice, the distinction between federalism and devolution greatly affects the relationship between central and local government. Thus the German government cannot transfer authority from one of the Länder legislatures, whereas the Westminster government can transfer power back from a devolved assembly. It can even close down a devolved assembly, as it has in the case of Northern Ireland.

Supporters of devolution claim that it has encouraged regional democracy, reflects the cultural diversity of the UK and allows for policy variations that have enhanced political debate (e.g. the refusal to introduce fees for higher education in Scotland, and free care homes for the elderly). However, critics of devolution refer to the so-called 'West Lothian question'.

The West Lothian question

The West Lothian question gains its name from the constituency represented by the MP who first raised this problematic issue back in the late 1970s. As a staunch opponent of devolution, Tam Dalyell argued that it was unfair for Scottish MPs to vote on matters of domestic policy affecting the rest of the UK, while English MPs could not vote on matters affecting Scotland. The West Lothian question arose in January 2004 when the government passed controversial legislation with the support of Scottish Labour MPs, whose constituents were unaffected by top-up fees.

The growing use of referendums

Since 1997 the government has set 34 referendums on a range of constitutional issues, most of which concern the issue of devolution. The use of referendums over the past nine years reflects a more 'European' approach to constitutional issues, and has to some extent been influenced by the UK's membership of the EU.

Referendums are common in several EU states, but are by no means universal (the German constitution actually forbids the use of referendums). At the time of writing, the government has pledged to hold a national referendum on our membership of the eurozone, although it has yet to set a date. This is obviously a direct result of our membership of the EU.

The key element of the UK constitution is parliamentary sovereignty, which can be defined as 'the power of Parliament to make or repeal any law it wishes'. As such no person or body has the right to override or set aside legislation passed by Parliament. Referendums could of course be seen as undermining parliamentary sovereignty, yet in practice the government can simply ignore it, or hold another until the 'right' result is achieved. Both the Danish and Irish governments held repeat plebicites on the ratification of EU treaties, and this option could be used by the present government if the people said no to joining the euro.

Individual and collective ministerial responsibility

Membership of the EU has weakened the traditional doctrine of individual ministerial responsibility. Since the Single European Act was ratified, the UK parliament has found it more difficult to hold the government to account, as decisions taken in the Council of Ministers are usually made on the basis of Qualified Majority Voting, and always in secret.

One must also take into account the impact of supranational

bodies. When EU legislation is implemented by national governments, the minister in charge of that department may be perceived as accountable for that policy, when in actual fact he or she had little influence over the decision taken. As for collective ministerial responsibility, this doctrine was suspended during the 1975 referendum on EC membership. It is clearly the case that if we had not joined the EC, collective ministerial responsibility would have remained unaffected.

The extent to which our constitution is written

The UK constitution is uncodified and largely unwritten. Since the UK joined the EC in 1973, the *acquis communitaire* has led the UK towards a *more* codified constitution, while stopping short of adopting a fully codified constitution. EU laws and treaties now form an important written element of our constitution.

Constitutional reform

Since 1997 the Labour government has implemented a radical programme of constitutional reform. The key elements have been:

- ➤ devolution;
- ➤ Lords reform;
- ➤ the incorporation of the European Convention of Human Rights into UK law.

Reform of the House of Lords has been influenced by EU membership, as the options for reform have been partly based on the existence of powerful second chambers in Germany and Spain. After faltering attempts since 1999, the government appears to have lost enthusiasm for Lords reform.

There is a deep-seated human rights culture within the EU, and that has to some extent affected the UK. A clear illustration is the incorporation of the European Convention on Human Rights into UK law in 1998. The Freedom of Information Act 2000 could also be considered. There is much that could be reformed in order to place Britain within the European mainstream. A written constitution, an elected second chamber and genuine federal powers for Scotland and Wales are just three possible areas. At the present time, major constitutional reform is not on the government's agenda.

THE GOVERNMENT'S POLICY TOWARDS THE EU SINCE 1997

Since 1997, the government has found common ground with its European partners in several areas. It has opted into the Social Chapter, signed two major treaties, managed to lift the ban on British beef and incorporated the European Convention on Human Rights into UK law. Britain is now more of a team player in Europe (Ladrech 2004: 55), and Tony Blair could claim to be the first intuitively pro-European Prime Minister since Edward Heath (Stephens 2004: 153).

The government has been able to pursue a more enthusiastic and constructive approach to the EU than the Conservatives did during the 1980s and 1990s. The Labour Party is more united on the issue of Europe than the Tories were under John Major and the size of the government's majority reduces the ability of backbench rebel MPs to cause trouble for the government. Blair has also established a good working relationship with the Swedish Prime Minister Göran Persson and the former Spanish leader José Maria Aznar, and found allies among many of the new member states.

Not everything, however, has gone in a pro-European

direction. In 1998 there was a high-profile diplomatic row with the French government over British beef, and in 2003 the EU was plunged into crisis over the US-led coalition in Iraq (which Britain supported). During the Luxembourg summit of 2005 there were bitter recriminations over the British rebate, and the UK's presidency of the EU was dogged by the issue of the EU's budget.

The UK's reluctance towards further European integration is not confined to Conservative governments. The Chancellor is firmly against harmonising tax policy across Europe, and in December 2003 the government held firm on several red liners during negotiations leading up to the EU Constitution. More importantly, we remain outside the eurozone. Despite Blair being in favour of entry, he remains reluctant to call a referendum and the issue is currently off the government's agenda. In common with John Major, Tony Blair has been forced to adopt a 'wait and see' policy due to opposition from the public, and to lesser extent from his own party.

TO WHAT EXTENT IS BRITAIN THE 'AWKWARD PARTNER'?

The academic Stephen George (1998) argues that Britain is the 'awkward partner' of the EU. There are several historical examples of Britain's apparent awkwardness (Geddes 2004: 2–3) and it is undoubtedly the case that our approach to European integration has been characterised by reluctance. The UK's continual reluctance or awkwardness towards the process of European integration could be attributed to several factors, such as late entry.

Britain joins late

By joining late, Britain could not negotiate from a position of strength, and thus lost the opportunity to influence the path of European integration. We therefore had little choice but to accept the rules of the Community which, in some cases, worked directly against British interests. Britain also failed to secure a satisfactory budgetary deal. On joining the UK became a net contributor to the EC's budget, despite the poor shape of the economy.

The significance of public opinion

The British are less supportive of European integration than other member states (Geddes 2004: 213). This is demonstrated through opinion polls and low turnout in European elections. For instance, in 1999, the UK recorded the lowest turnout in the whole of the EU.

The financial costs of membership shed further light on public opinion. Britain is the second largest contributor to the EU (*Telegraph*, 8/6/05: 1), which must surely have an affect on the UK's attitude towards Europe. It is also revealing that the issue of Europe barely figured in the 2005 general election campaign. Yet in the only nationwide referendum ever held in Britain, the public voted two to one in favour of continued membership of the EC. In addition, whenever one of the main parties has taken a firm Eurosceptic stance, it has lost the general election by a wide margin.

The press

It is undoubtedly the case that the British public have relatively little knowledge about EU institutions; the so-called 'knowledge deficit'. Our ignorance might partly be explained by the influence of Britain's (largely) American- and Australian-owned press.

Unique among the member states, three-quarters of all newspapers sold in the UK could be described as anti-European. As one might expect, most of those newspapers tend to focus on the negative effects of EU membership. For example, the *Sun*'s 'Guide to the EU Constitution' contained such dubious claims as 'Our army will have to follow EU orders' and 'We will lose control of our borders and have no say in who enters the country' (*Economist*, 'The world in 2005': 42). The press also criticise so-called Eurocrats for generating too much red tape and making ludicrous decisions, such as forcing fish and chip shops to change the name of their food to their Latin equivalent (Lawes 2005: 139). In fact there are just under 36,000 European civil servants (D. Leonard 2005: 90), fewer than the number of staff employed by a medium-sized city council (www.europa.eu.int/institutions/comm/index_en.htm). The Eurosceptic press also ignore the role of national bureaucracies, who often seize on loopholes or legal ambiguity to create added regulations. One such example is the Workplace Directive 891/654. The original document contained just 34 lines, but the UK Civil Service managed to turn it into 20 pages of regulations, plus more than 100 pages of explanatory guidance (MacDonald and Bowden 2005: 109).

The impact of the New Right

Since 1979, there has been a disparity between Britain and the rest of Europe over economic policy. The extent of this divergence was at its peak during the Conservative governments of the 1980s and 1990s, and symptomatic of that era was the Single European Act.

Mrs Thatcher signed the Act because she hoped that the single European market would lead to a free trade Europe. The other leaders firmly believed that a single market should entail a Social Chapter and closer union, and were somewhat baffled by Thatcher's description of the Social Chapter as Marxist.

The British preference for intergovernmentalism

The UK has always preferred intergovernmentalism to federalism, and has usually taken a pragmatic approach to European integration. Unlike many other member states, Britain has never equated its national interests with further integration, thus our preference for a Europe of the States is based firmly on our perceived national interests. The UK's global links are undoubtedly part of the reason for its reluctance to support a United States of Europe. Himself a supporter of a federal Europe, Winston Churchill once depicted Britain as 'with, but not of, Europe' (Geddes 2004: 24). It is an argument based on our special relationship with the USA, and our links to the 'kith and kin' of the Commonwealth. Britain is also an island separated physically from Continental Europe, we speak the world's second most popular language and have an imperial history. Yet if it were simply a case of geography (and to an extent language), the Irish would be equally hostile to the EU, and as for our imperial history, no less than eight European nations all had sizeable empires.

Perhaps a more substantive reason for Britain's hostility to closer union derives from a different understanding of the word *federalism*. In Continental Europe it means taking decisions at the most appropriate level, whereas the British have tended to associate federalism with a European superstate. In 2003 the government insisted that the draft EU Constitution should not contain the word federal, and in the early 1990s John Major had the 'f-word' removed from the text of the Maastricht Treaty.

As British policymakers have often pointed out, being a 'good European' does not mean signing up to every new initiative, nor does it mean European integration should always shift in the direction of a closer union. However, the UK's preference for intergovernmentalism under governments of both parties has regularly placed it in opposition to pro-federalist states such as France and Germany.

The significance of parliamentary sovereignty

Political debate in the UK is often based on the assumption that sovereignty cannot be shared. The reason for this is parliamentary sovereignty, a concept at the very core of the UK's constitution. One might add that at the time of joining there was little discussion from politicians as to what the phrase 'ever closer union' might entail. The Conservative government of Edward Heath even claimed that EC member-ship raised no question of any erosion of essential national sovereignty. It is therefore difficult to escape the view that our political elite were somewhat economical with the truth (Geddes 2004: 73).

Is Britain the only awkward partner?

The UK is *not* the only country to resist moves towards an 'ever closer union'. Consider the following examples:

- Denmark and Sweden have refused to join the eurozone;
- in 2005, both the French and the Dutch rejected the EU Constitution;
- during negotiations over the proposed EU Constitution many countries had their own red liners such as the Spanish over regional policy and Germany over asylum and immigration;
- Ireland has refused to join the Schengen Agreement;
- Spain, Denmark, Poland, Holland and Italy all supported the US-led coalition in Iraq;
- some western European countries (Norway, Switzerland and Iceland) have not even joined the EU.

The UK has also played an active role on several occasions. The British government has always been keen on the Single European Market, and instigated the European Security and Defence Policy (along with the French). The UK is also one of the main supporters of the Lisbon Strategy (along with Spain). Moreover, we have a good record of implementing EU directives, unlike many of our supposedly pro-European partners.

IS EUROPE DESTINED TO BECOME A SUPERSTATE?

The term 'superstate' is often used by Eurosceptics in a negative way. They associate the word with a United States of Europe, in which power is exercised by a central authority based in Brussels. Yet clearly the EU is not a superstate, nor does a federal Europe necessarily imply a centralisation of power, as federalism consists of sharing power between the EU, the member states and local government.

While the EU does have supranational powers, its institutions only exist because the member states believe there are clear benefits in pooling sovereignty. It is also the case that the most significant bodies within the EU are intergovernmental (i.e. the European Council and the Council of Ministers). In addition, if the EU were to approach the status of a superstate, then a written constitution would be a relatively straightforward and short document. Yet the EU Constitution is 325 pages long precisely because the EU does *not* centralise power to Brussels.

WHAT DOES ENLARGEMENT MEAN FOR THE FUTURE OF THE EU?

The enlargement of the EU in May 2004 was unprecedented. Never before have ten member states joined at the same time, and never before have new members been so relatively poor as those of Central and Eastern Europe.

The most likely outcome of an enlarged EU is a multispeed or à la carte Europe, with some member states negotiating opt-outs while the federalist-minded countries integrate among themselves. This is already the case with border control, European foreign policy and the single currency. Thus in the long term, enlargement has ultimately strengthened inter-governmentalism within the EU and therefore Europe does not appear destined to become a superstate.

THE FUTURE OF BRITAIN IN EUROPE

Some would argue that the direction of the EU has in recent years favoured the UK, and one of the main reasons for this is due to the enlargement of the EU. There are three factors behind this assumption:

1   Many of the new member states gained independence from the Soviet Union between 1989 and 1991, and are therefore reluctant to concede their hard-won national sovereignty.
2   Those countries have clearly benefited from the widening of the EU, which is a key concept for the intergovern-mentalists.
3   Due to their geographical position they may fear the influence of an over-powerful Germany. Forming an alliance with the UK serves their own national interests by providing a defence against Germany.

Britain has also benefited from the decline of 'old' Europe. The Franco-German alliance has undoubtedly weakened in recent years due to domestic economic problems, in contrast to the success of the UK economy since Black/White Wednesday 1992. Even the EU Constitution was considered a victory for the British view of Europe, particularly in France.

Another factor to consider is the trend within the EU towards supply-side economics. José Barroso was appointed by Britain and her allies due to his free trade sympathies against opposition from France and Germany. The ten new member states also favour low tax and supply-side economics, and even the French appear to be adopting a more flexible labour market. Yet it is perhaps the Lisbon agenda that has seen the most significant victory for Britain.

However, not everything is going our way. During the British Presidency of the EU in 2005, Tony Blair agreed to give up around one-fifth of the UK's rebate in order to pay for the cost of EU enlargement. As many of the other member states are understandably resentful at the favourable treatment awarded to Britain, this was not a surprise. Moreover, our economic position has been transformed since 1984, which does make the rebate much more difficult to justify. However, the UK retains a veto over any further changes to the rebate, and the government will continue to press for substantial reform of the CAP.

DO THE BENEFITS OF BRITAIN'S MEMBERSHIP OF THE EU OUTWEIGH THE COSTS?

The costs of EU membership include:

➢ loss of sovereignty, if one accepts the traditional view of sovereignty;

- ➤ a weakening of our national identity;
- ➤ some policies have worked against British interests, such as the CAP and the CFP;
- ➤ the free movement of people has made the problems of illegal immigration and drug trafficking more widespread;
- ➤ the UK is a net contributor to the EU.

The benefits of EU membership include:

- ➤ European integration has made war between the member states almost unthinkable;
- ➤ Britain is a member of the world's largest single market;
- ➤ as citizens of the EU, we are entitled to the four freedoms contained in the Rome Treaties;
- ➤ the pooling of sovereignty actually strengthens the power of national governments – for instance, the UK can influence the policies of another member state in some EU policy areas;
- ➤ we are part of an economic and political organisation that rivals the USA;
- ➤ poorer regions have gained extra funding;
- ➤ the UK is part of an organisation that has spread democracy throughout Europe.

15

Gordon Brown as Prime Minister

Gordon Brown became Prime Minister of Great Britain and Northern Ireland on 27 June 2007. For the man himself it represented the fulfilment of an ambition he had nurtured (and been denied) for several years. For the Labour Party it represented an opportunity to cast aside the less savoury aspects of the Blair legacy and unite behind a new leader in an attempt to secure an unprecedented fourth term. Yet for the country, Gordon Brown was something of an enigma. Despite the fact that he was Chancellor of the Exchequer for just over a decade, few political analysts could offer a wholly convincing answer to the question, 'How would Gordon Brown's approach to the position of Prime Minister differ from that of Tony Blair?' (Giddens, 2007; Bower, 2004). However, at the time of writing it is now possible to offer an evaluation and analysis of Gordon Brown's premiership. I wish to consider each aspect of the syllabus, beginning with race and ethnicity.

RACE AND ETHNICITY

Three issues are relevant to any discussion of Brown's premiership thus far in relation to race and ethnicity. They are Britishness, immigration and the government's response to Islamic terrorism.

One of the central tenets of Gordon Brown's political compass is a strong emphasis upon 'Britishness'. Indeed he has spoken about the subject more often than any other Prime Minister of recent times. For instance, during his speech to the TUC he called for 'British jobs for British workers', and in his 2007 party conference speech he made no less than 81 references to Britain or Britishness (*Times*, 25/9/07:1). He has also endorsed a much more overt celebration of national identity – including a British Day and a call for the British flag to be flown in every garden.

Brown's emphasis upon 'Britishness' holds clear resonance to the issue of multiculturalism, but it also represents quite a sharp distinction between himself and Tony Blair. Whereas Tony Blair once conceded that he did not fully understand what the term multiculturalism actually means, Gordon Brown is more than willing to offer his thoughts upon this thorny – and often greatly misunderstood – concept. Gordon Brown's emphasis upon Britishness suggests that he takes a conservative with a small 'c' perspective upon multiculturalism. However, the reason for Brown's emphasis upon 'Britishness' might well be down to purely tactical considerations.

As a Scottish MP leading the United Kingdom in the post-devolution era Gordon Brown finds himself in an unprecedented situation. Voters (especially in England) may well perceive Gordon Brown's status as a Scot who can vote on matters affecting England – whilst having no direct influence over domestic issues within *his own* constituency – as both contradictory and untenable. The Scottish Nationalist Party's victory in the May 2007 devolved assembly election only exacerbates the Prime Minister's difficulties, and if he is to neutralise a potentially damaging situation he must provide a convincing answer to the West Lothian question. Thus far, the 'answer' appears to be an emphasis upon Britishness, but whether this is a wholly convincing answer is wide open to debate.

On the issue of immigration Gordon Brown has adopted a very similar strategy to that of Tony Blair. As Gordon Brown was the most significant Cabinet member during the Blair era, and one of the key architects of New Labour, this is not entirely surprising. During his first 100 days in office Brown's stance on immigration has consisted of:

> continued support for the concept of citizenship both as a subject taught within schools and as an official certificate from the authorities. In common with Blair, Gordon Brown believes that citizenship can help integrate members of our increasingly diverse society;
> pressing ahead with the controversial ID cards scheme;
> a pledge to create more effective border patrols;[1]

Gordon Brown has yet to convince the public that his government can effectively manage the level of immigration to the UK, and on this controversial issue he is clearly vulnerable to a resurgent Conservative opposition. David Cameron has criticised the present government for letting in too many immigrants, a charge he can back up with official statistics which confirm that over a million foreign nationals have been granted citizenship since 1997 (*Times*, 23/5/07:1). In addition, the level of net migration has more than trebled since 1997.[2]

The third and final issue in relation to race and ethnicity is the government's response to Islamic terrorism, which once

---

[1] Whilst making the pledge on border patrols the government conceded that it will take until 2014 for all visitors to the UK to undergo a passport check.

[2] Gordon Brown has much to do in order to heal divisions within British society. In an opinion poll taken by the Policy Exchange think-tank shortly before he came to power, well over a third of young British Muslims said they wish to live according to Sharia law (*Guardian*, 31/1/07:4), whilst in a report commissioned by the Democratic Audit, 1 in 5 people in England said they would consider voting BNP (*Daily Telegraph*, 19/4/07:6).

again represents continuity with those policies pursued by Tony Blair. As such, Brown could be said to be pursuing a combination of both 'tough' and 'tender' policies. In the case of the former, the Prime Minister has spoken in favour of extending the period terrorist suspects could be held without trial, endorsed the use of control orders and pledged to allocate an extra £86 million for the intelligence and counter-terrorism services. In terms of a more tender approach, Gordon Brown has maintained government-sponsored programmes designed to strengthen links with Islamic groups, such as 'Tackling Extremism Together', and is supportive of organisations such as the recently-created Commission on integration and social cohesion. He has also encouraged LEAs to twin schools so that children of different faiths can socialise together from an early age. Revealingly, Gordon Brown's appointment of Jacqui Smith as Home Secretary reflected a slightly softer tone of language used by the government when she stressed the need for 'a calm response' to the July 2007 incident at Glasgow airport rather than a rush towards new legislation. She also stressed the need for 'co-operation between the government and the opposition' (http://news.bbc.co.uk/1/hi/uk_politics/6260252.stm). This shift of language marks a departure from the tougher rhetoric of the Blair era. However, the broad direction of Brown's premiership has been a continuation of New Labour policies.

LAW AND ORDER

When Gordon Brown took over at Number 10 he inherited a situation in which the level of crime had steadily fallen since the mid 1990s but the public remained deeply worried about crime and anti-social behaviour. In an opinion poll taken just before he became Prime Minister, 70% of those questioned said that Britain was a more dangerous place in which to live than when Labour first came to power (*Observer*, 11). To analyse Gordon Brown's approach to this crucially important issue we need to understand his position within the New Labour project.

Central to the New Labour project is an emphasis upon tough measures to deal with public concerns in this area and, along with Tony Blair, Gordon Brown has taken a largely authoritarian stance upon issues relating to law and order. One of his first decisions in relation to law and order was to press ahead with ID cards despite rumours of scepticism towards the scheme while he was Chancellor. It was an early signal of Brown's intention to renew the government's emphasis upon law and order, a stance maintained by the PM's support for extending the length at which terrorist suspects can be detained without trial from the existing level of 28 days. Further signs of Brown's largely authoritarian approach to law and order were in evidence during his first party conference speech as Prime Minister, in which he pledged to:

➢ extend stop-and-search powers of the police
➢ impose a 5-year mandatory sentence for anyone carrying a gun
➢ withdraw licences from retailers who repeatedly sell alcohol to those under the age of 18
➢ give authorities the power to deport any newcomer to Britain caught selling drugs or using a gun
➢ review 24-hour drinking[3]
➢ provide 10,000 handheld computers to help police cut down on paperwork.

---

[3] Shortly after coming to power Gordon Brown reversed the government's stance on supercasinos due to concerns over the link between gambling and crime/ anti-social behaviour. Coupled with a reconsideration of the government's previous decision to declassify the status of cannabis, Gordon Brown's premiership represents a more moralistic approach to politics than his predecessor.

The PM's unmistakably 'tough' approach is designed to reassure the public, and as Brown was a central figure in the emergence of New Labour he seems fully aware of the electoral dangers of being portrayed as 'soft on crime'. Yet to the dismay of libertarians the Prime Minister has chosen not to place a high priority upon civil liberties, despite the fact that in Brown's Britain:

> the national DNA database is the largest in the world and contains almost a million samples from children (*Times*, 15/6/07:4);[4]
> there are an estimated 5 million surveillance cameras in the UK, roughly 1 for every 12 people. This is the highest density of surveillance cameras in the world (*Guardian*, 27/3/07:17);
> control orders can be issued with no evidence, no trial and no right of appeal. Suspects are therefore guilty until proved innocent;
> under the Serious Organised Crime and Police Act, Maya Evans was arrested by 14 police officers for reading out in public the names of soldiers killed in Iraq. 78 police officers were also employed to remove the anti-war protestor Brian Haw just outside Parliament, and in that same year an 80-year-old army veteran was manhandled out of the Labour Party conference for expressing opposition to the war in Iraq under the notorious Section 44 of the Terrorism Act 2000;
> the actions of the authorities in relation to certain cases – such as that of Abu Bakr – have been compared to those of a police state (*Guardian*, 19/3/07:33), a

---

[4] In September 2007 Sir Stephen Sedley proposed that every man, woman and child in the country should be obliged to provide DNA samples for the national database.

sentiment shared by (of all people) the Archbishop of York (*Guardian*, 6/2/07:29).

Gordon Brown is also set to continue with the Orwellian-sounding Children's Index, which is due to be created sometime in 2008. Another issue to consider in relation to law and order is that of overcrowded prisons. The prison population reached breaking-point soon after Brown came to power. Overcrowded prisons are a major problem because shunting inmates from one prison to another undermines the rehabilitation process as prisoners lose touch with their families and leave drug-detox schemes. Overcrowding can also lead to prisoners sharing a cell, which can cause problems (such as the murder of Zahid Mubarak at the Feltham Young Offenders Institution by a racist psychopath). It also places extra strain upon prison wardens, an issue highlighted by the Prison Officers Association who called their first-ever strike on 29 August 2007. One could also argue that the Labour government has exacerbated the problem with the introduction of over 3,000 new offences since 1997, coupled with a failure to build an adequate number of prisons during Brown's period as Chancellor (and Prime Minister). If his pronouncements on other law and order issues are anything to go by, Brown's response to the issue is likely to be authoritarian rather than a focus upon liberal measures such as rehabilitation.

WELFARE STATE

During the Blair era Gordon Brown was widely perceived as a politician sceptical of the alleged merits of marketisation within the public services. This view was based upon Brown's endorsement of the Wanless report (2002), his initial opposition to foundation hospitals in 2003 and his praise of the public service ethos amongst workers in the state sector. Therefore, the assumption was that Gordon Brown would be a more left-wing leader than Tony Blair, an assumption Brown himself often played up to. However, during the early months of Brown's premiership the government has done remarkably little to reverse, or even criticise, the trend towards marketisation within the public services.

It is undoubtedly the case that Gordon Brown – a man even his opponents would concede holds a considerable intellect – offers little academic challenge to the influence of the New Right's critique of the welfare state. The fact that Gordon Brown was criticised by the left of his party during the run-up to taking over from Tony Blair (i.e. from both John McDonnell and Michael Meacher) is in itself rather telling. Indeed, it is worth recalling that, while he was Chancellor, Gordon Brown championed the Private Finance Initiative and firmly supported a flexible labour market as the most effective response to globalisation. Moreover, during his period as Chancellor, Gordon Brown allocated significant funds to the welfare to work programme, a strategy which borrowed heavily from policies implemented by the 'new' Democrats in the United States (and which were in themselves influenced by the New Right's critique of the welfare state), and he was much more supportive of selective benefits than any of his Labour predecessors. The prominence of New Right-influenced means for social justice ends has undoubtedly continued since Brown became Prime Minister. Thus whilst his public pronouncements and background suggest a man of the left, Gordon Brown's political stance is much closer to Tony Blair's than is sometimes assumed. For a politician who was once a virulent critic of Thatcherism (Brown, 1989) he has travelled a remarkably long way along the political spectrum.

Although portrayed by his critics on the right as a roadblock to market-based reform, Gordon Brown has maintained Blair's emphasis upon parental and patient choice as a key method by which to improve standards throughout public services. The PM's mix of Thatcherite policies with an emphasis upon social justice is essentially the same combination that characterised Blair's premiership and served him so well during three election victories. What differences exist with the Blair era are largely stylistic rather than those of ideological substance and, whilst Brown is less inclined to conduct the debate in terms of marketisation, his focus upon a more personalised approach to the welfare state is no different in substance from that of Tony Blair.

HEALTH AND EDUCATION

During his speech to the 2007 Labour Party conference Gordon Brown pledged that his government would ensure:

➢ one-to-one tuition for problem children;
➢ a personal tutor for every pupil through their time at secondary school;
➢ further-education grants to students up to the age of 18;
➢ greater assistance for the poorest young people throughout their education.

In that same speech Gordon Brown also placed the NHS at the heart of his political outlook. His government is now pledged to provide 5,000 hospital matrons with the power to overturn hospital cleaning contracts, to extend bowel cancer screening until the age of 75 and to extend screening for breast cancer by 6 years. Brown also said that every suspected case of breast cancer would be treated as urgent and promised a major 'clean-up' of hospitals in order to tackle the problem of superbugs. In contrast to health and education, Gordon Brown has said little in relation to other areas of welfare provision, although he has pledged to extend paid maternity leave to 9 months and provide one-to-one support for deprived teenage mothers for the first 2 years of their child's life.

His proposals in the field of welfare provision may, however, prove difficult to fund. The significant increase in public expenditure from 1999 to 2007 is set for a slowdown. For example, in the 2007 Comprehensive Spending Review the government pledged to increase health spending by 4% per year in real terms (in contrast to 7% per year since Labour first came to power). Public spending on state education is also facing a similar slowdown. This problem is compounded by a predicted slowdown in the level of economic growth. Gordon Brown may therefore find it somewhat difficult to deliver on his promises.

HOUSING

While it is the case that Gordon Brown undoubtedly continues with many policies of the Blair era, there is at least one area of welfare provision in which he differs from his predecessor. Since taking over as Prime Minister Gordon Brown has placed a far greater emphasis upon housing than Tony Blair did, and after years on the political backburner it seems that the priority awarded to housing policy will increase. Since Gordon Brown took over as PM the government has pledged to:

> increase investment on new social housing to £8 billion;
> spend £4 billion renovating social housing over the next 3 years;
> move towards a target of creating 2 million new homeowners by 2010;
> build 10 new eco-towns.

Gordon Brown's interest in the issue of housing may in part be influenced by a loss of support for Labour within their traditional heartlands. In many of these areas working-class voters have either stayed at home or registered a protest vote for other parties (including the British National Party). Housing is undoubtedly an important issue within many deprived communities and Brown has, at least in this regard, taken a stance largely associated with the left.

Gordon Brown has also pledged to make the issue of affordable housing a key element of his premiership. On this issue he certainly faces a very difficult challenge. According to official statistics, in 2007 the average home in England cost 7 times the level of average income, and if nothing is done to resolve the situation the next generation of first-time buyers is likely to face house prices equivalent to 10 times average income (*Times*, 7/6/07:1). In order to tackle this problem the recent Barker review recommended the construction of an extra 70,000 houses and flats per year (*Times*, 6/6/07:16), but a major building programme cannot be implemented without facing opposition from both the public and environmental pressure groups.

NORTHERN IRELAND

The transformation from a troubled province characterised by sectarian hatred to one in which some form of normality is slowly emerging is a very welcome development within British politics. Whilst problems undoubtedly remain, Gordon Brown inherited a relatively stable political situation in which little is expected from a British Prime Minister because the power-sharing executive formed on 8 May 2007 now runs the affairs of Northern Ireland. Therefore in the foreseeable future it seems highly unlikely that Gordon Brown will be expected to play an overtly political role within the province. Moreover the high degree of consensus amongst the main parties on the issue of Northern Ireland means that Gordon Brown is unlikely to face much criticism from the Tories or the Liberal Democrats.

THE ECONOMY

If one word summarises Gordon Brown's political credo more than any other it is 'prudence'. Rarely has a politician been so closely associated with the values of caution and sobriety. Indeed the word 'prudence' could have been invented for Gordon Brown. During his decade at the helm of economic policy Gordon Brown was a prudent Chancellor, and many political pundits formed an expectation that Brown's premiership would also be characterised by a cautious mentality.

For a Prime Minister so closely associated with caution, Gordon Brown has faced an unexpectedly high number of crisis situations such as terrorist attacks, flooding and an outbreak of foot-and-mouth disease. In the context of the economy yet another case in point stands out – that of Northern Rock.

The Northern Rock crisis (September 2007)

In response to lengthy queues outside many branches of Northern Rock the government aimed to reassure investors that the Bank would not go bust. To back up these assurances the Treasury (along with the Bank of England and the FSA) provided financial support to Northern Rock to ease its liquidity crisis. The intervention appeared to calm the public and a major crisis was largely averted. As an added measure the Chancellor, Alistair Darling (himself a close ally of Gordon Brown), said that the government would increase protection for savers by guaranteeing deposits of up to £35,000. This represented a substantial improvement on the previous situation.

The government's response to the Northern Rock crisis can be interpreted in two ways. The first appears to be one of decisive (if somewhat delayed) action in the face of a crisis that may well have ruined Labour's carefully cultivated mantle as the party most trusted to manage the economy – a mantle that owes more to Gordon Brown than anybody else. The second interpretation is one of a government prepared to intervene in response to a crisis despite Brown's public pronouncements in favour of the free market and his personal association with the granting of independence to the Bank of England. The Northern Rock crisis of September 2007 could therefore be seen as a classic illustration of a government placing politics *above* economics.

Whilst it is still too early to assess fully the long-term impact of the government's handling of the Northern Rock crisis, opinion polls suggest that Gordon Brown came out of the crisis with his reputation intact. In a Populus poll published shortly after the Northern Rock crisis the public placed greater trust in Gordon Brown/Alistair Darling than David Cameron/George Osborne by a significant margin (http://ukpollingreport.co.uk/blog/archives/category/voting-intention). This may well suggest that in the event of an economic downturn the public is likely to stick with the present government rather than switch to the opposition, a view that echoes the situation during the 1992 election when the Conservatives were re-elected during a downturn in the economic cycle and Brown was himself on the losing side. From a purely political standpoint a crisis comparable to Black Wednesday was avoided, and that in itself is one of Brown's most notable 'achievements' thus far as Prime Minister.

On the issue of the economy, the public's assessment of Gordon Brown will inevitably be influenced by what he did during his time as Chancellor. Over the course of a decade two decisions really stand out in terms of their political significance – the surprise decision to grant independence to the Bank of England and a refusal to take Britain into the Eurozone. Both decisions were taken by Brown, *not* Blair. As such, Brown deserves some credit in terms of managing the economy. Indeed, according to the chief economist of the OECD, Jean-Philippe Cotis, Britain could be described as a 'goldilocks economy' – having got the balance right between economic growth and low inflation (*Guardian*, 12/3/07:27). This ringing endorsement from an important institution clearly strengthens Brown's hand, and he can of course remind voters of David Cameron's association with Black Wednesday (Cameron was a special advisor to the then Conservative Chancellor, Norman Lamont).

Having said this, the Chancellor Alistair Darling faces a number of problems that were left unresolved during Brown's tenure at Number 11. Perhaps the most important of these in political terms is tax. Since 1997 the level of taxation has increased by over £3,000 per household (*Observer*, 43), often via stealth measures. Shortly before Brown took over as Prime Minister, Britain's tax burden reached its highest level since the mid-1980s (*Daily Telegraph*, 6/3/07:1) and surpassed the OECD average (*Guardian*, 12/10/06:26). Having said this, the Conservatives have found it difficult to score any political points against Brown on the issue of tax due to their reluctance to argue the case for tax cuts. During the 2005 general election the Tories' modest proposals for tax cuts were depicted by Labour as a large-scale plan to slash and burn public services. While the substance of Labour's charge was highly exaggerated, it does seems likely that the charge did some political damage to the Conservatives. Perhaps because of this the Tories rejected most of the findings of an internal Commission published in November 2006 to cut government spending by £21 billion, and an incoming Tory government has pledged to stick with Labour's spending plans for three years.

The Conservatives may have more scope to attack Gordon Brown's economic record as Chancellor (and now Prime Minister) as there are several other economic problems facing the UK economy. For example:

> since 1997 productivity growth has declined from 2.3% to 1.6% (Goodlad, April 2007 *Talking Politics*: 139);
> the trade gap has widened considerably since Labour came to power;
> our balance of payments have been transformed from a small surplus in 1997 to a deficit in 2006 of £55 billion (*Guardian*, 15/3/07:35);
> over a million jobs in the manufacturing sector were lost during Brown's period as Chancellor (*Guardian*, 15/3/07:35);
> the IMF has predicted a major collapse in the housing market (*Times*, 18/10/07:1);
> over 650,000 jobs currently go unfilled due to a skills shortage in the economy (*Times*, 11/9/07:14);
> the government's finances have been transformed from a surplus in 1997 to a significant deficit of £38 billion (£4 billion more than Gordon Brown initially predicted). More importantly, the Chancellor, Alistair Darling, scaled back predictions for economic growth from 2.5%–3% to 2%–2.5%.

As the man who was Chancellor for over a decade, Gordon Brown possesses a deep-rooted awareness of economic issues and an acute sense of its importance to the country and its relationship to electoral support for himself and his party. One of the truisms of political discourse is that economic success often translates into electoral success. As such, the stakes remain high in this crucial area.

THE EUROPEAN UNION

By far the biggest issue facing Gordon Brown's premiership in relation to the European Union is the EU Reform Treaty. Thus far Brown has refused to hold a referendum on the Reform Treaty despite considerable pressure from the public, the Labour movement and the opposition parties. It is not hard to see why. A defeat for the government (which would almost certainly be the case) might damage the Labour Party's standing in the polls and provide a major boost for the Conservatives. A referendum might also expose divisions within the Labour Party in a scenario akin to the 1975 referendum on Britain's membership of the European Community, an event that many argue marked the origins of Labour's bitter divisions of the early 1980s between social democrats and democratic socialists.

Brown's argument is that the Reform Treaty is different from the EU Constitution and thus the Government's manifesto pledge to hold a referendum on the Constitution is no longer valid. Moreover, previous governments have refused to hold plebiscites on other EU Treaties such as Maastricht (under the Tories) and Amsterdam (under Labour). However, the House of Commons European Scrutiny Committee has claimed that the EU Reform Treaty is 'substantially equivalent' to the constitution and said it was 'likely to be misleading' for the Government to claim that the Treaty no longer had the characteristics of a Constitution (http://www.channel4.com/news/articles/uk/treaty+plans+spark+calls+for+eu+referendum/898052). Although Brown is justified in his argument that Britain is a representative democracy and therefore elected representatives should decide on such matters, it is an argument unlikely to convince the public. In a similar vein, the PM also ignored Sir Menzies Campbell's call for a referendum on Britain's existing membership of the EU. Thus, for all his rhetoric about 'a new style of politics', the Prime Minister continues to ignore calls to give the people a direct say over the future of Britain's relationship with Europe.

During his time as Chancellor Gordon Brown gained a reputation as something of a Eurosceptic. This was based upon his opposition to Britain joining the Eurozone, his allegedly aloof attitude during meetings with his European counterparts and his strong endorsement of the Anglo-Saxon economic model. Since becoming Prime Minister, Gordon Brown has done nothing to dissuade people from this widely-held assumption and, while he has tried to portray David Cameron as yet another right-wing Eurosceptic Tory leader, the reality is that Brown and Cameron dispute remarkably little in the realm of European issues. Indeed, the only substantive dividing line on European matters concerns calls for a referendum on the EU Reform Treaty.

The electoral salience of Europe has always been difficult to gauge. In recent years the issue of Europe appears to enter the public's consciousness only when something dramatic occurs (such as withdrawal from the Exchange Rate Mechanism or the controversy over the launch of the €). As such, Gordon Brown may well escape from such a difficult issue as the Reform Treaty relatively unscathed, although his reputation as a politician offering an end to spin has already taken a sizeable knock.

CONCLUSION

Somewhat fittingly, it was a former Prime Minister (Harold Wilson) who once said that 'a week is a long time in politics'. If that is truly the case, then the length of time Gordon Brown has been Prime Minister is already of some significance. Since taking over from Tony Blair, Gordon Brown has identified policies, themes and ideas that will shape the conduct and direction of his premiership. However, the change

349

from Blair appears to be principally one of style rather than major political substance.

Since taking over from Blair, Gordon Brown has presented himself as a reassuring figure reminiscent of a national leader acting 'above' party politics. This was in evidence from the very beginning of his premiership. Just three days into his new post Gordon Brown was forced to deal with a major terrorist attack on Glasgow airport. He won praise for his handling of the crisis, and coupled with a sure-footed response to an outbreak of foot-and-mouth and a statesman-like approach to large-scale flooding in certain parts of the country his approval rating was initially high.

During the course of his premiership Gordon Brown has attempted to appeal to floating voters whilst reassuring the party's core vote. Distancing himself from George Bush has helped the government reconnect with disaffected former Labour voters, whereas connecting with Conservative and Liberal Democrat voters has required a more consensual rather than tribal approach to politics. Reaching out towards Tories and Lib Dems in order to establish a 'government of all the talents', including Patrick Mercer (a former Tory frontbencher who lost his post after appearing to suggest that racism directed at black people within the armed forces was no more than 'harmless banter') and the former Lib Dem leader Paddy Ashdown, initially appeared to pay electoral dividends. A decline in the appeal of the Liberal Democrats and an apparent move away from the centre by David Cameron also helped Brown portray himself as a leader governing in the national (rather than party) interest. Yet from the perspective of October 2007 any discussion about Gordon Brown is inevitably drawn towards his decision *not* to call a general election.

At the time of writing, conventional wisdom states that Brown lead his troops to the brink of calling an election only to call the whole thing off in response to a set of bad opinion polls. However, politics is currently in an extraordinarily turbulent stage and the negative publicity surrounding Brown could eventually fade away due to events that may in part have been instigated by the recent election fever. For instance, the Liberal Democrats have replaced their unpopular leader Sir Menzies Campbell and any resurgence in the polls for the third party is expected to chip away at support for David Cameron's Conservatives. Secondly, George Osborne's proposals on inheritance tax – which were announced at the Tory party conference to an enthusiastic reception and were in part instigated by the prospect of an autumn election – have been (and will be) challenged by the government who claim that the sums do not add up. The government's tactics on this issue appear to consist of reminding voters of the 'boom and bust' era by claiming that Tory proposals on the economy would inevitably result in economic instability. If the public are persuaded by these (and other) arguments then Gordon Brown may yet secure an historic fourth term for Labour and a mandate from the people. We shall see...

Glossary

Accountability Where elected representatives are answerable to the electorate, usually via an election. Accountability also consists of the government being scrutinised by elected representatives within the legislature, such as via committees and question time. Accountability is a vital concept within any representative democracy.

Acquis communautaire The existing body of EU laws and directives, accumulated over 50 years of European integration.

Additional member system A hybrid of both FPTP and PR, which makes it unique amongst the electoral systems used in Britain. AMS is used to elect representatives to the Welsh Assembly, the Scottish Parliament and the Greater London Assembly. Under this system the electorate has two votes each: one for a candidate and one for a party.

Adversarial politics A political system characterised by a considerable ideological disagreement between two or more political parties. Under this system, policies put forward by the government are subject to hostile scrutiny by the opposition. In addition, the opposition parties usually take a different opinion to that of the government, even when the individual MPs might personally agree with what the government is trying to do. At Westminster, Britain has one of the most adversarial systems in the democratic world, in part encouraged by the layout of the House of Commons.

Asylum seeker Someone who flees from a country because

of persecution on the grounds of political/religious beliefs and/or ethnicity. A refugee gains asylum status when his/her case is considered successful by the authorities.

Authority The right of a person, or institution, to make political decisions. Authority is closely related to the concept of power. According to the sociologist Max Weber, there are three types of authority (traditional, charismatic and rational-legal).

Awkward partner A term that depicts Britain's reluctant approach towards closer European integration. The phrase is associated with the academic Stephen George.

Black Wednesday A term used to describe the events of 16th September 1992, when Britain pulled out of the Exchange Rate Mechanism after the Chancellor Norman Lamont had been forced to raise interest rates from 10% to 15% in the space of a few hours. It represented a major turning point in British politics. After Black Wednesday the Major government never really recovered, and Labour gradually established itself as the party of prudent economic management. As the long-term effects of Black Wednesday have been largely positive, some economists describe it as White Wednesday.

Boom and bust A term coined in the late 1980s/early 1990s to describe the weak performance of the UK economy, which oscillated from rapid economic growth to deep recession.

Bureaucracy A reference to the administrative functions of a state/organisation. The term is often used in a negative way.

Centralisation Where power is concentrated at the level of central government. Governments of both main parties have tended to centralise power over a wide range of policy areas.

Child poverty A situation in which children live in relative poverty, often due to their parents being unemployed. Since

1997 the government has considerably reduced the level of child poverty. In 2006, the Conservative party pledged their support for the government's target to end child poverty by the year 2020.

Citizenship An individual's membership of a state. The concept of citizenship usually applies a range of rights and responsibilities on behalf of both the state and the individual. For example, the citizen should participate in the political process, obey laws, etc. and in return the state should provide protection against terrorism, foreign invasion and the destructive effects of lawlessness.

Civil liberties A range of moral rights that consist of personal freedoms protected and guaranteed by the state on behalf of their citizens, such as freedom of association. Civil liberties are usually enshrined in a constitution.

Coalition An alliance formed between two or more political parties in order to form the executive. Coalitions are common in the devolved assemblies, but are relatively rare at Westminster.

Co-decision In the context of the European Union, those decisions that are made jointly by the European Parliament and the Council of the European Union. The range of decisions taken on this basis has increased significantly since the 1990s.

Collective ministerial responsibility The convention that ministers should maintain the government's collective position, at least in public. If a minister cannot accept collective ministerial responsibility, he or she should, in theory, resign.

Consensus A broad agreement amongst the main parties over basic principles and ideas, rather than over precise policy details. In the UK there is a bi-partisan consensus over many political issues ranging from membership of the EU, the use of market forces and principles within the welfare state and the preservation of a national health service 'free' at the point of use.

Consensus politics Where political parties aim to reach cross-party agreement in order to move the legislative process forward. Most legislatures throughout the world including the EU Parliament, the US Congress, and the devolved assemblies of Scotland, Wales, London and Northern Ireland are designed in a curve formation. It has been argued that this tends to encourage a more consensual style of politics, rather than the adversarial character of Britain's House of Commons.

Constitution A constitution is a system of rules which describes the structure and powers of government, the relationship between different parts of the government, and the relationship between the government and the citizen. The aim of a constitution is to allocate power within a state. The British constitution contains the dignified part (i.e. the House of Lords and the monarch), whose role is primarily symbolic and ineffectual; and the efficient part (i.e. the House of Commons and the Prime Minister), who take the important political decisions. Some have argued that, with the growth of Prime Ministerial power and the notion of party government, the House of Commons has actually become part of the dignified element of the UK's constitution.

Convention An unwritten assumption relating to a certain code of behaviour. Conventions form a crucial element of the UK's constitution. Examples include collective ministerial responsibility and individual ministerial responsibility.

Democratic deficit A lack of accountability, openness and legitimacy within the institutions of the European Union.

Dependency culture A term associated with the New Right in which the welfare state undermines individual responsibility and self-reliance. It is argued that claimants become trapped within the benefits system with little or no incentive to escape.

Devolution The transfer of power from Westminster to a local authority or regional assembly. Devolution has been at the core of Labour's programme of constitutional reform.

Devolved assemblies exist in Scotland, Wales, Northern Ireland and London.

Double majority A proposal contained in the EU Constitution which states that EU laws should only be passed when 55% of the member states, representing at least 65% of the EU's combined population, vote in favour.

Elected dictatorship A reference to Britain's powerful executive branch. The term is associated with the former Conservative politician Lord Hailsham.

Elected mayors A number of British cities now elect a mayor to represent their interests. This has been a feature of UK politics since 1997.

Electoral systems There are three main types of electoral system; majoritarian, proportional and a combination of the two known as a hybrid. In Britain, there are five electoral systems currently in use – the highest number in the world.

European Convention of Human Rights A collection of rights and freedoms outlined at the Council of Europe in the late-1940s. The ECHR is now incorporated into UK law. Since 2000, all legislation has to comply with the ECHR.

European Union An organisation consisting of 27 member states who have joined together to work towards the goal of ever closer union. The European Union consists of both intergovernmental and supranational institutions.

Europhile Those supportive of European integration.

Eurosceptic Those hostile to European integration. Eurosceptics often refer to themselves as Eurorealists.

Exchange rate A measure of the value of national currencies on the foreign exchange markets.

Exchange Rate Mechanism An exchange rate system that aims to ensure a degree of currency stability before an applicant state joins the Eurozone. Britain left the ERM in 1992.

Executive The executive is a branch of government formed by those who implement government policy, such as the

Cabinet. In the case of the UK, the head of the executive is the Prime Minister.

Exports Those goods and services going out of an economy.

Factortame A legal case heard in the early 1990s at the European Court of Justice which demonstrated how the UK had lost sovereignty to the European Union. As a result of the case, the ECJ ruled that the Merchant Shipping Act contravened existing EU law.

Federal state Unlike a unitary system, authority is divided (or shared) between several co-ordinate agencies. The central (or federal) level holds the more important responsibilities, but state/local government has a great deal of power within its constitutionally allocated spheres of responsibility. Several EU member states favour a United States of Europe, but Britain is opposed to the creation of a federal Europe.

Federalism In the context of the European Union, a federal Europe would consist of a United States of Europe in which power would be divided between various levels of government. The EU would do what is appropriate for a central government – such as setting monetary policy, whilst national governments would retain power over policies such as education and health. The local level would deal with issues closest to the people, such as local transport. The EU would also display the symbols of a federal state such as a single currency, a flag, a common passport, etc.

Fiscal policy Macro-economic decisions that deal with public spending, and the level of taxation. Fiscal policy is decided upon by the government.

Foundation schools State schools that operate independently from the government. In 2006 the government's attempt to establish independent state schools was supported by the Tory party in the face of a large-scale rebellion from the Labour backbenches.

Freedom of Information Act (FOIA) An attempt by the

Blair government to strengthen the concept of open government within the UK. However, the Act has been criticised as relatively weak. In 2006, the government announced plans to limit the public's access to information under the FOIA.

Government The term government can be applied to either the party that forms the executive, or the various institutions of the state. There are three branches of government; the legislature, the executive and the judiciary.

Green paper A consultative document issued by the government during the passage of a Bill.

Habeas corpus The right that no person shall be detained without some form of trial, or jury. The Government has restricted this fundamental and ancient civil right in relation to cases involving terrorism (e.g. the imposition of control orders).

Hereditary peers Members of the House of Lords who have inherited their position. Since 1999, just 92 hereditary peers are left in the House of Lords.

Human rights Human rights are those rights to which we are entitled due to the virtue of being human. They are universal, inalienable and absolute – and could be considered a secular version of God-given natural rights.

Hung parliament The result of a general election in which no party has an absolute majority of seats.

Hybrid electoral system A combination of both proportional and majoritarian electoral systems. The only example of a hybrid system used in the UK is the Additional Member System (AMS).

ID cards A controversial initiative introduced in 2006 to address various problems causing public concern (e.g. illegal immigration, crime, bogus asylum seekers and the threat of terrorism).

Immigration Where people migrate towards a country in

order to seek residency and/or employment. Immigration can either be legal or illegal.

Imports Those goods and services entering the economy.

Individual ministerial responsibility A convention in which ministers are held to account for their own actions, and/or the decisions implemented by their government department. In theory a minister should resign if he/she has acted in an improper manner.

Inflation A measure of the rate of increase in prices within the economy. Inflation is expressed as a percentage.

Institutional racism A term derived from the MacPherson report (1999) into the murder of Stephen Lawrence to describe deep-seated racial prejudice within the police force. Since then the term has been applied to those organisations that demonstrate a noticeable degree of racist behaviour.

Interest rates A measure of the cost of borrowing. In recent years, interest rates have stood at relatively low levels. Interest rates are decided upon by the Monetary Policy Committee of the Bank of England.

Intergovernmental organisations These organisations allow member states to co-operate on agreed matters whilst maintaining their national sovereignty. The two main intergovernmental institutions within the EU are the European Council, and the Council of the European Union. Various other international organisations, such as NATO, operate on an intergovernmental basis.

Intergovernmentalism Co-operation between the governments of the member states in which decisions are based upon unanimity. The goal of intergovernmentalists is a Europe of the states, as opposed to the federalist aim of a United States of Europe.

Internment Detention without charge or trial, primarily in relation to terrorist suspects.

Islamophobia A hostile perception of Muslims based upon prejudice and ignorance.

Judicial independence The ability of judges to act independently of the legislature and the executive.

Judicial neutrality The absence of political or personal bias amongst judges. In theory, judges should conduct their activities on the basis of judicial neutrality.

Judicial review Where courts consider a case in which a minister acted beyond his/her powers.

Judiciary The judiciary is a branch of government concerned with enforcement and implementation of the law. In theory, the judiciary is independent of the other two branches of government.

Law Lords The most senior judges in the UK, although citizens can take their case to the European courts. The importance of the Law Lords is likely to decline if proposals for a Supreme Court are implemented.

League tables The publication of results recorded by schools and hospitals in order to encourage competition, and provide parents and patients with a degree of choice. League tables are one aspect of the marketisation agenda.

Legislature A law-making body such as Parliament or Congress. The legislature is one of the three branches of government.

Lobby fodder A term used to describe the limited influence of individual MPs, particularly on the actions of the executive. Since 2001, the term has fallen out of favour due to the growing propensity of Labour MPs to rebel against the government.

Lobbying The process by which pressure groups try to influence policy-makers.

Loyalism A political perspective whose goal is to secure the union between Northern Ireland and the United Kingdom via extra-constitutional means, such as the use of force and terrorism. There are various loyalist groups within Northern Ireland.

Majoritarian electoral systems Under a majoritarian system a candidate or party requires over 50% of the votes cast. Examples of majoritarian systems include supplementary vote, additional vote and second ballot. Only the first of those examples is used in the United Kingdom.

Mandate A mandate is gained via a general election by the party with the most seats. The government claims a mandate from the people for the duration of its time in office. At each general election, the government of the day seeks to renew its mandate.

Manifesto An outline of various policies put forward by a political party. In theory, the governing party should implement its manifesto over the course of a parliamentary term, but in practise they often fail to do so.

Marketisation The use of market forces and market principles within the welfare state. As the term suggests, marketisation takes the private sector as its model. Opponents of marketisation claim that it represents the 'privatisation' of public services, whereas supporters claim that market-based reforms result in efficiency gains and a greater level of personal choice.

Migration The movement of people into and out of a country.

Monetary policy Those macro-economic decisions that affect the money supply and the level of interest rates. Monetary policy is decided upon by the Monetary Policy Committee of the Bank of England.

Multiculturalism A confusing concept that means different things to different people (even Tony Blair admitted that he did not fully understand what multiculturalism means). Part of the confusion lies in the fact that there are three perspectives on the issue (liberal, conservative and Parekh). In everyday usage, the term is often linked with the liberal perspective on multiculturalism; which places an emphasis upon tolerance and respect for all faiths and beliefs, and states that all views should be accepted and encouraged unless they endanger the freedom of others.

National Health Service The provision of health care 'free' at the point of use and according to need, regardless of a person's ability to pay.

New Right A political ideology closely associated with Conservative politicians such as Sir Keith Joseph and Margaret Thatcher, and right-wing theorists such as Friedrick Hayek and Charles Murray. The New Right greatly influenced economic and welfare policy during the 1980s and 90s.

Official Secrets Act A notorious piece of legislation that contributes to a deep-seated culture of secrecy within the British political system.

Ofsted A government agency set up to monitor standards within state education. Ofsted was created as a result of the 1988 Education Act.

Open government The availability of official records and information to the public. In a liberal democracy, it is argued that the public have the right to access information from the government. The aim of the Freedom of Information Act 2000 was to encourage a more open form of government.

Parallel lives A term derived from the Ouseley report (2001) in reference to the problem of Whites and Asians leading separate lives from each other, with little or no inter-racial contact. The Ouseley report was the government's response to race riots in several northern cities during the summer of 2001.

Parenting orders A legal punishment issued against the parents of children who play truant.

Parliamentary sovereignty Parliament is the only body that can make law for the UK. No other authority can overrule, or change, the laws that Parliament has made. In theory the British Parliament can make, amend and repeal any law it wishes.

Party whips MPs/peers chosen by the leaders of their political party in order to enforce party discipline.

Positive discrimination Attempts made to improve the

representation of various groups within society, often in an attempt to reverse the effects of negative discrimination. The term is also known as affirmative action, particularly in the United States.

Postcode lottery Where the quality of welfare provision differs greatly from one area to the next. The term can also be applied to the disparity in life chances between one region and another.

Post-war consensus The period from 1945 to 1979 in which the main political parties shared a broad agreement on basic social, economic and political issues. The consensus centred around Keynesian economics, the welfare state and a tripartite bargaining process between the government, big business and the trade unions.

Poverty trap Where families and individuals face great difficulty moving out of poverty due to poor life chances.

Power-sharing executive In the context of Northern Ireland, an attempt to reconcile differences between Unionists and Republicans and bring both sides into government.

Prime Minister's Questions (PMQs) A method by which the Prime Minister is held to account by the House of Commons. PMQs are held every Wednesday when Parliament is in session.

Privatisation The transfer of assets from the public sector to the private sector.

Qualified Majority Voting A system of voting used in the Council of the European Union. Each member state has a set number of votes based on the size of their population.

Referendum A vote by the electorate on a specific proposal which allows the people to register opinions on constitutional or policy issues. A referendum usually provides two options to a question, yes or no. Referendums are the most common illustration of direct democracy.

Rehabilitation Measures designed to socialise offenders back into society.

Republicanism A political perspective that advocates the creation of a 32-county Irish republic and the end of the union between Northern Ireland and the British mainland. There are several strands of republicanism within Ireland, primarily those who support the Good Friday Agreement (e.g. the IRA/Sinn Fein) and those who believe the armed struggle is the only way to remove the British presence within the north of Ireland. Examples of groups that hold the latter view include Continuity IRA and the INLA.

Salisbury convention An unwritten code of behaviour in which the un-elected Lords will not block a proposal made in the government's manifesto. This is because the government holds a clear mandate from the people.

Scrutiny The means by which the executive is held to account, usually by the legislature. In the UK there are six main areas of scrutiny; select committees, public bill committees, the ombudsman, opposition days, PMQs/Question Time and the House of Lords.

Separation of powers Where the power of each branch of government is limited and checked in some way. The separation of powers is a key element of any liberal democracy. The United States political system operates on the basis of the separation of powers.

Single-member constituencies Where one representative is elected to serve a geographical area. Single-member constituencies are used for the elections on the basis of FPTP.

Social engineering Attempts by the government and various other institutions to create socially desirable outcomes (e.g. the government's target to get 50% of all young people into higher education by 2010).

Social justice Attempts made to address the problem of social exclusion and inequality within society.

Sovereignty The principle of absolute and unlimited power, and the defining feature of a state. In the UK Parliament is sovereign, because it alone has absolute legislative power.

State An organisation, usually a country, that exercises through its institutions power over its citizens. There are several institutions of the state such as the police and the army.

Statute law An Act of Parliament.

Stealth taxes Tax revenue raised by indirect taxation, partly because it is less likely to cause a public backlash than an increase in the level of direct taxation. Since the 1990s the use of stealth taxation has greatly increased.

Subsidiarity The principle by which decisions should be taken at the most appropriate level. Subsidiarity has been integral to the EU since ratification of the Maastricht Treaty.

Superstate A negative term used by opponents of a federal Europe, who claim that a United States of Europe would centralise power into the hands of an unelected and unaccountable Brussels elite.

Supranational institution An institution independent of, and above, the member-state. Such an institution has the power to impose decisions upon member-states such as the UK. As such, any decision made by a supranational body takes precedence over national law. Many of the EU's institutions are supranational such as the Commission, the European Court of Justice and the European Central Bank.

Terrorism Defined under Section 1 of the Terrorism Act 2000 as 'the use or threat of action ... designed to influence the government or to intimidate the public ... and the use of or threats made for the purpose of advancing a political, religious or ideological cause.'

Thatcherism A radical form of conservatism associated with the New Right. Policies associated with Thatcherism include privatisation, the sale of council homes and de-regulation.

The term gains it name from the former Prime Minister Margaret Thatcher (1979-90).

Third Way A theoretical perspective that combines the pursuit of social justice with a neo-liberal stance on economic issues. The idea of rights and responsibilities is a key element of the Third Way, in which the welfare state provides a 'hand up not a hand out'. The Third Way also consists of stakeholding – where businesses have a responsibility to various groups, rather than just their shareholders.

Trade union An organisation created to promote and defend the interests of its members. Trade unions have played a key role in the development of the Labour movement.

Ultra vires Where a cabinet minister has acted beyond their legally specified powers.

Unanimity Decisions taken on the basis of consensus amongst representatives of the member states, in which the national veto is retained. The alternative to unanimity is Qualified Majority Voting.

Uncodified constitution A constitution that is not specified in one single authoritative document. Unlike most other countries, Britain has an uncodified constitution.

Unionism A political perspective that strongly supports the maintenance of the United Kingdom. In the context of Northern Ireland, Unionists wish to secure the union between the province and the mainland. The main unionist party is the Democratic Unionist party.

Unitary state A state in which power is centralised into a central authority, such as the Westminster Parliament in the UK. Devolved or regional assemblies can exist, but any powers they possess will have been granted to them by the central authority, and could be withdrawn by that authority.

Vote of no confidence Where the main opposition party in the House of Commons calls a vote of no confidence in the government of the day. In 1979 the then Leader of the Opposition Margaret Thatcher called for a vote of no confidence in the Labour government of Jim Callaghan. The government lost the vote, and in accordance with the British constitution, a general election had to be called.

Welfare state A wide range of benefits and services provided in order to meet the welfare needs of its people.

Welfare to work A series of measures designed to get welfare claimants back to work via changes to the tax and benefit system. It combines the pursuit of social justice with an acceptance of New Right theory.

West Lothian Question A constitutional anomaly in which Scottish MPs can vote on matters in England and Wales which do not directly affect their constituents. In January 2004, controversial legislation on variable fees for higher education was passed with the support of Scottish Labour MPs – although a majority of English MPs voted against it.

Winners bonus Under FPTP the party with the largest number of seats can gain an artificially high majority. Labour have benefited from the winner's bonus since 1997, as did the Conservatives during the 1980s.

Works of authority Those books are cited by politicians during times of constitutional debate and conflict, such as Walter Bagehot's *The English Constitution* and Dicey's *An Introduction to the Study of the Law of the Constitution*. Works of authority are one source of the UK's uncodified constitution.

Bibliography

A-Brown, Y. (1999) *True Colours: Public Attitudes to Multiculturalism and the Role of the Government* (IPPR, Guildford & Kings Lynn).

Audit Commission (2000) *Another Country: Implementing Dispersal Under the Immigration and Asylum Act 1999* (HM Government, London).

Bainbridge, T. (1998) *The Penguin Companion to European Union* (2nd Edition, Penguin Books, London).

Bartholomew, J. (2004) *The Welfare State We're In* (Politico's, London).

Beckett, F. and Hencke, D. (2004) *The Blairs and their Court* (Aurum, London).

Black, J. (2004) *Britain Since the Seventies: Politics and Society in the Consumer Age* (Reaktion Books, London).

Bomberg, E. and Stubb, A. (2003) *The European Union: How Does it Work?* (Oxford University Press, Oxford).

Booker, C. and North, R. (2003) *The Great Deception: The Secret History of the European Union* (Continuum, London).

Bower, T. (2004) *Gordon Brown* (HarperCollins, London).

Briscoe, S. (2005) *Britain in Numbers: The Essential Statistics* (Politico's, London).

Brown, G. (1989) *Where There's Greed: Margaret Thatcher and the Betrayal of Britain's Future* (Mainstream Publishing, Edinburgh).

369

Budge, I. *et al.* (2001) *The New British Politics* (2nd Edition, Pearson Education Limited, Harlow).

Buller, J. (2004) Foreign and European policy, in S. Ludlam and M.J. Smith (eds) *Governing as New Labour*, pp.193–210) (Palgrave Macmillan, Hampshire and New York).

Connolly, B. (1995) *The Rotten Heart of Europe: Dirty War for Europe's Money* (Faber & Faber, London).

Cootes, R.J. (1984) *The Making of the Welfare State* (2nd Edition, Longman, Essex).

Cowles, M.G and Dinan, D. (2004) *Developments in the European Union* (Palgrave Macmillan, New York).

Coxall, B. and Robbins, L. (1994) *Contemporary British Politics* (2nd Edition, Macmillan, London).

Coxall, B. and Robbins, L. (1998) *Contemporary British Politics* (3rd Edition, Macmillan, London).

Coyle, D. (2002) *Sex, Drugs and Economics: An Unconventional Introduction to Economics* (Texere, London).

Crosbie, A.M. (2004) *Britain's Hot Potato! A Boiled-down Guide to the European Union, the Constitution Debate, the Euro, and Us* (HBI Publishing, Wiltshire).

Cunningham, M. (2001) *British Government Policy in Northern Ireland 1969–2000* (Manchester University Press, Manchester and New York).

Davies, A. (1998) *British Politics and Europe* (Hodder & Stoughton, Oxfordshire).

Denver, D. (2004) European Parliament elections 2004, *Politics Review*, 14 (2): 17–19.

Dinan, D. (1994) *Ever Closer Union? An Introduction to the European Community* (Macmillan, Hampshire and London).

Driver, S. and Martell, L. (2002) *Blair's Britain* (Polity, Cambridge).

Edexcel (2005) *A Level Politics Syllabus* (Edexcel, London).

Fielding, S. (2003) *The Labour Party, Continuity and Change in the Making of 'New' Labour* (Palgrave Macmillan, Hampshire).

Friedman, M. (1990) *Free to Choose: A Personal Statement* (Thomson Learning, London).

Geddes, A. (2004) *The European Union and British Politics* (Palgrave Macmillan, Hampshire).

George, S. (1998) *An Awkward Partner: Britain in the European Community* (3rd Edition, Oxford University Press, Oxford).

George, S. and Bache, I. (2001) *Politics in the European Union* (Oxford University Press, Oxford).

Giddens, A. (1998) *The Third Way: The Renewal of Social Democracy* (Polity Press, Cambridge).

Giddens, A. (2007) *Over To You, Mr Brown* (Polity Press, Cambridge).

Giddings, P. and Drewry, G. (2004) *Britain in the European Union: Law, Policy and Parliament* (Palgrave Macmillan, Hampshire).

Glover, S. *et al.* (2001) *Migration: An Economic and Social Analysis* (Home Office, London).

Goodlad, G. (2007) Ten Years at the Treasury: Gordon Brown and the Economy *Talking Politics*, April: 137–139.

Grant, M. (2005) Is the Labour Party still a socialist party? *Politics Review*, 15(1): 24–27.

Grant, W. (2000) *Pressure Groups and British Politics* (Macmillan, London).

Grant, W. (2002) *Economic Policy in Britain* (Palgrave Macmillan, Hampshire).

Griffiths Report (1983) *NHS Management Inquiry Report* (DHSS, London).

Guiraudon, V. (2004) Immigration and asylum: a high politics agenda, in M.G. Cowles and D. Dinan (eds) *Developments in the European Union*, pp. 160–180 (Palgrave Macmillan, New York).

Hall, M. (2005) The race card: asylum and immigration in contemporary British politics, part 1, *Talking Politics*, April: 151–152.

Hayek, F. (1944) *The Road to Serfdom* (Routledge, London).

Heywood, A. (2005) *Key Concepts in Politics* (Palgrave, Hampshire and New York).

Hitchens, P. (2003) *The Abolition of Liberty: The Decline of Order and Justice in England* (Atlantic Books, London).

HM Statistical Office (2005) *Budget 2005 Summary* (HM Statistical Office, London).

Home Office (1997) *No More Excuses* (Home Office, London).

Hoskyns, C. and Newman, M. (2000) *Democratizing the European Union* (Manchester University Press, Manchester).

Huntington, S.P. (2002) *The Clash of Civilizations and the Remaking of World Order* (Free Press, London).

Hutton, W. (1995) *The State We're In* (Jonathon Cape, London).

Hutton, W. (2002) *The World We're In* (Little, Brown, London).

Jones, B. *et al.* (2001) *Politics UK* (4th Edition, Pearson Education Limited, Harlow).

Jones, M. and Lowe, R. (2002) *From Beveridge to Blair: The First Fifty Years of Britain's Welfare State 1948–98* (Manchester University Press, Manchester).

Joyce, P. (2001) *Teach Yourself 101 Key Ideas Politics* (Hodder & Stoughton, London).

Kingdom, J. (2003) *Government and Politics in Britain* (3rd Edition, Polity, Cambridge).

Ladrech, R. (2004) Europeanization and the member states, in M.G. Cowles and D. Dinan (eds) *Developments in the European Union*, pp. 47–64 (Palgrave Macmillan, New York).

Lawes, C. (2005) The referendum on the European constitution, *Talking Politics*, April: 135–139.

Leach, R. (2004) *Europe A Concise Encyclopaedia of the European Union* (4th Edition, Profile Books, London).

Leonard, D. (2005) *Guide to the European Union* (9th Edition, Profile Books, London).

Leonard, M. (2005) *Why Europe Will Run the 21st Century* (Fourth Estate, London).

Lowe, R. (1999) *The Welfare State in Britain since 1945* (2nd Edition, Macmillan, Hampshire).

Ludlam, S. and Smith, M.J. (2004) *Governing as New Labour* (Palgrave Macmillan, Hampshire).

Lynch, J.E. (2004) Blighty: at home in a foreign land, *Talking Politics*, April: 154–157.

Lynch, P. (2004) British politics and Europe, *Politics Review*, 13(4): 17–19.

Lyons, A. (1999) *The Government and the Economy* (Hodder & Stoughton, Oxfordshire).

MacDonald, J. and Bowden, A. (2005) *Dare We Trust Them? A New Vision for Europe* (Book Guild, Lewes).

Macpherson of Cluny, Sir William (1999) *The Stephen Lawrence Inquiry: Report of an Inquiry by Sir William Macpherson of Cluny* (HMSO, London).

McCormick, J. (2004) *Understanding the European Union: A Concise Introduction* (Macmillan, Hampshire & London).

McNaughton, N. (2003) *Understanding British and European Political Issues* (Manchester University Press, Manchester).

McNaughton, N. (2003) A2 Resource Pack: *Government and Politics Key Political Issues Edexcel Route A* (Philip Allan, Oxfordshire).

Mote, A. (2003) *Overcrowded Britain: Our Immigration Crisis Exposed* (Tanner, Hampshire).

Mulholland, M. (2002) *Northern Ireland: A Very Short Introduction* (Oxford University Press, Oxford).

Naughtie, J. (2003) *The Rivals Blair and Brown – The Intimate Story of a Political Marriage* (Fourth Estate, London).

Norris, P. (2005) Anti-terrorism measures in Britain: a fine line between democracy and authoritarianism, *Talking Politics*, April: 142–144.

Novak, M. (1999) *Is there a Third Way? Essays on the Changing Direction of Socialist Thought* (ILEA, London).

Nugent, N. (2003) *The Government and Politics of the European Union* (5th Edition, Palgrave Macmillan, Hampshire).

Ouseley, H. (2001) *Community Pride, Not Prejudice: Making Diversity Work in Bradford* (Bradford Vision, Bradford).

Parekh, Lord B. (2000) *The Future of Multi-Ethnic Britain: Report of the Commission on the Future of Multi-Ethnic Britain* (Profile Books, London).

Patten, C. (2005) *Not Quite the Diplomat: Home Truths About World Affairs* (Allen Lane, London).

Peele, G. (2004) *Governing the UK* (4th Edition, Blackwell, Oxford).

Peterson, J. and Shackleton, M. (2002) *The Institutions of the European Union* (Oxford University Press, Oxford).

Pierson, C. (1998) *Beyond the Welfare State? The New Political Economy of Welfare* (Polity Press, Cambridge).

Pilkington, C. (2001) *Britain in the European Union Today* (2nd Edition, Manchester University Press, Manchester).

Pinder, J. (1998) *The Building of the European Union* (3rd Edition, Oxford University press, Oxford).

Pinder, J. (2001) *The European Union: A Very Short Introduction* (Oxford University Press, Oxford).

Pitchford, R. and Cox, A. (1997) *EMU Explained* (Kogan Page, London).

Randall, N. (2004) Three faces of New Labour: principle, pragmatism and populism in New Labour's Home Office, in S. Ludlam and M.J. Smith (eds) *Governing as New Labour* pp.177–192 (Palgrave Macmillan, Hampshire).

Rathbone, M. (2006) Civil Liberties Under Labour *Talking Politics*, September: 17–21.

Reid, J. and Phillips, T. (2004) *The Best Intentions: Race, Equity and Delivering Today's NHS* (Fabian Society, London).

Reid, T. (2004) *The United States of Europe* (Penguin, London).

Rifkin, J. (2004) *The European Dream* (Polity, Cambridge).

Roberts, D. *et al.* (1999) *British Politics in Focus* (2nd Edition, Causeway Press, Ormskirk).

Sampson, A. (2004) *Who Runs this Place? The Anatomy of Britain in the 21st Century* (John Murray, London).

Savage, S.P. and Atkinson, R. (2001) *Public Policy Under Blair* (Palgrave, Hampshire).

Seldon, A. and Kavanagh (2005) *The Blair Effect 2001–5* (Cambridge University Press, Cambridge).

Solomos, J. (2003) *Race and Racism in Britain* (3rd Edition, Palgrave Macmillan, Hampshire).

Stadlen, M. and Glass, H. (2004) *The Politics Companion* (Robson Books, London).

Stephens, P. (2004) *Tony Blair: The Price of Leadership* (Politico's, London).

Stuart, G. (2003) *The Making of Europe's Constitution* (Fabian Society, London).

Toynbee, P. and Walker, D. (2001) *Did Things Get Better? An Audit of Labour's Successes and Failures* (Penguin, London).

Toynbee, P. and Walker, D. (2005) *Better or Worse? Has Labour Delivered?* (Bloomsbury, London).

Turner, A. (2005) *A New Pension Settlement for the Twenty-First Century: The Second Report of the Pensions Commission* (HMSO, London).

Turner, A.J. (2002) *AS/A Level UK Government and Politics Essential Word Dictionary* (Philip Allan, Oxfordshire).

Watts, D. (2000) *Britain and the European Union: an Uneasy Partnership* (The Politics Association, Manchester).

NEWSPAPERS AND PERIODICALS

The Observer supplement (2007) *The Blair Years 1997–2007*, May: 1–45.

Index

379

381

386

387